THE
DOLLS' HOUSE
SHOPKEEPER

LIONEL & ANN BARNARD

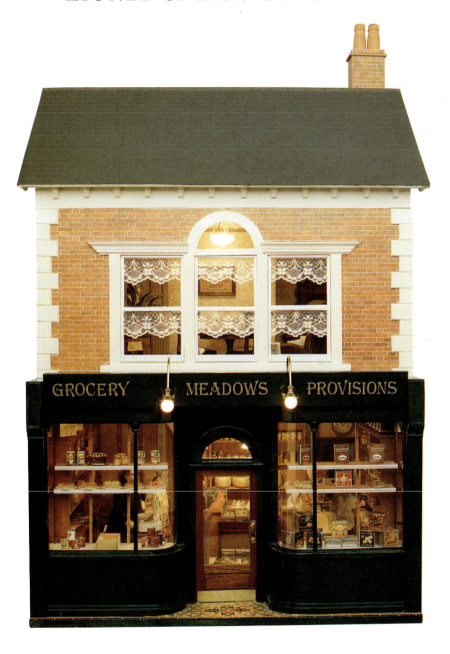

David & Charles

To Ann's father Cyril Roberts,

the inspiration for Meadows the grocers, and to

Lionel's mother, Phyllis.

A DAVID & CHARLES BOOK

First published in the UK in 2001

ISBN 0 7153 0966 8

Book design by Maggie Aldred
and printed in China by Leefung-Asco
for David & Charles
Brunel House   Newton Abbot   Devon

CONTENTS

INTRODUCTION

Whilst most miniaturists are re-creating life with dolls' houses, many are involved in making and stocking scale model shops: for every range of dolls' houses currently manufactured, as much as twenty percent are retail premises. This comes as no surprise to us as the sight of an old hardware store, or say, one selling pipes and tobaccos, complete with an original frontage, will attract visitors from miles around. A complete street of life-size shop fronts and contents were sold at a recent auction and more than one museum is devoted to shops and their contents. Model shops have also been used for both amusement and as useful teaching aids for children.

When we first started to make dolls' houses in $1/12$ scale we included one or two shops in our range and they always proved very popular. It wasn't long before we had to add some fixtures and fittings and then the goods with which to stock them. We researched extensively and continuously into periods, stock and architecture in order to make things correctly and noticed that information on full-sized shops was hard to come by and almost impossible in miniature. Whilst few books on old shop exteriors remain in print there is almost nothing on the older style interiors of anything except for some of the larger departmental stores.

The elegant interior of Meadows grocer's shop displaying a full range of high class provisions

Gamages and the Army & Navy stores would commission engravings or photographs of their counters laden with stock to place in their turn-of-the-century mail-order catalogues but there was little interest shown in the local boot repairers, milliners or village stores. Collections of photographs depicting village life and high streets are available, and a great deal of useful information can be gleaned on how shopkeepers dressed their windows, but little can be gathered on interiors as shops before 1940 were often very badly lit.

Most books on making dolls' houses have, for the most part, ignored the subject of shops and few have provided good, reliable information on how to make more than basic fixtures and fittings. For some time now we have been gathering material on this subject in order to satisfy customers who have been keen to find the right type of stock and fittings to complete their own miniature shops with some degree of accuracy. Hopefully the projects included here will provide some of that information and inspire the making of shops that are not the usual milliner or baker.

The book is divided into four main parts. The first part contains information on tools and materials required for making miniature shops. This is followed by a Basic Techniques and Lighting section, where we see how different decorative techniques can be used to bring an authentic look to projects. The Shopkeeper's Resource section follows and describes how to make a wide variety of fixtures and fittings for various shops – and not just those included in the projects as we recognise that many of you will already have kits waiting to be assembled or have purchased ready-made shops.

In the final part of the book we show you how to make five completely different shops. Jingles, our toy shop is set in a small shop with an unusual front window. Luscombes, which houses an ironmongers, makes great use of some of the excellent metal work from specialist makers. The Clarence, a tea room set in the Art Deco 1920s is different from other buildings with its extensive glass top and decorative skylight. Pickwicks, a Victorian book and print dealer set in a Tudor-style building has been given a winter feel for the outside scene and crammed with books and prints on the inside. Lastly, Meadows, the grocers and provision merchant, allowed us to use many different types of brightly coloured packaging.

The making of each shop project is described in detail, beginning with a list of the materials needed. Fixtures and fittings are included and instructions are given for making up anything unique. Standard shop stock and equipment can be made by referring to the Shopkeeper's Resource section.

We had great fun making up all the different shops and hope that you will too.

The making and stocking of miniature shops is not a new phenomenon as they have existed for hundreds of years and were made in large numbers during the nineteenth century. Usually quite small, about 12in wide, they consisted of an open display mounted onto a wooden base with the stock shown on the back wall. There was no top and everything was placed on view so that it could easily be reached and played with. Each of the display areas were fully stocked with counters, shelves and other fittings according to the trade they represented, such as hardware, milliners and pharmacies.

BASIC TOOLS AND MATERIALS

You cannot have too many varieties and sizes of small screws and panel pins to hand when starting to make a 1/12 scale building.

Use a good set square to make up a simple 90 degree bench jig before commencing work and you will save a lot of time later. Check set squares regularly as they can be inaccurate after being dropped.

Whilst experienced miniaturists and craft workers will probably have a number of tools and be familiar with most of the materials we shall be using, the following gives information on basic tools together with a background on materials for beginners.

Wherever possible we have used commercially available and ready-planed obeche and mahogany timbers and used jelutong mouldings for the miniatures, all of which are readily available from your local miniature shop or dolls' house fair. We have only used straightforward materials and lighting techniques, which should prove easy to follow.

SCALE AND MEASUREMENTS

Throughout this book we have used the universally known and used scale of 1/12, or one inch to one foot. We appreciate that other scales are available to the model maker and that 1/24, or half scale, is gaining in popularity or that 1/16 scale was used extensively in recent years. However, we are convinced that 1/12 is the most popular scale in use throughout the world and a much easier scale for the beginner to make calculations with.

The measurements used throughout the book are given in imperial feet and inches as we find that most miniaturists are more comfortable with these than with millimetres and centimetres. We have not been tempted to give metric equivalents for any measurements as the two rarely mix and the result often leaves odd and unexplained millimetres or fractions on drawings and finished models. One exception to this rule is in the use of commercially produced sheet plywood and MDF (medium density fibreboard) as these are only produced in metric sizes, especially for the thickness. The materials lists therefore refer to the thickness of a sheet for these materials in millimetres but the cutting of lengths and widths will be made in imperial feet and inches. Inch or inches has been abbreviated to 'in' throughout.

Tools

Although most tool collections will prove adequate they can always be improved by making sure that knives and saws are sharp and adding some small drill bits for making miniatures. Generally speaking, cheap tools are unreliable, often inaccurate and give poor results; buying only those of good quality will pay in the long run and prove useful for many jobs other than miniatures.

Before starting any of the projects check all try squares for accuracy and keep knives and chisels as sharp as possible, that way they will give a cleaner finish when cutting timbers and are less likely to slip and injure the user. Power tools should always have guards in place during use and it is a good idea to check any electrical fittings, fuses, plugs and connections before storing away.

Hand Saws

Saws cut with the toothed section along the bottom edge and the teeth vary in length and are alternatively offset according to the type of cut required. The following are described in order of size, the largest first.

Rip Saw With coarse teeth these saws are designed for cutting up large pieces of timber and will almost certainly be required for cutting sheet MDF or plywood. Use carefully to avoid an excessive rag or rough edge under the sheet as you cut. Supporting the sheet on trestles or a suitable work bench will make it easier to handle.

Tenon Saw Tenon saws are easily identified by the supporting bar along the top of the blade. They are smaller than rip saws and have a fine set on the teeth making them ideal for cutting smaller pieces of timber. Standard tenon saws will have a blade about 10in long and have some 12–15 teeth per inch, making them very useful for cutting smaller sheets and joints in timber. A Gent saw is a smaller version of a tenon saw with correspondingly smaller teeth.

Fretsaw and Piercing Saw Used for cutting shapes and holes from sheet timber, the design of this tool makes it extremely useful for cutting apertures such as windows and doorways. The blades are available in several grades and are easily changed should they break. The main difference between the two saws is that the fretsaw has a larger frame allowing more 'reach'. The use of a V-block will assist in the cutting of delicate parts. Mechanical versions known as vibrating or scroll saws are useful but not necessary.

Pad or Keyhole Saw This is an ideal saw for cutting out any apertures such as windows and provides a useful alternative to setting up a powered router or attempting to cut with a craft knife. The toothed blade tapers to a point and can be inserted into a hole drilled into the timber sheet to provide a start: two holes are required for cutting out squares and rectangles. The teeth on these blades are generally coarse and the surfaces will need cleaning up afterwards. Blades are fitted into a separate handle and can be renewed when blunt.

Razor Saw Razor saws are miniature versions of tenon saws and the teeth can number as many as 52 per inch. Both the thickness of the blade and the set is extremely fine indeed. The result is a very sharp and extremely useful saw giving a small rag on

cutting and thus is ideal for cutting small pieces of timber used in miniature furniture and accessories. These saws are sold in three sizes, choose the deepest for working with mitre boxes.

Table Saw Sometimes known as powered, table, bench or circular saw, they can take all the hard work out of cutting sheet timbers into useful sizes. The diameter of the blade determines the thickness of the material that can be cut, as the top part of the blade should appear above the table and the surface of the wood. Saws used for full-sized cabinet work have blades of 8in or more in diameter and can easily tackle materials up to 2in thick. Those used for modelling and miniature work are often attachments for lathes and have blades of approximately 4in diameter, which limits them to cuts of approximately $1/4$in in depth. The Minicraft and Dremel ranges are quite suitable for miniatures but are unlikely to cope with any timbers over $1/4$in thick. With the ability to set accurate stops on the table, the user is able to machine several pieces of timber knowing that they will all be the same size when cut. Use a push stick to move any materials between the fence and the blade. Housing joints can also be produced with this tool although a sufficiently large enough work table must be used for accuracy.

As with all powered tools, protective goggles and face-masks should be worn when producing dust in a confined space, and guards should always be fixed in place.

Router

Housing joints and apertures can all be cut with extreme accuracy using an electrically powered router with a plunging action and a guide. Tools with this action are particularly useful for cutting out window apertures as the timber is left with a nice clean edge.

Housing joints near the edge of timber sheet are cut using the router with a fixed guide, those beyond the scope of the guide will need fences clamped to the work.

Powered circular saws should always be used with the guard fitted as recommended by the manufacturer. Blades of less than 4in diameter are unlikely to cut materials above $3/8$in thick without difficulty.

When cutting sheet timber by hand using a craft knife remember that the thicker the material the stronger the blade should be. Keep saws and craft knives sharp and use a guard to protect the blades when they are not in use. Use a small surgical scalpel No.3 to cut fine guide-lines into timbers or to cut out labels and posters. The blades are extremely sharp and great care should be taken at all times.

Cutting out apertures will require the use of templates unless you are skilled and confident enough to use the router free hand. The powerful motion of the motor and the cutter will tend to make the tool drift to the left when used without fixed guides and it is recommended that these are used at all times.

Routers may also be fixed in a vertical position under the surface of a bench so that only the cutter is visible, in this case the work is run against a guide, or fence, and the cutter to produce the profile or cut required. They can also be fixed into a drill stand for profile cutting and any number of different profile and size cutters can be purchased to give a variety of effects. For work on the projects in this book only cutters that combine a bottom and side cut are necessary and those of 6mm and 9mm diameters should prove sufficient as wider cuts can be taken with more than one pass.

The usual safety rules apply when using powered tools – always use the guards supplied and wear goggles and masks if producing dust in a confined space.

Mitre Box

This tool enables accurate cuts to be made at 90 and 45 degrees. Available in many sizes, miniaturists will find the smaller table-top versions designed to take razor saws the most useful. Made in a variety of materials such as plastic, wood and aluminium, the latter gives lasting results if used with care. Placing a piece of scrap timber in the base of a mitre box will prevent cutting though the base and help preserve the life of the saw.

A bench jig used for clamping and sawing mitres, shown with two razor saws

Bench Jig

A simple bench jig combining 45 and 90 degree angle cuts will prove most useful for the home miniaturists. A simple jig can be made from pieces of scrap ³/8in thick timber

sheet offcuts but it must be assembled with accuracy if it is to give good results. The basic requirements are that it should contain at least one block set at right angles to the bed with another set at right angles to that for accurate clamping of materials.

Knives

There are a number of craft knives available and it is recommended that one with strong renewable blades be used for most general work. Knives are also available with snap-off blades, giving no excuse for not having a permanently sharp blade.

A No.3 scalpel, available with several differently shaped, replaceable blades, is one of the most useful tools available to the miniaturist as it allows very fine cuts to be made in a wide variety of materials. The blades can be discarded once blunt, however, they remain capable of cutting fingers so discard with care! Generally speaking the larger the section of wood being cut or trimmed the stronger the blade should be.

Plane

Use a metal-soled jack-plane for cleaning up and squaring off the edges of sawn timber sheet and use a small adjustable plane 5in or less in length for smoothing off the edges of small section timbers. With care these can be used for some miniature work. Plane blades should be kept accurately ground and sharpened and be set squarely in the body. Blades should always be withdrawn into the body of the plane after use.

Drills

When working on materials up to ¹/2in thick a small hand drill, used with the appropriate bit, will be more than adequate for most carcass work on a shop project. Electric drills powered by small 12 volt DC motors via a transformer are extremely useful for many aspects of work on both carcasses and miniatures and are readily available from specialist shops. Hand-held pin and Archimedian type drills are ideal for close miniature work, as the chucks are very small and easily centred.

Drill bits from ¹/₈in to ³/₁₆in and a screw counter-sink bit are used in most of the projects but a selection of smaller drill bits ranging in size from ¹/₃₂in to ¹/₈in will prove useful for all the miniature jobs listed. Drill bits are usually sold in metric sizes with imperial equivalents on the packaging. It is important that the chuck jaws of all drills are correctly centred and that drill bits are sharp and firmly held – blunt drill bits make for hard and inaccurate work. Electrically powered drills normally used for full-sized work should be used with care as too much power may result in damaged work surfaces.

Ruler and Set Square

A good quality metal ruler giving inches and metric equivalents is essential. Choose a 12in length for most jobs and a 6in length for measuring in small areas. 1in to 1ft scale rules are available from specialist ¹/₁₂ craft suppliers and may prove useful when working out a site plan or checking dimensions.

An accurate set or try-square will make all the difference to the miniaturists' work. The all-metal versions, also known as engineers' squares, are definitely the best and less likely to be affected by extremes of temperature.

Sliding Bevel

This is a very useful tool for setting out and marking complex angles and they are available in a variety of sizes. Use in conjunction with a protractor.

Caliper and Depth Gauge

This is a useful measuring tool and certainly one that any miniaturist should have. Many sizes are available but using one about 6in long with one set of inside and a second set of outside measuring jaws at one end and a 'tail' at the other is ideal. The body of this tool is usually marked with inches and millimetres and as the jaws are opened the tail moves. This is particularly useful for measuring the length of timber required to fit

the depth or width, for say a drawer carcass. In most cases there is little need to take the reading off the scale as the measurement can be transferred directly to the timber using the tail.

Chisels

Very useful for cleaning up edges, housing joints and cutting rebates, all chisels should always be kept sharp and used with hands behind the action being taken – never cut towards the body in any circumstances. One ¹/₄in and one ¹/₂in wide-bladed chisel will prove adequate for most work. Miniature chisels can be made up using watchmaker's screwdrivers with the blades ground and sharpened.

Small Tools

You will need a hammer, the smaller the better, a pair of pliers and an awl for making starter holes for drilling in blockboard and MDF. Fine tweezers are valuable for picking up and placing small pins and for arranging stock. Pliers, pincers and cutters will always prove to be useful additions to a tool kit. Select a few finely toothed 6in files for use on miniatures and white metal kits and include at least one round or rat-tailed file for enlarging and cleaning holes.

Abrasive Papers

Glass paper (popularly, though incorrectly, referred to as sandpaper) and emery paper can be purchased in several grades from coarse to fine and is used accordingly. In later chapters we refer to fine grade abrasive paper but most grades of garnet or cabinet papers will prove a useful alternative for delicate work. Using these in conjunction with a cork sanding block will give superior results to flat surfaces, finer pieces can be moved across a paper laid flat onto a suitable surface. In common with everyday usage we refer later to 'sanding' various

Miniature chisels made from watchmaker's screwdrivers are shown here alongside a standard chisel and awl

9

wooden parts but this means using glass paper.

Powered sanders with flat bases are ideal for work on the carcasses of buildings made from sheet material. Work *with* the grain on plywood and avoid using a power tool to sand the thinner edge sections.

Goggles, Gloves and Masks

Goggles should be worn when drilling or using circular saws, particularly when using powered machines. Face-masks are *strongly* recommended when spraying adhesives and spirit-based paints and whenever you are cutting or drilling MDF with power tools. Leather-palmed gloves will provide simple protection against splinters when cutting large sheets of plywood or blockboard.

Clamps and Cramps

Clamps or cramps are available in a variety of sizes and designs and most conform to the basic G shape. A selection of small clamps with jaws less than 2in will be useful in making up miniature pieces of furniture. Try not to over-tighten clamps and always use a piece of waste wood between the clamps and the work piece to avoid damage.

A selection of small G clamps with two adjustable sash cramps on the left

Cutting Mat

A flat, plasticised cutting mat is available in a variety of sizes with a specially formulated surface that 'heals' itself even after repeated cutting. Used in conjunction with a scalpel or sharp craft knife and a steel rule, clean and accurate cuts can be made to the thinnest paper stock without leaving a ragged edge. Constant cutting in one spot will eventually mark the surface so turn the mat around at regular intervals.

Materials

The materials and adhesives used in this book are generally available from timber merchants, the ironmongery departments of most superstores or your local decorator's merchants. The smaller dimension and section timbers used can all be sourced from specialist miniaturist suppliers.

Timbers

Although the projects in this book have been designed using only imperial measurements of feet and inches, timber and hardware merchants in the UK and Europe supply their goods almost exclusively in metric. We have therefore given the metric sizes that you will be offered by the merchants for plywood and MDF boards, followed by the imperial equivalent in brackets.

When cutting rebates, the two thicknesses of MDF sheets used in all these projects measure a nominal 6mm and 9mm and the closest imperial equivalents expressed as fractions are $1/4$in and $3/8$in, therefore the rebates are quoted in the instructions as metric followed by the imperial equivalent in brackets where appropriate. We suggest that an offcut of timber be used to check the width of all rebates *before* cutting them out, adjusting as necessary. Rebates are best cut out using a powered router or circular saw as both these tools will leave clean edges and bottom surfaces, however rebates can also be cut using sharp hand tools.

It is recommended that pilot holes should always be drilled out for screws (and often panel pins too) or the wood may split.

Obeche This is generally available but sometimes proves hard to find; any modelling timber of corresponding thicknesses may be used as an alternative but we do not recommend balsa for any of these jobs.

Sheet Timbers MDF (Medium Density Fibreboard) is a man-made board which is an excellent alternative to plywood as it is unlikely to warp and is easy to cut. When painting, varnishing or papering any 'sheet' wood such as MDF or plywood it is recommended that both sides are treated equally to avoid warping, particularly on materials of less than 9mm or $^3/8$in thickness. Common thicknesses are 3mm, 6mm, 9mm and 12mm, ($^1/8$in, $^1/4$in, $^3/8$in and $^1/2$in, approximately). These sheets have excellent finishes on both surfaces and can be reversed without problems. They are also very easy to machine and rarely need sanding or smoothing on the face surfaces.

Some publicity has been given to the risks of using MDF and the dust and formaldehyde given off when it is machine finished, e.g. sawn or drilled. The British Health & Safety Executive apparently consider the risk to be very low especially as some manufacturers are using low levels of formaldehyde. We recommend that if cutting MDF, or any other wood particle-based material with electric saws, routers or drills, that you wear a protective mask and ensure good ventilation or dust extraction. Consult your national health and safety organisation if appropriate.

Plywood is made up by bonding several wood veneers one on top of another and the best quality is usually faced with birch wood and resistant to water. Birch-faced plywood is a superior surfaced timber supplied in sheet form and can be used in lieu of MDF, however MDF is less expensive and more generally available. It is recommended that those parts that have to be machined or cut to provide apertures should be made from MDF to avoid warping.

Blockboard is made up with a scrap pine core with a thin wood veneer facing. Purchase plywood and blockboard sheets without knot holes or obvious defects and avoid boards imported from the Far East as these have a coarse grain, are liable to tear on cutting and require a great deal of filling.

Blockboard, MDF and plywood are all produced in standard 8ft x 4ft (2400mm x 1200mm) sheets. Common thicknesses are 6mm ($^1/4$in), 9mm ($^3/8$in) and 12mm ($^1/2$in). Offcuts can often be obtained from a timber merchant and some DIY stores stock smaller sheets with one dimension of 2ft or 4ft.

Hardboard is a useful man-made board usually 2mm, 3mm or 4mm thick and has a smooth upper surface and a patterned back. Thin sheets can be bent, with care. The use of hardboard is not recommended for carcasses except in exceptional circumstances.

Very thin plywood of $^1/32$in (1mm) thickness is used in aero and boat modelling. It is a very strong and flexible material, ideal for bending around sharp curves and can be purchased in small sheets approximately 1 foot square.

Modelling Timbers Jelutong, a straw-coloured timber, is the most easily worked wood used in modelling as it has a tight grain and will shape and carve easily. Unfortunately it is not always readily available and we recommend obeche as an excellent alternative.

Obeche is also light in colour with a grain similar to that of mahogany, and in most circumstances it is undetectable from jelutong. Both of these timbers are used extensively for making miniature furniture and architectural mouldings as they leave a good clean edge when sawn or cut and take stain easily.

Mahogany and walnut hardwoods are both used extensively in making miniatures and will give good results when stained and polished but care should be taken to use only those with fine-grain patterns.

Spruce often has a very defined grain that sometimes makes it difficult to work, as although light in colour, the grain is often darker and can show through coloured stains.

We do not recommend the use of balsa wood under any circumstances except for aero-modelling, as it is too soft and open-grained for miniature work.

Most modelling timbers are purchased in pre-planed and sanded sheets, usually 3in or 4in wide x 36in, in a wide variety of thicknesses. The common thicknesses are $^1/16$in (2mm), $^3/32$in (2.5mm) and $^1/8$in (3mm) but larger sizes can be purchased. Although not directly equivalent, both metric and imperial sizes are usually printed on the sheets. A number of specialist suppliers also stock a

Leave the protective coating supplied with Perspex and other transparent materials in place as long as possible as it will make marking out easier and protect the surface from unwanted scratches.

variety of square and moulded sections that can save a great deal of cutting and sanding.

Use a razor saw for hand cutting any of these modelling timbers as this tool leaves a very small 'rag' or rough edge under the cut.

Plastic Card

Plastic styrene sheet (also known as plasticard) is usually available in black and white from most model shops and in a variety of thicknesses, usually quoted in millimetres. This material is very soft and pliable under pressure and care must be taken to avoid the sheet moving whilst being cut. Scoring both sides then snapping along the cut line often proves the best way. A variety of mouldings, usually square or round tubes and beam extrusions, can be purchased ready-made. Use a plastic weld liquid, applied with a small brush, to fix parts together (see adhesives, below).

Perspex and Acetate

Used mainly to mimic glass, Perspex or Plexiglas, is an optically pure material that can be cut and shaped with a knife or saw. The best thickness for most miniature work is approximately $1/16$in but sometimes thicker or thinner materials can produce better results. Manufacturers only sell this in metric measurements and 0.7mm is a reasonable choice for most work. These materials may shatter and produce sharp edges when cut, so use goggles at all times.

Acetate sheeting supplied as clear is not quite optically pure and can take on the appearance of 'old' window glazing much better than its counterpart, Perspex. Available in much thinner sheets than Perspex, this material can easily be cut with a knife or scissors and as it is very flexible it can be used for 'curved' window sections.

There are many trade names for these transparent materials and modern processes have given slight variations in their chemical make up. Throughout the book we refer to 'acetate' and this should be taken to mean a suitable transparent plastic material.

Paper and Card

Art board can be purchased at most art shops in a variety of thicknesses, usually expressed as gsm or grammes per square inch. Paper stock does not usually exceed 120gsm. A wide selection of coloured finishes are available.

Panel Pins, Nails and Screws

Standard sizes found in ironmongers are in metric not imperial. When fixing carcasses together, $3/4$in (18mm) long panel pins will prove to be most useful but shorter pins should be used when working on thinner sections. Longer veneer pins and stronger nails may prove useful for some projects, so have a small selection to hand. A variety of sizes of cross-head screws have been used in the projects, all counter-sunk.

Panel pins will sometimes 'turn' when being hammered into man-made boards and this can be overcome by pre-drilling pilot holes. Pilot holes should always be drilled out for screws or the material may split.

Adhesives

Miniaturists should take care when using any adhesives, especially spirit-based adhesives and 'super glues'. It is recommended that all labels be read first and suitable precautions taken. In all circumstances avoid smoking and naked flames when using any spirit-based adhesive.

PVA Glue There are a variety of PVA glues available and not all of them are suitable for wood. Certain types of PVA are specifically designed for use with paper and card and the properties should be checked before use. Those formulated for wood will say so on their labels. PVA Tacky Glue will stick a number of materials together and provides a quick grab facility that is useful in some situations. Modelling PVA is best for assembling paper and card miniatures. Unless otherwise stated we have used a white PVA fast-acting wood glue for most items in the projects and Evo-stik Resin W proved more than adequate for most tasks. For all other work a clear, spirit-based glue is ideal.

Epoxy Glue   Different materials, such as plastics and metals, are difficult to glue together especially metal to metal, metal to wood or metal to plastic. In all these cases use five-minute rapid epoxy glue for strength. Parts to be joined should be cleaned with a de-natured alcohol first and clamped together wherever possible. Keeping the assembled parts warm will speed the curing times.

Spirit-based Adhesives   These clear glues, e.g. UHU and Clear Bostik, are very useful as they provide a permanent hard joint for many different types of materials. Spread over the two surfaces to be joined together, allow to dry until tacky and then place together for an instant bond.

'Super Glues'   We have mostly avoided the use of any of the so-called 'super glues' in the projects, as traditional adhesives have proved best for us, however they can be useful in some circumstances, provided the manufacturer's instructions are followed.

Plastic Weld Adhesive   This is specially developed for making two styrene plastic surfaces adhere. The adhesive works by literally dissolving the styrene sheets and fusing them together, being drawn into the joints by capillary action. Do not allow this adhesive to get onto your fingers whilst you are handling the parts or you may find fingerprints indented into the surface. Follow the instructions from the manufacturer regarding working with this product and obey those concerning smoking or using near naked flames.

Spray Adhesives   These adhesives are supplied in pressurised cans, used by artists and designers for fixing and positioning paper and card products. Spray Mount allows the materials to be re-positioned but it may not prove to be a permanent solution, especially if the surfaces are uneven. Display Mount or Photo Mount spray adhesives will prove a more permanent alternative.

Modelling Clay

Polymer clay, Fimo, Sculpey and Formello are the trade names of various coloured clays that can be mixed, worked and moulded then hardened in an oven. Used to make a variety of items, these products are especially useful for making flowers, vegetables, plants and fish.

Paints, Stains and Polishes

Emulsion Paints   Vinyl emulsions with a silk finish have been used for most of the exterior and interior painting as they have an easy-clean surface sheen and in some cases we have mixed a little of one colour with another to give a more appropriate shade. The emulsions have been applied directly to raw wooden surfaces, although the first coat may be diluted with 10 percent clean water to provide better adhesion.

Acrylics and Gouache Paints   Used by artists, these can be mixed together to produce any colour or shade and give a matt finish on drying. An acrylic glaze or scumble can be added to give a glaze. These too may be applied to bare wood and acrylics can be used on metal with some success.

Oil-based and Enamel Paints   These paints (e.g. Dulux and Humbrol) are very suitable for any number of jobs and there is a large range of colours and effects. Dilute with the manufacturer's thinners or white spirit. Prime new or bare wood before applying enamel paints. Enamels are at their best when used for painting metal and give a superior finish when used as gloss, but matt finishes are available too.

White spirit and enamel paints have low flash points and are extremely flammable, so avoid smoking and naked flames when using either of these materials.

Brushing a thin coat of PVA adhesive onto bare wood will allow plaster fillers to adhere more permanently. Wood and plaster fillers are also available pre-mixed in handy sized tubes, although you may find that these products dry out quickly.

Spirit-based Wood Stains These are ideal for ageing wooden furniture or faking finishes, obeche as mahogany, for instance and colours can be mixed and diluted using white spirit. Stain will only penetrate into the surfaces of wood that is clean – any spots or lines of glue will show as white. To avoid this, stain all parts in an assembly *before* gluing them together.

French and Button Polishes Available in small cans, these should be applied with a rag or brush, building up coat upon coat until a high gloss finish is obtained. Hard wax furniture polish should be thinly spread over the surface of the miniature with a soft cloth and when dry it should be buffed to give a soft sheen finish. There are a variety of polishes on the market and some contain a colouring agent.

Sanding Sealer This is used primarily in the aero-model hobby but is a very useful sealer for all miniature wooden projects as it acts as a primer and prepares the surfaces for painting as well as giving the surface a degree of strength. Based on cellulose, is it highly flammable and should *never* be used near flames or cigarettes.

Wall and Roof Materials

There are a number of brick, wall and tile finishes available commercially should you decide that you want a more authentic finish to a project. See also Creating Exterior Finishes, page 15.

Bricks for Walls The most easily obtainable material is one of the ready coloured, three-dimensional moulded fibre-glass sheets. These measure approximately 14in x 20in but sizes vary according to the manufacturer. The sheets can be purchased in a variety of brick bonds, or patterns in which the bricks are laid, the most popular probably being English bond, but Flemish and Garden can be used without being incorrect. However, it might be best to determine which bond reflects the area and period in which your project is set. All of these sheets can be cut using a steel rule and sharp craft knife and fixed using one of the PVA adhesives.

Thin sections of scale bricks can be purchased singly or in bags and laid to any bond pattern, again using a PVA glue to fix them to the building. The joints between the brick courses will need to be grouted. Bear in mind the additional weight of a hundred or so brick slips to a frontage.

Printed paper sheets of brick are a very inexpensive way to finish off walls and are easy to apply. There are probably only two readily available finishes, a plain red brick and a mellow brick. The latter is more accurate and therefore preferable. Glue on the sheets using wallpaper paste.

Several rough cast and other random brick finishes are made in fibre-glass sheets and Jingles toy shop shows how to achieve a rough finish using an abrasive paper.

Slate and Tiles for Roofs Roofs in the UK are usually finished with tiles or slates and whilst most slates look very similar, except in size, there are a variety of tiles. Plain, small, red-coloured tiles are best for wooden framed buildings but pantiles, which have a curved interlocking shape, are used extensively in some parts of the country.

Three-dimensional moulded fibre-glass sheets and printed papers can be purchased to mimic most types of slates and tiles but they are not capable of mimicking the pantile shape very well. Fix these two materials using the methods described above for bricks.

At least one manufacturer now offers thin pantiles made from compressed fibres that have been pre-coloured. The laying of these will require considerable attention to detail but should be well worth the effort.

Thatched roofs can be made using a product called 'coir' which can be purchased from a number of miniature outlets. Instructions for making thatch roofs are hard to come by and beyond the scope of this book.

GENERAL TECHNIQUES AND LIGHTING

The shop projects in the book have full instructions for construction and completion but you should also find this section valuable as it is full of useful hints and tips on aspects of finishing *any* shop project. The information here will be particularly helpful if you are planning to complete one of the many shop kits available from specialist suppliers.

In all cases we have used only straightforward and basic materials that can be found in most hardware stores or your favourite miniature shop. No special equipment is required but do read the section on Basic Tools and Materials before embarking on any of the projects. These are not meant to be comprehensive but they will give you some useful ideas and guidance on basic procedures.

CREATING EXTERIOR FINISHES
Using Paint

The easiest way to finish the exterior walls of a shop project is with a suitably coloured emulsion paint applied with a brush or a mini roller. Foam rubber art rollers can be purchased in a number of different widths up to 3in wide.

Start by preparing the surfaces well, filling and rubbing down to remove any blemishes and masking off any window and door frames that are to be painted a different colour. Apply the paint with even strokes and if you are using a roller use a small artist brush as well to take the colour right up to the edge of any frames or corners. Brushes may leave slight criss-cross marks but sponge rollers used with a light touch

will give a fine textured effect that looks very effective (see the upper sides of Luscombe's ironmongery). Keep a small pot of any specially mixed colour for touching up any surfaces as it may be difficult to obtain a perfect match later.

Unless you want a perfect finish to the walls why not introduce a little modelling to the surfaces by streaking a little darker paint to indicate cracks, especially under windowsills. Look at any real building over fifty years old and you will soon see that the most obvious places to reproduce this effect are wherever rain water runs.

Choose a different colour emulsion or acrylic paint, such as a white broken with a little brown ochre, for any door and window frames. Generally speaking, it is not a good idea to use coloured gloss paint as the finish will appear too bright and too hard and this could be visually out of scale. Use instead an oil-based paint with a satin or sheen finish for painting shop doors and the main window fittings. It will be necessary to prime and undercoat these surfaces before applying the paint but any of the water-based acrylic products will be suitable. If you have an unsteady hand, mask off any glazing or abutting woodwork before painting.

Remember to apply paint to sides as well as fronts of buildings and to overlap the paint onto any surfaces that will later be covered with paper or fibre-glass sheets in order to give a neat finish.

Using Brick and Tile Effects

Brick is one of the most predominant finishes for outside walls and the cheapest and the easiest way to achieve this effect is to use

> *White metal kits make inexpensive and accurate additions to your stock. Paint with car spray colours and add highlights with enamels.*

15

one of the commercially produced printed papers. Some of these are a little crude and too obvious to use on a scale model but with a little care the 'mellow' brick paper can look effective. Be sure to clean up the surface first and remove any unsightly bumps and dents, smooth off with a fine abrasive paper and wipe down with a soft, damp cloth. Cut the paper to size and use good quality wallpaper paste to size the walls first. Paste the paper evenly, making sure that the whole of the surface is covered and wait at least two minutes for the paste to penetrate thoroughly. The paper will stretch when wet and shrink back as it dries; applying paper before it has stretched will almost certainly result in bubbles forming below the surface.

A very useful and effective alternative is one of the moulded fibre-glass sheets. These sheets are produced to give various brick patterns, or bonds, and are available in more than one colour finish. Prepare the surfaces in the same way as for paper and

lightly prime with a PVA glue diluted with about 10 percent clean water. Use a good quality PVA glue spread over the surface of the fibre-glass sheet or the wall surface and press into place as accurately as possible as there will be very little chance to re-position it once in place.

Try not to overdo this effect as using it for just half of the frontage will prove much more striking than pasting bricks onto every available surface, unless, of course, you are trying to accurately reproduce an actual building. (See the photograph, below, of the various outside wall finishes and also take a look at the lower sides of Luscombe's ironmongers.)

Covering a Roof

There are a number of ways to cover a roof, whether it is to be tiled, pantiled, slated or finished with shingles. Unlike walls, roofs have different pitches, gables and joints at various angles to take care of and so you will need to plan runs of tiles so that they look natural. It is advisable to spend a little time working this out on a plain sheet of paper before cutting out expensive sheeting.

As with wallpapers there are printed roof papers available in slate and a variety of tiles and pantiles, the latter in red or green. This finish is applied in exactly the same way as for the brick papers described above.

Fibre-glass sheets are also available in slate and tile patterns, all ready coloured. Apply in the same way as paper, making sure that tile runs appear natural and apply in the same way as you would for the brick sheets (see above and also the roofs for Meadows grocer's shop and Pickwick's book shop).

Wooden shingles are supplied with many American dolls' house kits and are more applicable to the houses in that country than those in the UK. Unless the shop or

Examples of brick and roof sheets shown on a cutting mat with miniature paint rollers and a scalpel

house is large the shingles will tend to dominate it as they are usually too thick for 1/12 scale. A useful wooden slate effect is available in strips from some outlets – again though, these look best when applied to large projects rather than small.

Making a Card Roof

To produce a finer and more scaled finish to a roof, thin card can be used to make your own slates or tiles. This has the advantage of being easily cut or shaped and it can also be bent around awkward gulleys and joints in more than one section of the roof. The finished surface will need painting to make it look realistic but this is easily achieved and it has the advantage of looking totally unique to your project. Use an art board sheet with a thickness in the region of 130gsm, available from any good art shop and choose a base colour suitable for the project in mind. For instance, use red for tiles and grey for slate (see Jingles toy shop roof).

To make a card roof, begin by marking up the card sheet into 3/4in wide strips across the longest dimension using an HB pencil and, turning the card at right angles draw a second set of lines, again dividing the card into 3/4in strips (see Fig 14 for Jingles toy shop roof, page 57). These dimensions are given as a guide, however they can be changed to give different tile or slate effects.

Cut the card into strips along the length, first placing it onto a cutting mat. Use a steel rule and sharp knife to keep the lines straight and accurate. Now, take each of the strips and, using your craft knife and steel rule, cut up each of the marked divisions approximately 9/16in to leave each tile attached by a minimum of 3/16in. Reserve sufficient of the long strips uncut to support the first run of tiles, re-cutting these to 3/8in wide. All the tiles on a real roof are rarely perfect, especially on older buildings where they may have been hand-made. Modern tiles and concrete slates are mass-produced by factories and that gives them that boring,

but perfect look. Lay one or two strips down and gently trim the edges of some of the tiles and cut small pieces from some corners. This will give the roof some character showing that it has been weathered or has had workmen clambering about.

Before gluing the tiled strips onto the roof a series of guide lines can be drawn to help avoid crooked rows of tiles. The first line should be 3/8in from the front edge and 3/4in from that row onward.

Using a quick grab adhesive, attach the 3/8in wide uncut strip flush along the front edge of all the roofs to be covered with tiles. The idea of this is to raise the leading edge of the first row of tiles in order to throw off the 'rain'. Select a strip of tiles with a whole tile on the end that is to be placed at the outer edge of the roof and glue this down on top of the uncut strip, overlapping the roof edge by about 1/8in along the face. If your project has a straight roof without joins try to make each end have either a whole tile or a half. Glue on the third strip (that is, the second row of cut tiles) staggering the joins, with the first tile being a half width and overlapping the second row by 3/16in. Repeat this procedure until you reach the top or apex of the roof.

On some roofs the outer tiles alternate between a whole width and a half width, on others the variation is a whole width and one and one half widths. To achieve this it will be necessary to mark up separate sheets or produce and add wide 'edge' tiles in singles, adding a strip of normal width tiles to these (see Jingles toy shop roof).

To produce a simple ridge tile, trim a 1/2in wide uncut strip of card and gently score the underside so that it will fold over the apex of the roof. Use a sharp pencil to score lines at 1in intervals all along the strip and cut through these marks for extra effect before gluing down.

Painting Roofs

There were as many variations on red roof tile colours as there were tile makers in the

Many different paint effects can be achieved by using small amounts of sponge rather than paint-brushes.

If you look at real buildings you will find that they are often imperfect in some way – a guttering hanging off, a small crack in the plasterwork, a plant growing out of the eaves or some bad repairs to brickwork in the wrong colour or brick bond. Introducing just one or two of these to your shop will make a world of difference.

The marking and cutting out of irregular shapes will be easier if you make a template first. Draw the pattern onto a sheet of clean paper and transfer this to thin acetate or stiff card and cut out using a sharp craft knife.

United Kingdom, so it becomes impossible to give a perfect colour mix and you might want to produce yours as grey slates rather than tiles. For a basic red tiled roof first paint the roof with small amounts of black and white acrylic paints applied in a random fashion with a nearly dry brush. Try not to make this a regular pattern or cover the roof but push 'splashes' of paint into cracks and crevices. Mix up small amounts of brown and black acrylic paint with sufficient amounts of a suitable red to cover the roof and apply over the whole of the roof including the splashes. You should notice that the spots of colour show through to give a broken effect. Adding tiny spots of white for bird lime or green for moss and lichen will enliven the roof and make it look more realistic (see Jingles toy shop roof).

INTERIOR DECORATION

The type of interior finish will need to reflect the type of trade you have selected for your shop. A pretty wallpaper might look very good in a milliners but be completely out of place in a butchers. The choice of colours and finishes is enormous but we can give some guidance here. Remember that for foodstuffs you need, by and large, a bright and easily cleaned surface. However, this is not always so, just look at Meadows the grocers for a very fancy but appropriate wallpaper. Shops that are intended for purchases of a more personal nature, clothing and hats for example, need to be cosy, warm and above all elegant and restrained. No clashing colour schemes and as much comfortable furniture as you can manage in the space available. A butcher will have some of the walls tiled, as might some grocers. Ironmongers and most practical shops need to have plain paint finishes. Unusual shops such as The Clarence tea rooms can have unusual paint finishes and colour schemes according to the style of the period.

Flooring is an area that is quite important in a shop project and will vary according to the trade. Food shops used a large amount of glazed encaustic tiles for floors laid into elaborate geometric patterns (see Meadows the Grocers). These floors were often covered in a layer of fine sawdust in order to pick up street dirt and dropped food, which was then swept out at the end of the day. The more practical shops would have left the floorboards bare, as rough workman's boots would soon destroy any linoleum that had been laid. The ladies shops would have run to carpet but shops selling cloth and materials by the yard were more likely to have had polished floorboards.

CUTTING OUT APERTURES

The shop models in the book have various apertures, mainly for windows and doors. The fastest and most accurate way of cutting any window aperture within a sheet of MDF or plywood is to use a powered router with a 'plunging' mechanism and a set of guides or templates. There are a number of these tools available, each capable of taking one or more shaped cutter. Good quality cutters, particularly those tipped with tungsten carbide will leave a smooth, clean edge that will require very little finishing. To cut through sheet timber of 9mm ($^3/_8$in) or less the cutter needs to be at least 9mm diameter, although it may be possible to do it using smaller cutters and several passes. Powered routers are liable to 'wander' and holding a straight line can therefore be difficult, thus the use of guides and specially cut templates is very much recommended. These tools always leave rounded corners at each right angle and they should be squared off using a sharp chisel.

A useful alternative is to use a powered jig or scroll saw. These tools hold short saw blades in a vertical position and using a reciprocating action can saw through quite thick material. They do need competent guidance however to hold a straight line.

For those wishing to cut apertures out of MDF and plywood sheet by hand the best method is to use a pad or keyhole saw. Start in the normal way by marking up the hole using a try square. Use a sharp craft knife to score along all the lines and do this on the under side too if you are confident that it will match those on the top surface. Drill a 3/8in wide hole into two opposite corners, say bottom left and top right, and gently saw away from one hole first along one line then along the other. Repeat this action from the second hole and the centre of the aperture should drop out.

USING WHITE METAL KITS

These useful and usually very accurately modelled kits can and do make very attractive additions to any shop, especially when modified or altered in some way to make your version different from the standard. There is a range of shop fittings, such as cash registers and scales (see Luscombes and Meadows) and many pieces that can be used for stock in a number of trades.

The component parts of these kits are produced by pouring hot liquid metal into moulds and this sometimes results in small slivers of waste material, called flash, appearing along the edges. Clean all this off with a sharp craft knife or file before proceeding and dry fit all the parts together before attempting the final assembly. Check all right-angled parts with a small try square and correct with a file as necessary, then clean out any 'blind' holes with a drill bit or rat tail file. At all costs avoid scratching the surfaces that show, as this will be difficult to smooth over or fill later. Check the manufacturer's instructions at this point and paint any parts that may prove difficult to reach after assembly.

The components can be assembled using a two-part epoxy adhesive or a low-melt solder – the latter will require the use of a special flux but it does give a stronger joint. Clean off all the surfaces with de-natured alcohol and lay the parts out onto a clean, flat surface ready for assembly. Prop any upright pieces together using Blu-Tack or Plasticine and build up following the manufacturer's instructions using one of the

adhesives suggested above.

It is important to clean off flux residues from soldered parts using warm soapy water. Rinse clean and allow them to dry thoroughly before painting. Remove any excess epoxy glue with a sharp craft knife.

Applying a primer coat of paint will assist the adhesion of the final coating and give superior results. For bright, hard finishes brush on a suitable coloured enamel paint or spray finish using products produced for automobiles. Acrylic paints are a good alternative but give a flat colour.

LIGHTING

Successful lighting is an important component of any realistic dolls' house or shop scene. There are many wonderful lighting systems including one that works by remote control and several that give flickering effects. We have deliberately chosen not to deal with anything more than the straightforward basics here as listing and explaining every device and fitting available would be a book in itself. There are lighting specialists who issue booklets and videos to help the miniaturist use their fittings. Look in the various dolls' house magazines for sources.

Preparing for Lighting

Cutting and drilling for lighting systems is much easier whilst all the parts are still laid flat on a work bench, so plan ahead. Hidden lighting means hidden wiring and you will need to work out the best way to organise the wiring. Perhaps you will need to cut special grooves or drill holes in awkward places. For example, is copper tape going to be easily concealed? Which is the best way to run the wiring – along the base of the walls or along the joint of ceiling and walls?

Positioning centre lights is not difficult, simply drill a small hole into the floor, before it is attached to the building, and cut a shallow groove across it to the back wall. A small hole will then need to be drilled through the wall for the wiring to pass out to the back of the building and this can

When drilling into MDF or white metal, use a pointed metal punch to make a starter hole for the drill. Fine grade oil will assist when drilling into metals.

easily be disguised with a skirting board. Work out now how you will connect any lamps attached to the fascia to your transformer or power source. Meadows the Grocer has two lamps connected in this way and uses a combination of round wire supplied with the lamps and copper tape on the walls. In this case a small amount of wire may be visible but in the case of Pickwicks book shop it is simply passed under the building.

Throughout this book we have used the standard UK 12 volt DC system, with both round wire and flat copper tape. In order to use this method of lighting it is necessary to step down, or reduce, the household circuit of 240 volts to a safe 12 volts. There are other lighting systems using three and four volt power supplies, either stepped down from 240 volts or used via a battery, the principles of wiring and circuits remain the same as for 12 volt – using batteries for a 12-volt system is expensive and unnecessary. Bulbs with different ratings cannot be successfully mixed within one circuit without introducing components beyond the scope of this book. Under *no* circumstances should dolls' house circuits be connected directly to the main supply.

Power Sources

In Britain, transformers simply change the household supply of 240 volt to a safe 12 volts via a convenient wall socket. The standard output rating is 1 ampere (or amp) although 2 amp models are available. The size of unit required will depend on the number of bulbs, not lamps, used and the total rating of all the bulbs, generally 1 ampere models will light 15 to 18 standard 65MA (milliampere) bulbs without noticeable dimming. Choose a transformer with an automatic safety cut out, in case of overload, and rated for a constant 12 volts. Transformers made for calculators and other electrical equipment often have outputs of less than 1 amp and a voltage rating that is variable within a setting, although this may not be detectable without metering. Models

that give out 9 volts will make the bulbs dimmer than usual but prolong their life; conversely an output of 16 volts will drastically shorten their working life and it is worth paying a little more for the correct model.

Batteries We do not recommend the use of batteries to achieve 12 volts on the grounds of cost, size and convenience.

Round Wire This is the basic wire to be found in the average lighting system. Usually made from copper and coated with a protective plastic sheath, it is purchased as two wires joined together to form a twin flex. This wire is also connected to bulb holders and other wiring systems using screw fittings or solder. The flex is very small but needs to be hidden from view by using specially cut channels or running behind mouldings or under carpets.

Copper Tape A great deal of mystery surrounds this tape although it is in fact easy to use and make connections to. A very versatile material, it can be easily hidden beneath wallpaper and run up walls, across ceilings or floors and is easily joined together. Supplied as a very flat pure copper strip it is usually 3/16in wide x 0.00125in thick and is wound onto a circular coil and coated with a self-adhesive inner side protected with a peel-off paper cover. Standard reels have one single strip but, as with round wire, two strips are required to make a circuit. Several manufacturers supply copper tape reels with two strips set at a constant distance apart. The only disadvantage of the double tape is that it is mounted on a thin carrier sheet and covered by a second, making tape runs thicker and more detectable under wallpapers than single tape, which uses no carrier. Single tape runs can be run in any direction as long as two are used for each circuit. Joints to runs of tape can be soldered or forced using hollow brass eyelets. It is easier to solder single tape to single tape than to join two pieces of double tape.

Before applying wallpaper over tape runs it is advisable to coat the surface of the tape with a matt varnish or cover it with thin adhesive tape, as the copper may react with chemicals contained in the paste and show as staining through the paper when dry. Most double tapes are already coated but if any part has been bared then re-covering it is recommended.

Lamps or Lights

Lamps come in a variety of shapes and designs – from a simple round ceiling globe to intricate chandeliers and wall fittings. Some have a single bulb and others have many, each actual bulb counting towards the rating or transformer required. Most are supplied with two wire tails that can be as long as 18in, and fitted with a removable two-pin plug. The methods of fitting lamps to walls and ceilings vary and some of these are explained later. Specialist lighting makers may supply their own fittings.

The soft glow of wall lighting creates an inviting ambience in The Clarence tea rooms

Bulbs

Replaceable 12 volt miniature bulbs are available in a number of physical sizes but not all lamps are capable of taking a replacement easily and therefore you should check with the supplier before purchasing bulbs. Renewing bulbs may mean dismantling wiring and lamps or, in some cases, returning the unit to the manufacturer. Most bulbs used with dolls' house systems are rated at 65MA, and approximately fifteen bulbs can be run from a 1 ampere transformer (15 x 0.65 = 0.975amp).

Grain of Wheat Bulbs These are very useful little bulbs; supplied with a two-wire tail of 4in or more in length they need to be fed through a lamp shade.

Candle Bulbs These are fitted with a tiny screw thread matching the bulb holder. They are sometimes difficult to tighten or remove but can be eased out with the help of a small diameter plastic tube.

Pea Bulbs Fitted with a screw thread matching the bulb holder, pea bulbs may be removed in the same manner as candle bulbs.

Other Lighting Components

Eyelets Small brass eyelets are used to join two runs of tape together; larger eyelets are used to take two-pin plugs found at the end of lamp wiring. Drill a small pilot hole into the carcass material before hammering home the eyelet.

Power Strip This is a simple extension unit, providing a convenient way of connecting to the transformers and giving a number of plug-in outlets for lamps.

Brass Pins These are useful for making simple joins and fixing lamp wires to copper tape. Simply wind the bared wire around the pin, clean off the surface of the tape and hammer home.

Grain of wheat, candle, pea and flicker are all types of bulb available in 12 volt in Britain but the fittings on these all vary. Check what you need before asking for replacements. 12 volt bulbs used with a 9 volt transformer will last longer, while using a 16 volt transformer will drastically shorten the life of the bulbs. Do not mix bulbs rated at 3.6 volts with 12 volts in the same circuit.

THE SHOPKEEPER'S RESOURCE

As with all miniature models, shops only come truly alive when they are dressed with all the paraphernalia of real life. This section provides instructions for making an interesting and wide range of fixtures and fittings that would be suitable for most dolls' house shops. Many of them can be mixed and matched, such as the decorative display units. This section also includes some small items of stock to help fill your shop.

When making the fixtures and fittings described in this section, use a PVA wood glue when gluing or adhesive is mentioned, unless stated otherwise. Using a jig or a clamping system will allow pieces to be glued at right angles to each other without marking the faces of the timber.

FITTING OUT

Before proceeding any further make a full-sized floor plan of your shop. Make adequate notes of where stairs or walls are and leave an allowance for doors to open in the correct direction. Cut out a series of paper templates for counters and shelves and move these

around the plan to find the best location and layout for your shop. Don't place counters and shelves in such a way that the assistant cannot get behind them. Hanging signs and lights should not be so low that the miniature customers will bump their heads. Once you are satisfied that you have a working layout you can compare yours with those in the five shop projects featured in the book to see if there is anything that you have missed out or might incorporate. There is no reason why some of the designs and sizes provided here can't be altered to fit your shop – it is usually just a matter of altering one or two measurements.

Angled Counter

This counter, found in Luscombe's ironmongers, is a good counter for many different shops, although it is probably best suited for a hardware establishment. Robustly built, it has a big top for larger items and an angled front that allows customers wearing hobnailed boots to stand close without damaging the timber. There is a shelf at the back for catalogues and ledgers. A drawer could be added if required. It has been made from a standard 6in length of pre-planed mahogany but it could be made from obeche and stained any colour desired.

MATERIALS

- Mahogany pieces as follows:
  Top 1/8in x 2 1/2in x 6in
  Front 1/8in x 2 13/16in x 5 5/8in
  Side 1/8in x 2in x 2 3/4in, 2 off
  Shelf 3/32in x 1 13/16in x 5 3/8in

Cut the top from 1/8in thick mahogany 2 1/2in wide x 6in long and square off all the edges ensuring that they are all at right angles to each other (see Fig 1).

The useful angled-front counter, as used in Luscombes ironmongers

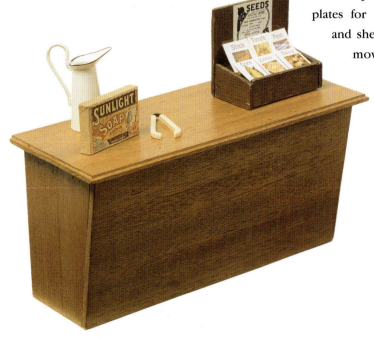

Set a circular saw for a $1/16$in depth of cut and cut a $1/16$in wide rebate along the two sides and the front of the top piece to form the moulded edge. Alternatively, place the top into a small bench vice and use a sharp razor saw to cut a $1/16$in deep slot on the outer edge of all three sides, $1/16$in from the top face. Lay the top onto a flat surface and make the corresponding right-angled cut, again using the razor saw or a scalpel with a steel rule as a guide. Remove the waste and clean up the rebate. Wrap a piece of fine abrasive paper around a small wood offcut and lightly round off the bottom outer edge of the rebate, being careful not to do this to the top.

Cut a strip of $1/8$in thick mahogany $2^{13}/16$in wide x $5^5/8$in long for the front of the counter and square off the edges as before. Place this into a bench vice with one long edge uppermost and then set an adjustable square to 10 degrees using a protractor. Use a small block plane to carefully produce a 10 degree bevel to the top edge, checking with the adjustable square. Remove this piece and turn it over so that you can make a second angled cut. Make sure that this second cut is correctly made to produce a complementary angle, that is, both cuts should face the same way, to make a lozenge shape not a pyramid.

Cut two sides, each $1/8$in thick x 2in wide x $2^3/4$in long. Using the adjustable bevel set at 10 degrees mark off each of the sides so that the top of each side remains at 2in and the base is $1^1/2$in (see Fig 1). You may substitute these measurements instead of using the adjustable bevel if you wish. Cut off the waste, keeping the edges nice and square. Place the sides together and check that the sloping sides are equal, adjusting if necessary. Glue each of the two sides onto the front, so that they sit behind it. Check that they sit at right angles and support if necessary. The front should not show the edges of the two sides but appear as one piece. This assembly should now represent a wide U shape. When the adhesive has set, gently

sand off the sides so that they blend in with the front. Do not apply too much pressure or the edge may distort and the side(s) might become detached.

Turn the assembly over so that it sits on the two sides, now looking like a wide inverted U. Place this onto a flat work surface and glue on the top so that it is flush to the back of the counter – there should be a $3/16$in overlap of the top to the front and each of the sides.

Cut a shelf from $3/32$in thick mahogany, $1^{13}/16$in wide x $5^3/8$in long and check all the sides are at right angles to each other. Place this in a bench vice and use a block plane to shape one long edge to a 10 degree bevel to match the sloping front. Glue this into the back of the counter 1in down from the top, with the bevel matching the front.

To finish off this piece, gently smooth down all the surfaces and blend in all the joints. The surface of the counter should be aged and distressed at this stage if required. Rather than making large dents or cuts into the surface, use a black ink pen and add a number of small 'fake' knots and dents with tiny spots of ink to those surfaces that show, but try not to overdo this effect. Finish off with two or three coats of a good quality wax polish, buffing up each layer with a stiff brush to produce a soft sheen. The wood may be stained first to give it a more antique appearance, in which case it would be best to stain all the parts before assembly, not afterwards.

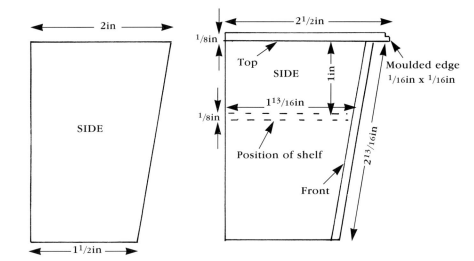

FIG 1
Angled counter

Counters can be given complicated moulded edges to tops by cutting them $1/16$in short all round and adding a commercial moulding, mitred at the corners.

Plain Counter with Drawer

This counter is used in Luscombe's ironmongers but is an ideal counter for just about any standard shop as it is very workmanlike and designed to last for years. At the rear there is a shelf and a large drawer for the shopkeeper to keep all the odds and ends, catalogues and ledgers. Constructed in a standard 6in length using pre-planed timber it has been made from mahogany but obeche could be used and stained any colour. If you wish, the drawer described here could be made as an addition to the Angled Counter on page 22.

MATERIALS

- Mahogany pieces as follows:
  Top $1/8$in x 2in x 6in
  Front $1/8$in x $2^5/8$in x $5^5/8$in
  Side $1/8$in x $2^5/8$in x $1^3/4$in, 2 off
  Shelf $1/8$in x $1^3/4$in x $5^3/8$in
  Divider $1/8$in x $1^3/4$in x $7/8$in
  Drawer front $3/32$in x $7/8$in x $1^1/2$in
  Drawer back $3/32$in x $1^1/2$in
  Drawer sides $3/32$in x $7/8$in x $1^9/16$in, 2 off
- Drawer base $1/16$in obeche x $1^9/16$in x $1^5/16$in
- $3/32$in diameter brass knob

The back view of the plain counter showing the drawer and shelf – complete with the shop cat

Cut the top from $1/8$in thick mahogany 2in wide x 6in long and square off all the edges ensuring that they are all at right angles to each other (see Fig 2, page 25). Create the moulded edge by following the instructions for the Angled Counter.

Cut a strip of $1/8$in thick mahogany $2^5/8$in wide x 10in long. From this cut the front of the counter $5^5/8$in long, squaring off edges as before. Cut two sides, each $1^3/4$in long. Glue the two sides onto the front, one at a time, so that they sit behind it when assembled. Check that they sit at right angles and adjust as necessary. (The front should not show the edges of the two sides but appear as one piece.) This assembly should now represent a wide U shape. When the adhesive has set, gently sand off the sides so that they blend in with the front. Do not apply too much pressure or the edge may distort and the side might become detached from the front. Turn the assembly over so that it sits on the two sides, place this onto a flat work surface and glue it to the top so that the top is flush to the sides at the back of the counter. There should be a $1/8$in overlap of the top to the front and $3/16$in at each of the sides.

Carefully measure off the inside dimension of the counter when viewed from the back, this should be $5^3/8$in, and cut a shelf from $1/8$in thick mahogany $1^3/4$in wide x $5^3/8$in long. The position of the shelf is $1/8$in from the top (see Fig 2A). To ensure that it sits level across the width of the counter make two pieces of any timber offcut 2in x $7/8$in wide. Turn the counter over so that it sits on its top and place an offcut at either end so that the shelf can rest temporarily on these whilst it is glued into position. Cut the divider $1/8$in thick x $1^3/4$in x $7/8$in and glue this $1^1/2$in from the right-hand side, flush to the back, keeping it upright and at right angles to the shelf.

The nominal size of the drawer aperture is $1^1/2$in x $7/8$in, and the completed drawer will need to be reduced by about $1/64$in all round to enable it to slide in and out easily.

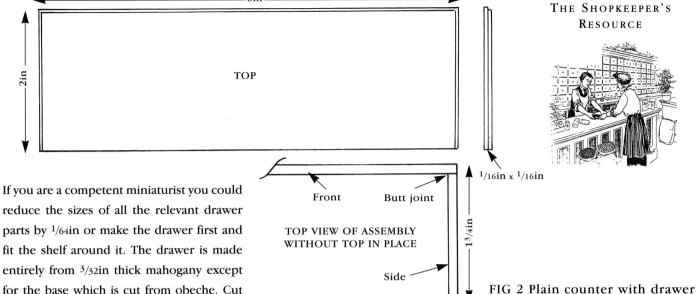

6in

2in

TOP

1/16in x 1/16in

Front   Butt joint

TOP VIEW OF ASSEMBLY
WITHOUT TOP IN PLACE

1³/4in

Side

FIG 2 Plain counter with drawer

If you are a competent miniaturist you could reduce the sizes of all the relevant drawer parts by ¹/64in or make the drawer first and fit the shelf around it. The drawer is made entirely from ³/32in thick mahogany except for the base which is cut from obeche. Cut the pieces as detailed in the Materials list on page 24 and square them all off. Find the dead centre of the drawer front and drill a ¹/16in diameter hole for the drawer knob (it will also prove very useful for retrieving a tight-fitting drawer during trial fitting).

Lay the parts out onto a flat work surface with the inner surfaces uppermost in the manner of the exploded drawing (Fig 2B). All the outer parts, except the base, are the same height and are assembled and glued around the base and for this reason it is important that the base is cut as accurately as possible and that all sides are at right angles. Dry fitting all parts before gluing will highlight any potential trouble spots and allow you to correct them before gluing the parts together. Clamp the parts together and assemble as follows: stand the back upright and glue the base to it leaving an equal over-lap either side, add the two sides and then the front. The sizes given provide for a near perfect fit into the drawer casing, especially on the height so the finished drawer may need a little sanding down to make it slide in and out easily – this is best done on a flat surface with a sheet of fine abrasive paper.

The surface should be aged and distressed at this stage if required, and then finished in the same way as for the Angled Counter on page 23.

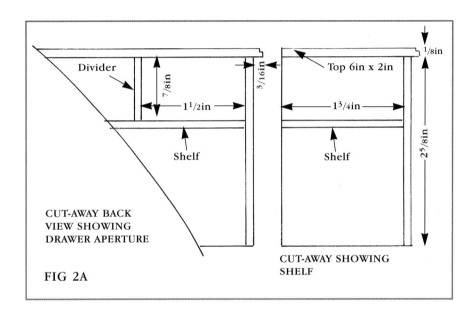

Divider

7/8in

1¹/2in

3/16in

Top 6in x 2in

1/8in

1³/4in

Shelf

Shelf

2⁵/8in

CUT-AWAY BACK
VIEW SHOWING
DRAWER APERTURE

CUT-AWAY SHOWING
SHELF

FIG 2A

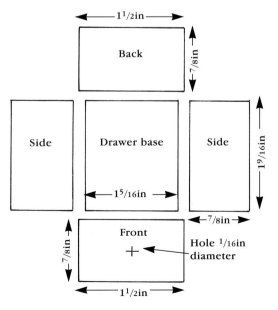

1¹/2in

Back

7/8in

Side   Drawer base   Side

1⁹/16in

1⁵/16in

7/8in

7/8in

Front

Hole ¹/16in
diameter

1¹/2in

Exploded view of drawer parts   FIG 2B   25

Glass-Topped Counter

This counter was used in Jingles toy shop, but would be ideal for any number of trades dealing with fine pieces, such as a milliners or sweet shop.

MATERIALS

- Mahogany pieces as follows:
  Front frame – A & B $1/8$in x $3/8$in x $5^3/8$in each
  C & D $1/8$in x $3/8$in x $2^7/8$in each
  Side $1/8$in x $1^3/4$in x $2^7/8$in, 2 off
  Base $1/8$in x $1^3/4$in x $5^7/8$in
  Top frame – E & F $1/8$in x $5/16$in x $6^1/4$in each
  G & H $1/8$in x $5/16$in x 2in each
  Shelf supports $3/32$in x $1/8$in x $1^5/8$in, 2 off
- Glazing 0.7mm acetate 6in x 6in (for front, top and shelf)

The framework is best produced using a circular saw to cut away timber sections. If this tool is not available to you and you don't feel confident enough to cut it with a hand saw we suggest you use $1/16$in thick timber as a base and glue on an additional $1/16$in thick layer to produce the required rebated profiles (see the small detail of Fig 3).

This toy shop counter clearly shows off stock to best advantage

The front framework is made up of pieces A, B, C and D. Piece A is cut from $1/18$in thick mahogany, $3/8$in wide x $5^3/8$in long. A rebated strip $1/8$in wide x $1/16$in deep is machined away from one long face of the material to leave $1/4$in (see Fig 3). Frame pieces C and D are cut in the same way, $2^7/8$in long. Piece B is cut to the same length as frame A but a rebated strip $1/4$in wide x $1/16$in deep is machined away to leave a $1/8$in strip.

Glue pieces A, B, C and D together with butt joints, using a suitable flat surfaced bench jig, with the rebates on the inside and pointing to the centre, to form a rectangle. The amount of material at each joint is quite small at this stage and care must be taken when handling. Check that all is square.

Cut the base from $1/18$in thick mahogany, $1^3/4$in deep x $5^7/8$in long and mark up a $1/8$in x $1/8$in notch into the two front corners. The front locates against the rebates cut into uprights C and D with the notch providing a fit against the remainder of C and D.

Cut the two sides from $1/8$in thick mahogany, $1^3/4$in x $2^7/8$in high. Lay the framework face down with the rebates showing uppermost and glue the two sides on each outer edge, flush at the sides. Glue the base into place at the same time. The front edge of the base rests into the rebate of frame B and is therefore $1/8$in above the bottom. Leave this part-assembly until the glue has set really hard and it is safe to handle without damage or distortion.

Cut the two shelf supports from $3/32$in thick mahogany, $1/8$in x $1^5/8$in and glue in position $1^1/8$in above the base.

The top frame is made from pieces E, F, G and H (see Fig 3A). Begin by preparing a strip of $1/8$in thick mahogany $5/16$in wide x 18in long and machine a $1/16$in wide x $1/16$in deep rebate down one side. Cut two pieces E and F, $6^1/4$in long with a 45 degree mitre at each end. Cut two more pieces, G and H, 2in long with matching mitres at both ends. Place piece E with the rebate uppermost onto the top of frame A with a $1/8$in overlap to the front and glue into this position.

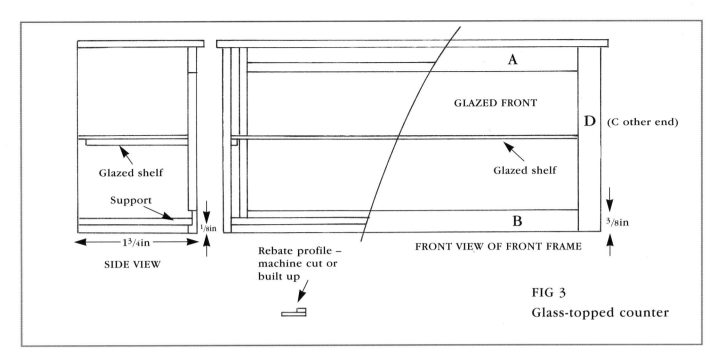

FRONT VIEW OF FRONT FRAME

FIG 3
Glass-topped counter

SIDE VIEW

Glazed shelf

Support

1/8in

1³/4in

Rebate profile –
machine cut or
built up

GLAZED FRONT

A

D (C other end)

Glazed shelf

B

3/8in

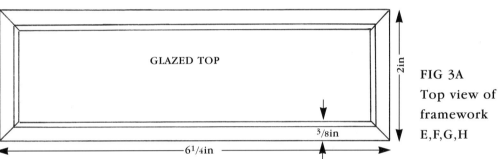

GLAZED TOP

2in

6¹/4in

3/8in

FIG 3A
Top view of
framework
E,F,G,H

Hold with a suitable clamp and add pieces G, H and F to form a rectangular top with the rebate uppermost.

To finish off the piece gently smooth down all the surfaces and blend in all the joints. Brush on a clear or dark furniture polish and buff up to a soft sheen using a stiff brush. The wood may be stained first to give it a more antique appearance in which case it would be best to stain all the parts before assembly, not after.

Adding the Glazing

The first piece of acetate to cut is the piece that fits into the front frame, checking that your measurement matches 2⁵/16in x 5⁵/8in and adjusting if necessary. Place the acetate inside the counter to rest in the rebates of the frame A through to D, sitting on top of the base. The acetate shelf can be cut to fit between the supports and flush to the front glazing 1¹/4in deep x 5⁷/8in wide. The top piece of acetate should be 1¹/16in x 5³/4in. Check this before cutting to make sure yours is a snug fit and drop it into the rebates formed in the top by parts J through to M. Your counter is now finished and ready to be stocked.

Counter with Sneeze Top

This counter is used in The Clarence Tea Rooms. The benefit of this unit is that the 'glassed'-in area shows off the delicate cakes available at The Clarence, allowing the customers to choose without actually touching the goods. These are known in the shop fitting trade as 'sneeze counters' – for obvious reasons. The counter could also be used in a grocer's or other shop where food requiring protection is sold.

MATERIALS
- 1/8in thick obeche pieces as follows:
  Front 5in x 1¹/2in
  Side 1³/8in x 1¹/2in, 2 off
  Top 5in x 1¹/2in
- Styrene plastic card top inlay 1/16in thick x 1¹/2in x 5in
- Commercial moulding 3/32in thick x 5/16in x 9in (total)

27

A sneeze-topped counter protects a range of cakes and delicacies

strip to fit along the front of the counter, mitring each end at 45 degrees. The inner part of the moulding should measure 5in long. Cut two pieces of moulding for the sides, with matching mitres. Glue these three pieces onto the counter so that 1/16in sits above the surface (see Fig 4).

This part of the counter can now be painted. In The Clarence Tea Rooms it was painted to match the walls and decor, however any paint finish would be acceptable. It could be stained a dark antique colour if required.

To make the white top, cut the piece of 1/16in thick styrene plastic card 5in x 11/2in to fit snugly behind the edge of the moulding.

Making the Sneeze Top

Following Fig 4A cut the front and two sides from the 0.7mm acetate sheet. Now cut the two 1/8in wide shelf support strips and glue these into position using a plastic weld adhesive (see page 13 for handling). Cut the top from acetate, 1in x 5in. Use a bench jig to glue the front and top to the two sides as shown in Fig 4A, noting that the sides are placed 1/8in from each end of the top. Check the measurement between the two sides and cut the shelf to this length x 11/4in wide. Glue onto the shelf supports.

Now simply place the 'glass' sneeze counter on to the white styrene top inlay and fill with cakes and delicacies to complete.

- Sneeze top parts from 0.7mm acetate, 24sq in approx.
- Plastic weld adhesive

Cut a strip of 1/8in thick obeche x 11/2in wide and cut the front and two sides from this – 5in long for the front and 13/8in long for each side (see Fig 4). Lay all three pieces onto a bench jig and use a PVA adhesive to glue together so that the sides lay on top of the front to form a wide upturned U shape. Cut the top 5in x 11/2in wide and glue this down onto the part-assembly of front and sides. Smooth off any rough edges and blend the edge of the front into the sides.

Cut a piece from the 5/16in wide moulded

FIG 4
Counter with sneeze top

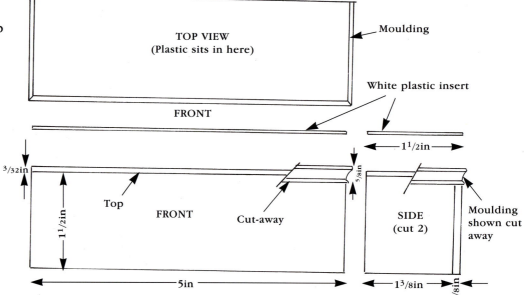

TOP VIEW
(Plastic sits in here)

Moulding

White plastic insert

FRONT

3/32in

11/2in

Top

FRONT

Cut-away

5/8in

11/2in

SIDE
(cut 2)

Moulding shown cut away

5in

13/8in

1/8in

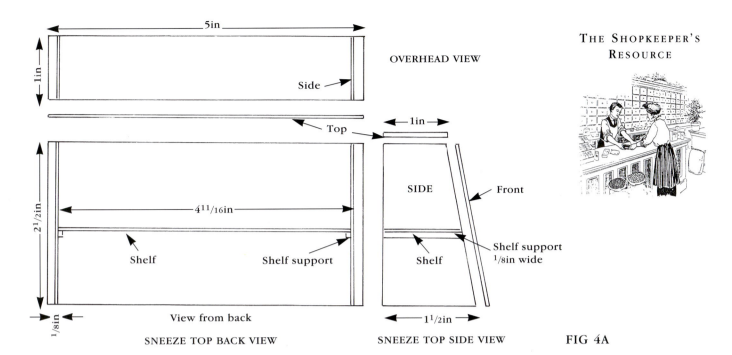

5in

1in

Side

OVERHEAD VIEW

Top

1in

SIDE

Front

$2^1/2$in

$4^{11}/16$in

Shelf

Shelf support

Shelf

Shelf support
$1/8$in wide

$1/8$in

View from back

$1^1/2$in

SNEEZE TOP BACK VIEW

SNEEZE TOP SIDE VIEW

FIG 4A

Delicatessen Counter

This fixture can be found in Meadows grocer's shop in two different lengths but it is suitable for any shop serving food. It is a bold unit, rather taller than some but an ideal height for showing and serving from. The sneeze counter simply sits on the top. The counter can be made up to any reasonable size simply by extending the lengths of the relevant parts.

MATERIALS

- Mahogany pieces as follows:
  Front $1/8$in x 6in x $2^3/4$in
  Side $1/8$in x $1^5/8$in x $2^3/4$in, 2 off
  Top $3/32$in x $1^7/8$in x $6^1/4$in
  Top moulding $1/16$in x $3/16$in x 12in
  Front and side column mouldings
  $3/32$in x $1/4$in x 12in (total)
- White styrene plastic card top inlay $1/16$in x $1^5/8$in x $5^3/4$in
- Sneeze top parts from 0.7mm acetate 24sq in
- Plastic weld adhesive

Cut the top from $3/32$in mahogany, $6^1/4$in x $1^7/8$in, squaring up all the sides and removing any rough edges. Cut the front from $1/8$in thick mahogany, 6in x $2^3/4$in, and two sides $1^5/8$in x $2^3/4$in. Square up the sides on all pieces and glue the two sides onto the

back of the front, flush top and bottom to form an upturned U-shaped assembly. Glue the top down onto this assembly with $1/8$in overhanging the front edge.

Prepare the 12in mahogany strip for the front and side column mouldings as one piece as it will be easier to machine cut the reeded slots into this rather than four separate pieces. Use a circular saw to run a $1/32$in deep slot, $1/32$in from the edge (see Fig 5).

The delicatessen counter, with sneeze top covering cut meats and cheeses

29

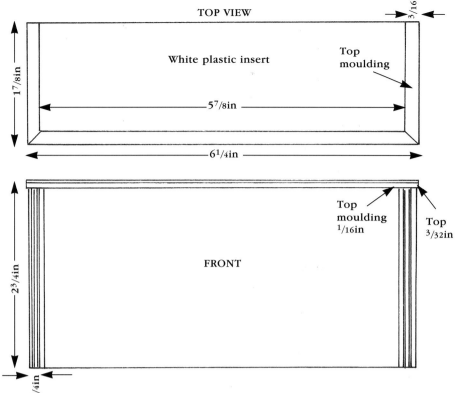

TOP VIEW

White plastic insert

Top moulding

$17/8$in

$57/8$in

$61/4$in

$3/16$in

FRONT

Top moulding $1/16$in

Top $3/32$in

$23/4$in

$1/4$in

FIG 5
Delicatessen counter

Brush on a clear or dark furniture polish and brush up to a soft sheen using a stiff brush. The wood may be stained first to give it a more antique appearance in which case it would be best to stain all the parts before assembly, not after.

Make the top inlay from $1/16$in white plastic card sheet, $15/8$in x $53/4$in, and lay this behind the top moulding to fit flush on all three sides.

Making the Sneeze Top

Using 0.7mm acetate throughout and plastic weld for gluing, start by cutting out the front, $11/2$in (trimmed as required) x $53/4$in, and two sides each $11/8$in x $13/8$in (see Fig 5A). Cut the angled front onto both sides as shown in the diagram. Cut the top from acetate, 1in x 6in. Use plastic weld adhesive to glue all the parts together being very careful not to let it run outside the area being assembled (see page 13 for handling). Lay the front down onto a clean surface and glue the two sides into place flush with the outer edges. Support them in an upright position and check with a small set square. Once this assembly has set sufficiently to allow it to be handled you can glue on the top. The best way to do this is to lay the top down onto a flat working surface and place the front and sides onto it leaving a $1/8$in gap at the front and both sides.

Once all the parts are dry and set, the sneeze top can be placed on the counter and the unit filled with foodstuffs.

Turn the strip around and cut a second matching slot on the same side but opposite edge. Cut the strip into four pieces each $23/4$in long. Glue two of these to the front at each end overlapping by $3/32$in and add the second pair behind them, this time on the sides to form a corner moulding.

Cut a 12in strip of $1/16$in thick mahogany $3/16$in wide. Cut one length to fit the front edge of the counter, mitring each end at 45 degrees. Cut the two side pieces each with one 45 degree mitre and glue all three down as a framework on the top, flush with the outer edges.

To finish off this part, gently smooth down all the surfaces and blend in all the joints.

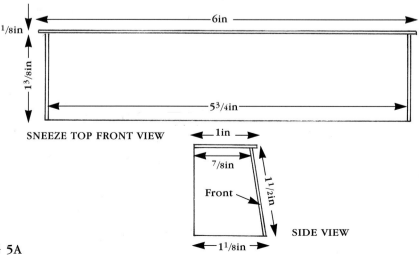

6in

$1/8$in

$13/8$in

$53/4$in

SNEEZE TOP FRONT VIEW

1in

$7/8$in

Front

$11/2$in

$11/8$in

SIDE VIEW

FIG 5A

Display Unit with Shelves

This unit is made up in two parts, the top sitting on top of the base unit. The top unit can used with the fancy display bases (see page 33).

MATERIALS

BASE UNIT

- Mahogany pieces as follows:
  Back $1/8$in x $2^7/8$in x $5^1/4$in
  Side $1/8$in x $1^3/8$in x $2^7/8$in, 2 off
  Top $1/8$in x $1^1/2$in x $5^1/2$in
  Bottom $1/8$in x $5^1/4$in x $1^1/4$in
  Shelf $3/32$in x $1^1/4$in x $5^1/4$in
  Divider $3/32$in x $1^1/4$in x $2^1/2$in
  Skirt board $1/16$in x $3/8$in x $5^1/2$in

TOP SHELVING UNIT

- Mahogany pieces as follows:
  Back $1/8$in x $5^1/4$in x $4^1/2$in
  Side $1/8$in x 1in x $4^1/2$in, 2 off
  Top $3/32$in x $1^1/4$in x $5^1/2$in
  Pelmet $1/16$in x $3/8$in x $5^1/2$in
  Shelf $3/32$in x 1in x $5^1/4$in, 3 off
  Divider $3/32$in x 1in x $3^1/2$in

MAKING THE BASE UNIT

Cut the back from $1/8$in mahogany, $2^7/8$in x $5^1/4$in. To make this in one piece it may be necessary to have the grain running horizontally as timber is usually sold in widths up to 4in. Alternatively glue two pieces together with a simple butt join, each $2^5/8$in wide x $2^7/8$in with the grain running vertically.

Cut two sides from $1/8$in thick mahogany, each $1^3/8$in wide x $2^7/8$in high, (grain running vertically) and glue these to the outer edges of the back to form an upturned U shape. Check that they are at 90 degrees and support in a bench jig until the glue has set.

Cut the top $1^1/2$in wide x $5^1/2$in long and use a sharp block plane to shape the front edge into a gentle curve. Glue this into position, covering the back and the two sides, flush at either end (see Fig 6 overleaf).

Cut the bottom $1^1/4$in deep x $5^1/4$in long, to fit between the two sides. Glue this into

position to form a shelf spaced $1/4$in from the bottom all round. Use a $1/4$in piece of waste timber to check. For a firm assembly, clamp the parts together whilst the glue sets.

Cut the skirt board from $1/16$in mahogany, $3/8$in wide x $5^1/2$in long, and glue it on to cover the front edge of the bottom shelf.

Cut a 8in length of $3/32$in mahogany x $1^1/4$in wide to cut the shelf and divider from, the shelf $5^1/4$in long and the divider $2^1/2$in.

Join these two pieces together using a halving joint as follows (see Fig 6A). Find the mid point of the length of the shelf at $2^5/8$in and the divider at $1^1/4$in. Mark these using a small set square and a sharp craft knife. Cut out a $3/32$in wide slot down the centre mark of the shelf, using sharp razor saw (cutting $3/64$in either side of the line) to half the width, or $5/8$in. Repeat with the divider at the centre point, again $5/8$in long. Push the two parts together down the matching slots to form an unequal cross. Separate, apply a little glue to one slot and re-join, maintaining them at right angles. Slide this assembly into the base unit and glue into position to complete.

A wide selection of dry goods fill the shelves of these display units. The divisions and shelves are set wide apart to allow bulky items like these to be shown and stored

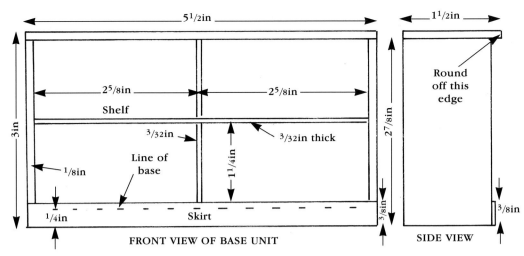

FIG 6
Display unit with shelves

Top unit labels: 5½in · 1½in · Round off this edge · 2⅝in · Shelf · 2⅝in · 3in · 3/32in · 3/32in thick · 1¼in · 2⅞in · 1/8in · Line of base · 1/4in · Skirt · 3/8in · 3/8in · **FRONT VIEW OF BASE UNIT** · **SIDE VIEW**

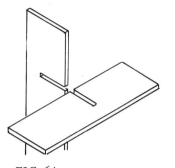

FIG 6A
Halving joint

MAKING THE TOP SHELVING UNIT

Cut the back from two pieces of 1/8in thick mahogany x 2⅝in x 4½in and glue together to form one piece 4½in x 5¼in with the grain running vertically. Cut the two sides 1in x 4½in and glue these either side of the back, checking that they sit upright at right angles to form a U shape. Cut the top from 3/32in thick mahogany, 1⅛in x 5½in and glue this onto the top edges of the back and sides to leave an overlap at the front of 1/8in. Cut three shelves from 3/32in mahogany each 1in wide x 5¼in long and from the same piece of 1in wide timber cut the divider 3½in long (see Fig 6B).

Using the same technique for making halving joints as described for the base above, take a steel rule to find the mid point of the length of the shelves at 2⅝in. Mark this using a small set square and a sharp craft knife. Take each shelf and use a sharp razor saw to cut out a 3/32in wide slot down the centre mark (cutting 3/64in either side of the line) to half the width, or 5/8in.

The divider is then divided into three parts: the first is at the very bottom; the second 1in above this, the cut being made above this line; the third is at 2½in above the bottom, the cut again being made above the line. Cut all the halving joints as described above. The bottom of the divider

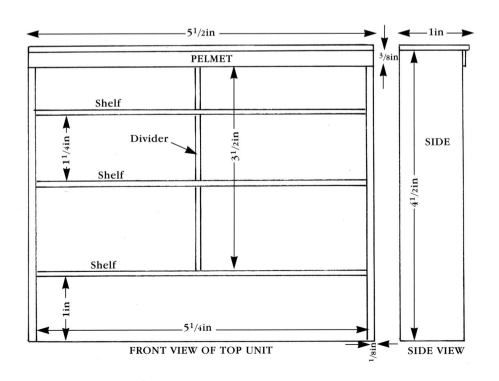

Bottom unit labels: 5½in · 1in · PELMET · 3/8in · Shelf · 1¼in · Divider · 3½in · Shelf · SIDE · Shelf · 4½in · 1in · 5¼in · 1/8in · **FRONT VIEW OF TOP UNIT** · **SIDE VIEW**

FIG 6B

is cut with a piece just $^3/_{32}$in wide being removed for $^5/_8$in of the width. Push the four parts together down the matching slots to check for correct assembly. Separate and apply a little adhesive to the slots and re-join the parts maintaining them at right angles. Slide this assembly into the shelf unit and glue into position to complete. Use small pieces of waste timber to maintain even distances between the shelves on each side.

Cut the pelmet from $^1/_{16}$in thick mahogany, $^3/_8$in wide x $5^1/_2$in long, and glue this across the top, effectively locking the central divider into place.

To finish off both units, slightly smooth over all the butt joints using a fine abrasive paper wrapped around a suitable block and then apply a coat of wax polish, buffing this to a soft sheen with a stiff brush. Both parts may also be stained to give a more antique appearance, in which case we recommend that all parts are stained before assembly.

Fancy Display Bases and Shelving Units

These attractive units were produced for Meadows the Grocers. The two base units are interchangeable with two top shelving units as they are not fixed together. The extra depth gives the opportunity to display more bulky items of stock. None of the drawers shown in the illustrations actually open, the unit being fitted with 'dummy' drawer fronts complete with knobs. Note that each of the four units has its own list of materials.

BASE UNIT 1

MATERIALS

- Mahogany pieces as follows:
  Back $^1/_8$in x $2^7/_8$in x $5^3/_4$in
  Base $^1/_8$in x $1^1/_4$in x $5^3/_4$in
  Side $^1/_8$in x $1^3/_8$in x $2^7/_8$in, 2 off
  Top $^1/_8$in x $1^1/_2$in x $6^1/_4$in
  Skirt $^1/_{16}$in x $^3/_8$in x 10in (total)
  Shelf $^3/_{32}$in x $1^1/_4$in x $5^3/_4$in
  Divider $^3/_{32}$in x $1^1/_4$in x $2^1/_2$in, 2 off

Cut the back from $^1/_8$in thick mahogany $5^3/_4$in long x $2^7/_8$in high and check that the sides are square to the top and bottom. (If necessary glue two pieces of timber together to produce the width of $5^3/_4$in with the grain running vertically.) Cut two sides each $^1/_8$in thick x $1^3/_8$in x $2^7/_8$in and glue these to either side of the back to form an upturned U shape. Cut the base $^1/_8$in thick x $1^1/_4$in x $5^3/_4$in long and glue this inside the back and against the two sides leaving a $^1/_4$in space at the bottom. Cut the top $^1/_8$in thick x $1^1/_2$in wide x $6^1/_4$in long and glue it on to the top of two sides and back, leaving a $^1/_8$in overlap at the sides and $^1/_4$in at the front (see Fig 7 overleaf).

Cut the skirt from $^1/_{16}$in thick mahogany x $^3/_8$in wide and measure one piece for the front, cutting both ends at 45 degrees for a mitred joint. Cut the two side pieces with one end square and the front end mitred to match the front. Glue the three pieces to the bottom edge at the front.

These two fancy display units have been placed together to house bottled goods and containers. The designs for the units were based on original illustrations taken from a grocer's manual of shop fittings

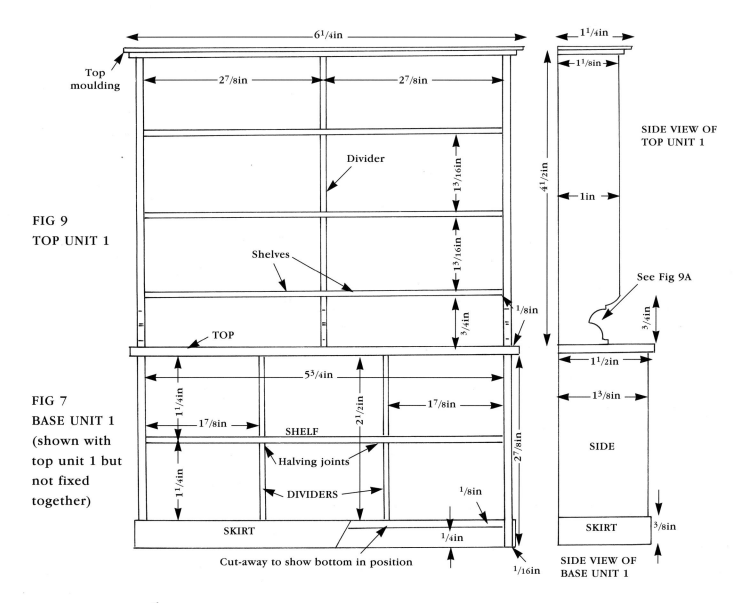

FIG 9
TOP UNIT 1

FIG 7
BASE UNIT 1
(shown with
top unit 1 but
not fixed
together)

Top
moulding

$6^{1}/_{4}$in

$2^{7}/_{8}$in $2^{7}/_{8}$in

Divider

$1^{3}/_{16}$in

$1^{3}/_{16}$in

Shelves

$^{3}/_{4}$in

$^{1}/_{8}$in

TOP

$5^{3}/_{4}$in

$1^{1}/_{4}$in

$1^{7}/_{8}$in

$2^{1}/_{2}$in

$1^{7}/_{8}$in

SHELF

$1^{1}/_{4}$in

Halving joints

DIVIDERS

$^{1}/_{8}$in

$2^{7}/_{8}$in

SKIRT

Cut-away to show bottom in position

$^{1}/_{4}$in

$^{1}/_{16}$in

$1^{1}/_{4}$in

$1^{1}/_{8}$in

SIDE VIEW OF
TOP UNIT 1

$4^{1}/_{2}$in

1in

See Fig 9A

$^{3}/_{4}$in

$1^{1}/_{2}$in

$1^{3}/_{8}$in

SIDE

SKIRT

$^{3}/_{8}$in

SIDE VIEW OF
BASE UNIT 1

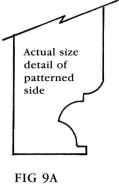

Actual size
detail of
patterned
side

FIG 9A

FIG 7A

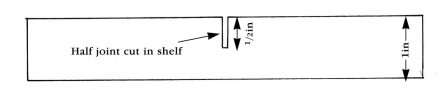

Half joint cut in shelf

$^{1}/_{2}$in

1in

Prepare one long strip of $^{3}/_{32}$in thick timber $1^{1}/_{4}$in wide for the shelf and two dividers. The shelf is $5^{3}/_{4}$in long to match the back and the dividers are $2^{1}/_{2}$in each. The shelf and the dividers are joined together using halving joints (see Fig 7A below and Fig 6A, page 32).

Use a steel rule to find two points along the length of the shelf at $1^{7}/_{8}$in from each end. The point on the dividers is dead centre at $1^{1}/_{4}$in. Mark these points using a small set square and a sharp craft knife. Take the shelf and use a sharp razor saw to cut out a $^{3}/_{32}$in wide slot down the centre of each mark (cutting $^{3}/_{64}$in either side of the line) to half the width, or $^{5}/_{8}$in. Repeat with the dividers at the centre point, again $^{5}/_{8}$in long. Push the three parts together down the matching slots to form six divisions. Separate and apply a little glue to the slots in the shelf and re-join the parts maintaining them at right angles. Slide this assembly into the base unit and glue into position to complete the construction.

To finish off base unit 1, gently smooth down all the surfaces and blend in all the joints. Brush on a clear or dark furniture polish and brush up to a soft sheen using a stiff brush. The wood may be stained first to give it a more antique appearance in which case it would be best to stain all the parts before assembly, not after.

BASE UNIT 2

MATERIALS

- Mahogany pieces as follows:

  Back 1/8in x 53/4in x 3in

  Sides 1/8in x 11/2in x 3in, 2 off

  Top 1/8in x 1in x 61/4in

  Base 1/8in x 13/8in x 53/4in

  Skirt 1/16in x 3/8in x 10in (total)

  Long shelf 3/32in x 13/8in x 53/4in

  Upright supports 3/32in x 13/4in x 11/4in, 6 off

  Drawer front 3/32in x 1in x 13/4in, 3 off

  Short shelf 3/32in x 11/4in x 13/8in, 2 off

- Brass knobs 3/32in diameter, 12 off

Cut the back from 1/8in thick mahogany, 53/4in long x 3in high and check that all sides are at right angles to each other. Cut the two sides from the same thickness material 11/2in x 3in high and shape the front edge slope as shown in Fig 8. Glue these to the sides of the back to form an upturned U shape. Cut the base from 1/8in thick mahogany 13/8in x 53/4in and glue into position leaving a 1/4in space at the bottom. The top is cut 1in wide x 61/4in long from 1/8in thick mahogany and is glued on flush at the back with a 1/8in overhang at the two sides.

Cut six uprights supports from 3/32in thick mahogany 11/4in deep x 13/4in high. Glue one onto each of the inner surfaces of the two side pieces. Glue two further pieces so that they are 1in away from each side and so

that the drawer fronts will cover them. The final pair of uprights are glued so that they are 1in apart and dead centre, or 23/8in away from the inner surface of each side.

Cut the long shelf from 3/32in mahogany, 13/8in x 53/4in, and glue this to the back and sides and on top of the six uprights.

The three sets of drawer fronts are all cut from 3/32in thick mahogany, 1in wide x 13/4in high. Divide the face of each of these into four horizontal spaces; dead centre and 7/16in from top and bottom (see Fig 8A overleaf). Use a circular saw with a 1/32in width saw blade or a sharp razor to make a 1/32in deep cut across these lines to produce the divisions between the 'drawers'. Mark each

This base unit can be used alone or combined with one of the fancy top units

FIG 8

Base unit 2

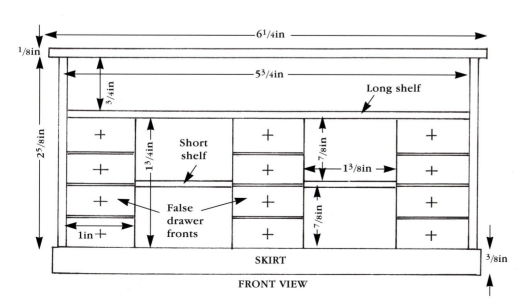

FRONT VIEW

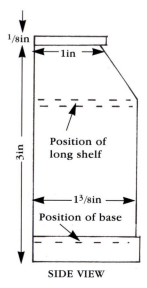

SIDE VIEW

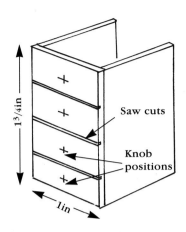

FIG 8A
Drawer fronts added
to uprights

drawer front at the dead centre and drill a $1/16$in diameter hole into which the knob can be fitted. Glue the drawer fronts onto the front face of the uprights.

Cut a 10in length of $1/16$in thick mahogany x $3/8$in wide for the skirt, cutting a long front piece with mitres at each end cut at 45 degrees. Cut the two side skirt pieces with matching mitres and glue these onto the front and sides of the unit.

Add the twelve $3/32$in diameter brass knobs to the drawer fronts gluing these into place with rapid-set epoxy cement. Then finish off the unit in the same way as base unit 1 on page 34.

TOP SHELVING UNIT 1
MATERIALS
- Mahogany pieces as follows:
  Back $1/8$in x $4^1/2$in x $5^3/4$in
  Side $1/8$in x 1in x $4^1/2$in, 2 off
  Top $3/32$in x $1^1/8$in x $6^1/4$in
  Top moulding $1/16$in x $1/4$in x 10in
  Shelves $3/32$in x $7/8$in x $5^3/4$in, 3 off
  Divider $3/32$in x $7/8$in x $4^1/2$in

Cut the back from two pieces of $1/8$in mahogany, $2^5/8$in x $4^1/2$in, and glue together to form one piece $5^3/4$in x $4^1/2$in with the grain running vertically. Cut the two sides $1/8$in thick x 1in x $4^1/2$in, and use a piercing saw and V-block to cut the pattern into the bottom front edges as shown in the side view of Fig 9, page 34. Fig 9A shows this actual size so you can trace it. Glue these either side of the back, checking that they sit upright, are at right angles and form a U shape.

Cut the top from $3/32$in thick mahogany, $1^1/8$in x $6^1/4$in long, and glue this on so that it overlaps at the sides and front by $1/8$in. Cut the top moulding from $1/16$in strip mahogany $1/4$in wide with 45 degree mitres at the two corners. Glue into position so that it overlaps at the sides and front by a further $1/8$in (see Fig 9).

The three shelves and the divider are cut from $3/32$in thick mahogany, all $7/8$in wide. The shelves are then cut with $3/32$in wide

halving joints dead centre (see Fig 7A, page 34 and Fig 6A, page 32). The bottom end of the divider is first shaped with a piercing saw and V-block to the same pattern used for the two sides. The divider is then cut with matching halving joints measured as follows. The first or bottom shelf is at $3/4$in, the second shelf leaves $1^3/16$in between it and the first. The third shelf leaves $1^3/16$in between it and the second (see Fig 9). Apply glue to the joints in the shelves and slide the assembly together. Maintain the shelves at right angles and glue this into the unit, flush with back and sides. Finish off the unit in the same way as base unit 1, page 34.

TOP SHELVING UNIT 2
MATERIALS
- Mahogany pieces as follows:
  Back $1/8$in x $4^1/2$in x $5^3/4$in
  Sides $1/8$in x 1in x $4^1/2$in, 2 off
  Top $3/32$in x $1^1/8$in x $6^1/4$in
  Top moulding $1/16$in x $1/4$in x 10in
  Base $1/8$in x $3/4$in x $5^3/4$in
  Shelf (A) $3/32$in x $7/8$in x $5^3/4$in
  Shelf (B) $3/32$in x $7/8$in x $5^3/4$in
  Divider $3/32$in x $7/8$in x $3^7/32$in
  Drawer front $3/32$in x $1^3/16$in x $1^7/8$in, 2 off
  Drawer front centre $3/32$in x $1^3/16$in x $1^3/16$in
  Drawer divisions $3/32$in x $3/32$in x $1^3/16$in, 2 off
- Brass knobs $3/32$in diameter, 3 off
- Drawer labels, 3 off

Cut the back, sides and top in the same manner as for Top Unit 1 and to identical dimensions but leave the sides plain. Assemble and glue the four parts together, as for top unit 1.

Cut the base from $1/8$in thick mahogany, $3/4$in wide x $5^3/4$in long, and glue it in flush at the bottom against the sides and back.

The top moulding is cut from $1/16$in mahogany strip x $1/4$in wide with 45 degree mitres at the two corners and glued into position so that it overlaps at sides and front

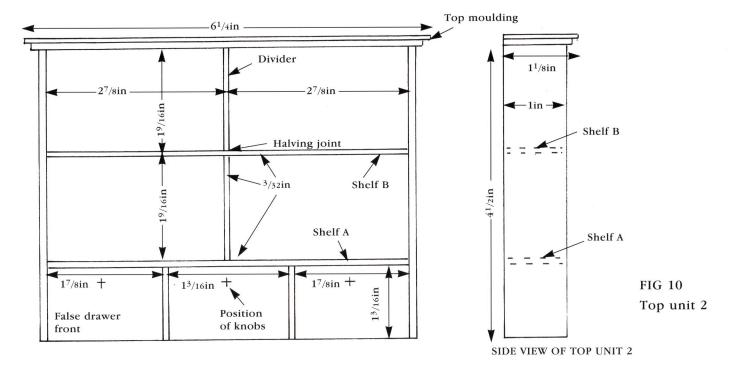

Top moulding

6¹/₄in

Divider

2⁷/₈in   2⁷/₈in

1⁹/₁₆in

Halving joint

³/₃₂in   Shelf B

1⁹/₁₆in

Shelf A

1⁷/₈in +   1³/₁₆in +   1⁷/₈in +

1³/₁₆in

False drawer front   Position of knobs

1¹/₈in

1in

Shelf B

4¹/₂in

Shelf A

FIG 10
Top unit 2

SIDE VIEW OF TOP UNIT 2

by a further ¹/₈in (see Fig 10).

Cut two shelves, A and B, from ³/₃₂in thick mahogany, each ⁷/₈in wide x 5³/₄in long. Shelf A is glued into position exactly 1³/₁₆in above the bottom to match the depth of the drawer fronts. Shelf B is marked at the centre point and a halving joint cut (see Fig 7A, page 34 and unit 1, above). The divider is cut ³/₃₂in thick x ⁷/₈in x 3⁷/₃₂in long and this too is marked and cut with a halving joint dead centre. Fit shelf B and the divider together, applying glue to one side of the joint and gluing into position, taking care that the assembly is square.

Cut three drawer fronts from ³/₃₂in thick mahogany x 1³/₁₆in high with the grain running horizontally on each. Cut the outer two 1⁷/₈in wide and the third, or centre front, 1¹³/₁₆in. Two vertical dividing bars are cut from ³/₃₂in x ³/₃₂in square timber 1¹³/₁₆in long. Mark the drawer fronts dead centre, horizontally, ¹/₄in down from the top edge for the positions of the drawer front knobs and drill ¹/₁₆in diameter holes for these.

Glue the left-hand drawer front first, flush at the bottom and resting against the bottom, the top being flush with the underside of the first shelf. Now glue on the right-hand drawer front, and finally the centre drawer front. Glue the brass knobs on the drawer

fronts using a rapid-set epoxy cement.

Three labels ¹/₄in x ³/₈in wide, printed white on black, can be produced using a desk top publishing programme on a computer (or you could cut them from a magazine). Glue the labels into place. Then finish off top unit 2 in the same way as for base unit 1, page 34.

Awaiting fresh stock, the three top drawer labels on this unit can be altered to suit any trade

Decorative Base and Shelving Unit

This was used in Jingles toy shop but could be painted to match any shop interior.

MATERIALS

BASE UNIT

- Obeche pieces as follows:
  Back 1/8in x 27/8in x 53/4in
  Side 1/8in x 13/8in x 27/8in, 2 off
  Top 1/8in x 15/8in x 6in
  Base 1/8in x 11/4in x 53/4in
  Shelf 3/32in x 11/4in x 53/4in
  Divider 3/32in x 11/4in x 21/2in

TOP UNIT

- Obeche pieces as follows:
  Back 1/8in x 41/2in x 53/4in
  Sides 1/8in x 7/8in x 41/2in, 2 off
  Top 3/32in x 11/8in x 6in
  Shelf 3/32in x 3/4in x 53/4in, 2 off
  Centre shelf 3/32in x 7/8in x 6in
  Shaped shelf divisions 3/32in x 1in x 3/4in, 4 off
  Centre support 3/32in x 13/8in x 1/2in
  Pelmet 3/32in x 1/2in x 6in
- Baluster posts 21/2in long Centurion pattern (Houseworks No.7202), 4 off

MAKING THE BASE UNIT

Cut the back from 1/8in thick obeche 53/4in long x 27/8in high and check that the sides are square at the top and bottom. (If necessary glue two pieces of timber together to produce the length of 53/4in with the grain running vertically.)

Cut two sides each 1/8in thick x 13/8in x 27/8in and glue these to either side of the back to form an upturned U shape. Cut the base 1/8in thick x 11/4in x 53/4in long and glue this inside the back and against the two sides leaving a 1/4in space at the bottom.

Cut the top 1/8in thick x 15/8in wide x 6in long, rounding off the front top edge using fine abrasive paper wrapped around a suitable block. Glue this piece on the top of the two sides and back leaving a 1/4in overlap at the front (see Fig 11).

Prepare one long strip of 3/32in thick obeche 11/4in wide for the shelf and divider. The shelf is 53/4in long to match the back and the divider is 21/2in long. The shelf and divider are joined together using halving joints as follows (see also Fig 6A, page 32). Use a steel rule to find two points along the length of the shelf at 17/8in in from each end. The point on the divider is at 11/4in. Mark these points using a small set square and a sharp craft knife. Take the shelf and use a sharp razor saw to cut out a 3/32in wide slot down the centre of each mark (cutting 3/64in either side of the line) to half the width, or 5/8in. Repeat with the divider at the centre point, again 5/8in long. Push the parts together down the matching slots to form four divisions. Separate and apply a little glue to the slots in the shelf and re-join the parts maintaining them at right angles. Slide this assembly into the base unit and glue into position to complete.

The base unit is finished to match the top unit (see page 40).

Toy shops and milliners
often use decorative pieces
such as this to display
their wares

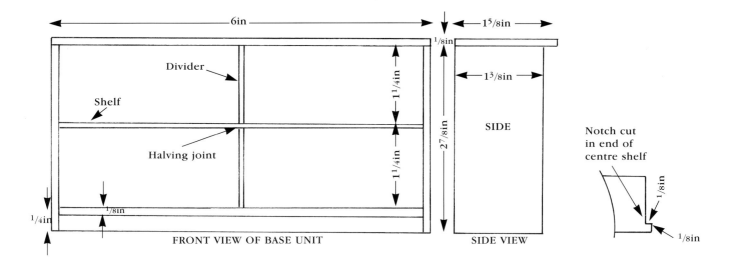

FRONT VIEW OF BASE UNIT

SIDE VIEW

Divider

Shelf

Halving joint

Notch cut
in end of
centre shelf

MAKING THE TOP UNIT

Cut the back from two pieces of $1/8$in thick obeche, $2^7/8$in wide x $4^1/2$in long, glued together to produce one piece $5^3/4$in wide x $4^1/2$in high. Cut the two sides from the same thickness $7/8$in wide x $4^1/2$in long and glue to them to the sides of the back to form the upturned U shape used in other shelving units. Cut the top $1^1/8$in wide x 6in long from $3/32$in thick obeche and glue this on

leaving an overlap at the front (see Fig 12).

Cut two narrow shelves from $3/32$in thick obeche, each $3/4$in wide x $5^3/4$in long and glue them into the top unit 1in from the bottom and $7/8$in from the top. The centre shelf should be cut $7/8$in wide x 6in long, with a $1/8$in x $1/8$in notch cut into the two front outer edges, as shown in the figure. Glue this into place 1in below the top shelf.

Cut and shape the four $3/32$in thick x 1in x

FIG 11
Base unit

FIG 12
Top unit (see side view overleaf)

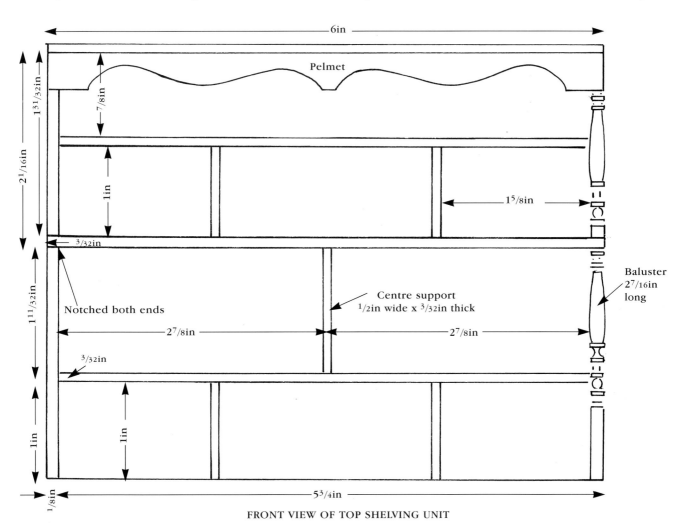

Pelmet

Notched both ends

Centre support
$1/2$in wide x $3/32$in thick

Baluster
$2^7/16$in
long

FRONT VIEW OF TOP SHELVING UNIT

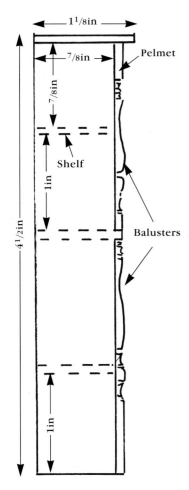

FIG 12
Top unit side view

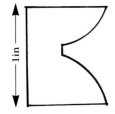

FIG 12A
Shaped shelf divider
(actual size)

³/₄in shelf dividers as shown in Fig 12A (actual size). Glue these into place 1⁵/₈in from each side. The smaller centre support is cut ³/₃₂in x 1³/₈in x ¹/₂in and glued dead centre between the bottom and centre shelf.

Cut the pelmet from ³/₃₂in thick obeche, ¹/₂in wide x 6in long, and shape it as shown in Fig 12 to give a net width of ³/₈in. Once cut, glue the finished pelmet onto the two sides and immediately under and flush with the top.

The four balusters are cut lengthways using a circular saw (or they can be planed down to the required thickness). Cut two of them down in height so that they fit just under the centre shelf. The second pair are cut down at the bottom to leave just ¹/₈in of square section and cut so that they fit immediately below the pelmet.

To finish off both the base and top unit, gently smooth down all the surfaces and blend in all the joints. Brush on a base sealing coat of matt white emulsion and apply a suitable colour top coat. The wood may be stained first to give it a more antique appearance in which case it would be best to stain all the parts before assembly, not after.

Set of Wall Drawers

This fixture is put to good use in Luscombe's ironmongers. We made this set six drawers high and six wide, all with false fronts. To make this up as 36 working drawers would be a complicated job, so we have devised this assembly with just one drawer shown partially open. Of course you may repeat this illusion as many times as you wish and also vary the degree that the drawer appears to be open.

MATERIALS

- Mahogany pieces as follows:
  Front ¹/₈in x 5¹/₂in x 4in
  Side ³/₃₂in x ³/₄in x 4in, 2 off
  Top ³/₃₂in x ³/₄in x 5¹¹/₁₆in
  Corner support ¹/₄in x ¹/₄in x ⁵/₈in, 4 off
  Moulding strip ¹/₈in x ⁵/₁₆in x 8in

  False drawer front ¹/₁₆in x ⁵/₈in x ⁷/₈in
  False drawer sides ¹/₁₆in x ³/₁₆in x 1¹/₂in
  False drawer bottom ³/₃₂in x ³/₄in x 5¹¹/₁₆in
- Brass knobs ³/₃₂in diameter, 36 off
- Printed labels ¹/₈in x ³/₈in, 36 off

Start by cutting a piece of ¹/₈in thick mahogany 4in high x 5¹/₂in wide for the front and make sure that all the sides are at right angles to each other. It is *very* important to be accurate here. Lay the front onto a flat surface so that the longest side lies from left to right. Divide the front into six equal divisions with five lines across the width (see Fig 13). Lay a 12in ruler across the width so that the 1in mark on the rule is level at any place on the left edge, now swivel the ruler until the 7in mark touches the right. Mark on the timber the line of each inch on the ruler and you will see that this gives six equal divisions. Use a set square to draw the lines across the width. Turn the front through 90 degrees so the longest side is now on your left, lay the ruler on this so that the 1in mark is level with the top and again swivel the ruler until the 7in mark touches the bottom, now on your right. Repeat the marking off as above and draw the lines using a set square and a sharp pencil. You can use this method to create more or less divisions as you wish. Lightly score along each of the lines with a sharp scalpel or craft knife using a steel straight edge.

Hold the front in a soft-jawed vice and use a razor saw to carefully mark the edge of the top and one end with all the divisions. These cuts are meant as a guide so make them quite shallow, about the depth of one saw tooth. Place the front onto a flat surface and carefully cut along each of the marks with a fine tenon saw (approximately ¹/₃₂in wide) to create all the rebated divisions between the drawer fronts.

Alternatively, if you have a circular saw with a fine blade (¹/₃₂in wide) set it to no more than a ¹/₃₂in deep cut, fix the guide for the first mark and run the timber over the

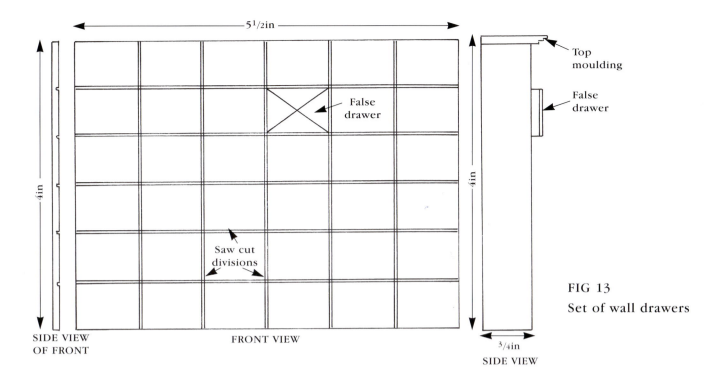

5¹/₂in

4in

False
drawer

Saw cut
divisions

SIDE VIEW
OF FRONT

FRONT VIEW

Top
moulding

False
drawer

4in

³/₄in

SIDE VIEW

FIG 13
Set of wall drawers

blade. Keep the guide in the same position and turn the timber round 180 degrees to make a cut at the opposite end. Repeat until all the lines have been rebated. *Safety point: You will have to do this with the saw guard removed so make sure the table is properly fixed into position and use a push stick to keep hands free of the operating area.*

Now mark up for the drawer knobs by laying the rebated front face up on a flat surface. Find the centres of all the drawer fronts, except the one(s) that is to appear as if open. We chose a space that looked most natural to us but it could be any. Use a ruler laid from corner to corner on each one and mark the centre point firmly with a sharp awl. Use a ¹/₁₆in diameter drill bit to drill all the holes for the shafts of the drawer knobs.

Making the False Drawer

To make the false front of the drawer, measure off the face of the blank drawer it is to cover and cut a piece of ¹/₁₆in mahogany, ⁵/₈in x ⁷/₈in (see Fig 13A, page 42). Find the centre and drill a ¹/₁₆in diameter hole for the drawer knob. Cut two spacer pieces (sides) of ¹/₁₆in x ³/₁₆in timber, each the length of one side of the drawer (in our case ⁵/₈in) and glue these onto the back of the drawer front, with the ¹/₁₆in side to the

drawer, flush with the outer edge. Measure off the distance between the two sides and cut a third spacer to fit at the bottom (this should be ³/₄in long but it may vary slightly if your cutting of the drawer front differs from our model). Glue this into place at the bottom of the drawer front, again on the back and between the side spacers. When the drawer front is placed over the blank

Many period shops kept goods and documents in sets of wall-mounted drawers. The sizes of the drawers would be designed around products or space available. These drawers could be used in an ironmongers, chemists or grocers.

41

space it should make it appear as if it is partially open. Increasing the depth measurement of the spacers will make the drawer appear to be further open and this can be adjusted to suit the project. Place this false drawer assembly to one side until the four sides of the drawer set have been added.

Assembling the Wall Drawer Set

The sides are made from $3/32$in thick x $3/4$in wide mahogany to match the front. Cut two pieces 4in long to match the sides and two pieces $5^{11}/16$in long for the top and the bottom. Lay the front onto a flat surface or jig, face down, and glue the sides around the front, adding the top and the bottom to form an empty box. Check all is square and clamp firmly until the glue has set.

Cut four $1/4$in x $1/4$in x $5/8$in long corner support blocks, and glue one into each corner. Leave to dry and then lightly sand off the sides so that the ends of the top and bottom pieces are flush to the sides.

To add the top moulding, cut a length of $1/8$in thick mahogany $5/16$in wide and use a vertically mounted miniature router or circular saw to make a horizontal cut, leaving a strip of $1/32$in x $1/32$in along one edge. Reset the saw and take a second cut $1/16$in wide x $1/32$in deep to produce a step moulding (see Fig 13). Cut the front moulding piece with two 45 degree mitred cuts and two side pieces with matching 45 degree cuts for the sides and glue all three pieces on top of this unit so there is an overlap of $1/8$in to the front.

Turn the assembly over so that the front is uppermost and colour the blank drawer space with matt black acrylic paint. Allow this to dry before gluing on the false front drawer assembly.

Glue in the drawer knobs. Add wax polish and buff to soft shine, allowing some polish to gather around the knobs to give an aged appearance. Now prepare thirty-six labels $1/8$in x $3/8$in, worded according to the trade it is to be used for. Using a clear, spirit-based adhesive, glue these on each 'drawer' front, placing them centrally over the knob.

False drawer parts

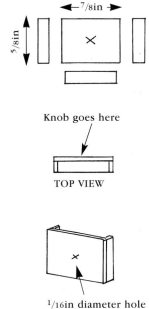

Knob goes here

TOP VIEW

$1/16$in diameter hole

FIG 13A
False drawer
construction

Print Holder

This was made for Pickwicks the bookseller, to house some of the many maps and prints.

MATERIALS

- Obeche pieces as follows:
  Sides $1/16$in x $1^1/2$in x $2^1/4$in, 2 off
  Ends $1/16$in x $5/8$in x $7/8$in, 2 off
  Legs $3/32$in x $1/8$in x $2^1/4$in, 4 off

Cut two sides from $1/16$in thick obeche. $1^1/2$in deep x $2^1/4$in wide, and square off. Cut two ends from $1/16$in thick obeche, $5/8$in x $7/8$in, cutting them to the triangular shape shown in Fig 14. Carefully glue one of these shapes to either end of one of the sides and allow this to dry, supporting it at right angles to the surface of the side. Glue on the second side to form the print holder.

Cut the four legs from $3/32$in thick obeche,

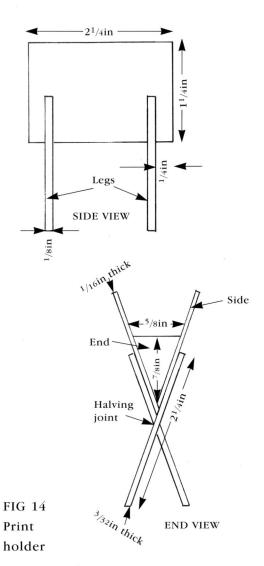

FIG 14
Print
holder

Ideal for large broadsheets and prints, this holder can be placed in any small space

¹/8in wide x 2¹/4in long, and mark each one at 1¹/8in, or dead centre. Cut matching halving joints (see Fig 6A, page 32) into each leg so that they will fit together and support the tray at the required angle. Trim the bottom of each leg so that it will sit flush on the floor and then glue onto the sides at ¹/4in in from the outer edges.

To finish off, paint the print holder a suitable colour to match the decor in your shop or leave a natural finish.

Bookcase

This bookcase was used in Pickwicks book shop but could be put to good use in almost any shop to hold different varieties of stock.

MATERIALS
- Mahogany pieces as follows:
  Side ¹/8in x ³/4in x 7in, 2 off
  Shelf ¹/8in x ³/4in x 2³/4in, 6 off

Cut two sides and six shelves to the measurements above, ensuring that the length of the sides match and that the lengths and widths of the shelves are all exactly the same.

Use a circular saw set to ¹/16in depth and cut six matching ¹/8in wide rebates in each side according to the measurements in Fig 15. Lay all the parts onto a suitable bench jig

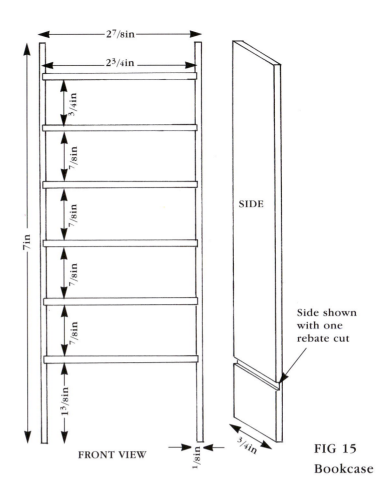

FRONT VIEW

SIDE

Side shown with one rebate cut

FIG 15
Bookcase

and glue the shelves into the rebates.

To complete, gently smooth down all the surfaces. Finish off with two or three coats of a good quality wax polish, buffing up each layer to produce a soft sheen. The wood may be stained first to give it a more antique appearance in which case stain all the parts before assembly, not after.

Packed with individual and false rows of books, these shelves cater for most sizes. Sets of shelves can be made to any height or width required

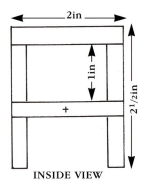

INSIDE VIEW

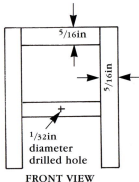

FRONT VIEW

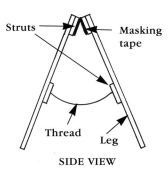

SIDE VIEW

FIG 16
Trestle table

An easily made trestle table is stacked with special editions and slip-cased books

Trestle Table

This was used in Pickwicks the bookseller but a trestle table is ideal for any trade, as it can be folded away when not in use.

MATERIALS

- $3/32$in thick obeche pieces as follows:
  Top $2^1/8$in x 5in
  Legs $5/16$in x $2^1/2$in, 8 off
  Struts $5/16$in x 2in, 8 off
- Cotton thread x 4in
- Masking tape

Cut the top from $3/32$in thick obeche, $2^1/8$in x 5in long. Check that the sides are square to each other and place aside for finishing.

To make one trestle, cut four struts $3/32$in x $5/16$in x 2in long and four legs $2^1/2$in long. Drill a $1/32$in diameter hole into the two bottom struts, dead centre of the length and width (see Fig 16). Lay one strut face down onto a flat surface with a second strut 1in below it. Glue one leg at each end face down onto the struts. Repeat the above to make the second set of legs.

Cut a 2in length of masking tape. Turn the assemblies over and fix the tape to the inside surface of the top strut, fold the tape over and place the second leg assembly onto it to fix the two together to make one trestle. Thread a short length of cotton thread through the holes in the bottom struts and tie off each end so that the legs will open to leave a gap of about $1^3/4$in, or an angle of $22^1/2$ degrees.

Make the second trestle in the same way, matching the distance between the legs exactly or the table will slope. Stand the two trestles 4in apart and place the top on.

Ladder

This ladder features in the book shop, Pickwicks, but it would be equally useful in many other shops, or it could be used as an item of stock in an ironmongers.

MATERIALS

- Mahogany pieces as follows:
  Sides $3/32$in x $3/8$in x $7^1/4$in, 2 off
  Rest $1/16$in x $3/4$in x $1^1/2$in
  Tread $1/16$in x $3/8$in x $1^1/4$in wide, 7 off

Cut two sides from $3/32$in mahogany, $3/8$in wide x $7^1/4$in long. Use a sharp razor saw to cut the bottom end at 20 degrees and the top front at a matching angle, allowing the steps to rest on a vertical surface (Fig 17).

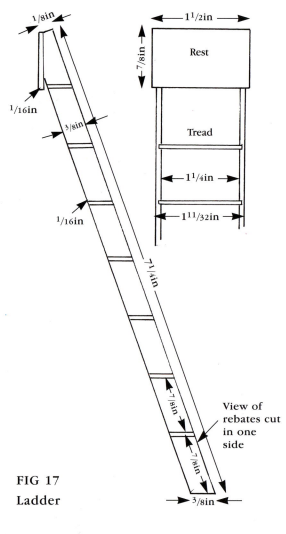

FIG 17
Ladder

Cut the ladder rest from $^{1}/_{16}$in thick mahogany, $^{3}/_{4}$in wide x $1^{1}/_{2}$in long. Place to one side until the ladder is assembled.

Cut seven treads from $^{1}/_{16}$in thick mahogany, each $^{3}/_{8}$in deep x $1^{1}/_{4}$in wide, ensuring that each one has identical dimensions or the ladder won't assemble correctly.

Lay the sides onto a flat surface and use an adjustable bevel and a sharp pencil to mark the divisions on each for the seven treads. Using a sharp scalpel and the bevel, mark $^{1}/_{32}$in either side of the division line for $^{1}/_{16}$in rebates. Cut the rebates using a sharp fine-toothed razor saw to cut to a depth of $^{1}/_{32}$in along each line. It is essential that these lines are parallel and that each side matches the other. Take a fine $^{1}/_{16}$in wide chisel and carefully remove the waste material to a depth of $^{1}/_{32}$in.

Lay one side onto a flat surface with the rebates uppermost and apply a little glue to each of the rebates. Place the end of one tread into each rebate, keeping them upright at all times. Apply a little glue to the rebates of the second side and lay this onto the other end of the treads to form the ladder. Clamp together lightly, checking that the assembly is evenly balanced and that the tops and bottoms are level with each other. Set aside and allow the glue to set. Add the front rest to complete the ladder.

Small Stock Items

There is a wealth of small stock items available commercially (see Suppliers for some addresses) but here we give simple instructions for making some of the basic items that will help fill out a shop.

DUMMY BOOKS

We have produced false rows of books for the bookseller in three different ways: all are effective and are an easy way of producing bulk stock.

Method 1

A coloured illustration of books was scanned into a computer and reproduced

just $^{7}/_{8}$in high to fit between shelves already made. This print was simply pasted onto a piece of 140gsm card and trimmed to the correct width and height. Any number of rows can be produced using this method and it is a quick and easy way to fill a book shop. For those without recourse to computer equipment, a colour photocopier can be used to reproduce the strips.

Method 2

Wooden blocks can be purchased which have been machined on the top and front edges to mimic books. Painted in various colours, the spines have a dash of gold paint to imitate a title. These are not very good when viewed close up but can be acceptable if placed at the back of a shop.

Method 3

Ready-printed book covers can be purchased from your local miniature shop. A

This ladder is suitable for a library or book shop, the rest on the front preventing damage to books

number are supplied with sheets of printed card which are cut and glued together, the book cover being bound around the assembled card pieces to make 'loose' books.

PACKAGING STACKS

These packaging stacks were made for Meadows grocer's shop, but could easily be made for any shop simply by changing the package fronts. Package fronts are available commercially in strips. Alternatively, if you have access to a computer and scanning equipment, you could scan in package pictures, reduce to the correct size and print off as many as you need.

MATERIALS

- Package front $7/8$in high x $11/16$in wide, 8 off
- $1/8$in thick obeche pieces as follows:
  Strip A $2^{3}/4$in x $1^{7}/8$in
  Strip B $2^{1}/16$in x $1^{3}/4$in
  Strip C $11/16$in x $2^{5}/8$in

Cut strip A to the size given above and lay it face down onto a flat surface. Cut part B and glue this on top of A to leave an equal amount either side but flush at the bottom (see Fig 18). Cut strip C and glue this on top of part B, again dead centre.

Paste or glue on four package fronts to the face of part A – three onto the visible part of part B and one onto the front of part C.

Simple stacks of packages soon fill shop windows and shelves

Colour the edges to match the packaging using acrylic paints or paste on a strip of matching colour paper. This unit should stand on its own as the base will be $3/8$in thick. Additional widths or heights can be made using this method, as required. Any assembly of less than two layers deep will probably require a back support.

This method can also be used to give the impression of a large amount of stock simply by placing one stack behind another.

HARDWARE STOCK

The stock described here was used in Luscombe's ironmongery, the various items being easy to make (see picture page 85).

Rolls of Asphalt

Use a sheet of dark-coloured, fine-textured abrasive paper used for automotive repairs (240 grit wet-and-dry is ideal) and cut it into 3in wide strips. Cut this into 4in lengths, roll these around a $1/4$in diameter roller, secure with a rubber band and glue the edge to form the roll. Write or print a suitable label $1^{3}/4$in wide and wrap this around the roll, gluing down the loose end.

Rolls of Fence Wire

Car body repair sheet, sold as expanded aluminium, can be purchased from most automotive shops. Cut with scissors or a sharp craft knife and steel rule, into 3in wide strips x 4in and roll these around a $1/4$in diameter roller. The material will hold its shape and doesn't need gluing together. Produce a suitable label as for the asphalt roll to complete.

Rolls of Wire

Strip the insulation off a 12in length of electric cable and wind the copper core into a 1in diameter circle. Use a pair of pliers to twist the two ends around the coil to secure.

Garden Hose

Take a length of electric cable and pull out the copper core. Coil up the empty tubing and tie off with a piece of cotton thread.

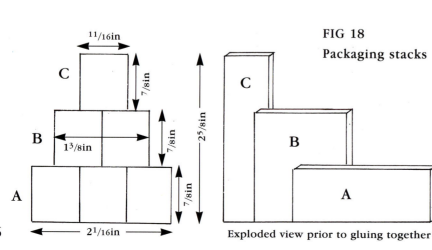

FIG 18
Packaging stacks

Exploded view prior to gluing together

SIGNAGE

One of the delights of owning a miniature shop is that you can use your own name for the fascia, or perhaps a shop you once knew. Choosing something to reflect the local character is recommended and we are sure that there are some names that are more relevant to your area than any other.

Unless you are very skilled, it will be difficult to produce a sign-written front by hand. If you want to try this, purchase a proper brush, called a 'pencil' and use Humbrol enamel paint thinned down so that it flows easily. It's best to practise on a spare piece of finished wood first.

There are firms selling ready-cut vinyl signs who can produce quite small lettering in a variety of fonts. Refer to The Clarence tea rooms and Jingles toy shop for more details on the methods of applying this lettering. Wooden laser-cut letters in one or two fonts are available (see Suppliers for Luscombes ironmongers and Meadows the grocer) and with a little care and attention these make really excellent signs, with the advantage that you can make up any name you want. For details on finishing and applying these cut-out letters refer to Luscombe's ironmongers and Meadows the grocer.

Lettered Signs

Lettered signs add a touch of period realism to a shop and examples of these can be seen in Luscombe's main window (see photograph on page 67). The signs can be made from small, $1/4$in cube-shaped, lettered glass beads – these are used to make up necklaces and can be purchased from jewellery finding shops. To be of use for these signs they need to be approximately $1/4$in across the face and with a small 'threading' hole through the centre. You will need sufficient letters to make up the sign required, such as 'IRONMONGERS' (eleven). A short length of piano wire with a diameter matching (or less) than the hole in the bead is also required. Proceed as follows with a 6in length of wire.

Using pliers, bend one end of the wire to 90 degrees to form the shape of a capital 'L', the shorter piece, or leg, being $1^1/2$in. Thread the letters onto the longer piece of the wire adding a touch of clear, spirit-based adhesive between all the beads to hold all the faces in the same plane. Now use the pliers to bend the other end of the wire up in the same direction as the first to form the second leg and cut it off to the same length of $1^1/2$in. Trim both ends of the wire shorter if necessary.

To attach the sign simply drill two holes, spaced to match the wire legs, with the diameter matching that of the wire and push them home adding a touch of clear, spirit-based adhesive to hold them in place.

USING COMMERCIAL ITEMS

We have provided instructions for basic fixtures, fittings and stock but there is, of course, a wealth of items available to miniaturists from individual makers, mail order outlets or your local dolls' house shop.

When looking for miniature stock remember that even in real life most small items are purchased from a shop and almost everything bought for $1/12$ scale can be used in a miniature shop. For example, in Luscombe's ironmongers you will see a wealth of tinware that was originally sold for bathrooms and kitchens. Jingles, the toy shop, is crammed with stuffed toys, small nursery items and games. Incorporating teddy bears and train sets into a toy shop instead of the nursery, and jugs and buckets into a hardware store instead of the garden, is a very straightforward way of increasing your stock. You will see many examples of commercially produced items throughout the book and some suppliers are given on page 174. It is impossible to list here all the sources and we suggest that readers check magazines for suppliers. It is certainly great fun to make as much as you can but using items for your stock made by experts will add a touch of realism to your project.

If you are building a British shop functioning before decimalisation in 1971, you will need to know some facts about British currency ('old money') before that date in order that your signs and prices look authentic.

One pound (£1) comprised 20 shillings (20s).
One shilling (1s) comprised 12 pence (12d).
One penny (1d) comprised either a one penny coin, or two halfpennies ($1/2$d), or four quarter pennies or farthings ($1/4$d).

An oblique or forward dash indicated a break in each division of money, e.g. £1/10/6 (meaning, one pound, ten shillings and sixpence); 15/10d (fifteen shillings and ten pence); 6/- (six shillings exactly, the dash denoting no pence); 5 $1/4$d (five and a quarter pence, spoken as 'fivepence farthing'.

JINGLES
AN EDWARDIAN TOY SHOP

An Edwardian toy shop was a place of magic, where a child's Christmas and birthday wishes could come true. There were fierce animals that could be cuddled at bedtime, teddy bears to soothe away problems and small aeroplanes that could fly. Trains that steamed through the night carried mail and passengers to strange places. There were dolls that could speak, but only when grown-ups left the room, rocking horses that might ride over the moon and brightly coloured marbles and exciting games for dull days indoors. A selection of sensible clothes for young children attracted caring mothers.

Keeping children amused and rewarded has meant that toy shops of some sort or another have probably been in existence ever since there were shops of any sort at all. Records show that dolls and toy animals have been found in all cultures and although providing them was initially the responsibility of the parents it must have eventually passed to a relative or member of the community

with more time or more skill, or both. Finding that making toys for other peoples' children paid, in thanks or money, must have led someone to create the first toy shop.

In the past, children probably had only a few toys and some of these were only played with on special occasions and holidays. Apart from extending the life of the toy it also gave it a special meaning and so it was probably rare, but not unknown, for a child to wantonly damage anything so precious. China and bisque dolls, delicate and easily broken, tended to be played with only on Sundays. Toys, like dolls' houses, were miniature replicas of contemporary life and in many cases were used to teach children the skills of everyday housekeeping.

'Jingles', the toy shop made for this project, is a simply constructed, single-story building designed to accommodate a large amount of stock in a comparatively small space. This frontage has some very pretty tracery in the upper part of the window, the delicate lace trim below it and the small panes inviting curiosity.

Ideally small, warm and welcoming, the shop should have counters and shelves within easy reach of children and almost every space should be utilised, even the ceiling could be used for suspending balloons and kites.

Architectural design is almost irrelevant when it comes to deciding
what sort of premises would best suit a toy shop but it should be child
friendly and something of an adventure to enter

A display of brightly coloured toys is essential. A decorative glass-fronted cabinet or counter would be useful, if only to keep sticky fingers off the more valuable and delicate toys, at least until they are paid for! The inclusion of small trays with divisions that only a child's fingers can gain entry to is also a good idea.

A period toy shop should be decorated with plain, warm colours, although much of the wall space is likely to be covered with over-crowded shelves. To add to the interest and entrance the customers, a pretty frieze illustrating part of a child's story can be pasted onto one or more of the walls. Materials and instructions are given in this chapter for the window box and the shelves. The counter and the cabinets can be made by referring to the Resource Section, pages 26 and 38.

MATERIALS

CARCASS

- 9mm MDF pieces as follows:
  Side $10^1/_2$in x 12in, 2 off
  Floor & top $14^5/_8$in x $9^3/_4$in, 2 off
  Skirt $1^1/_8$in x $14^1/_4$in
- Back 6mm MDF x 12in x $14^5/_8$in

FRONTAGE

- Front 9mm MDF x 15in x 12in
- 6mm MDF pieces as follows:

A toy shop can stock clothes for children as well as toys, displaying them in a pretty chest of drawers

Window former
  – A 9in x $1^3/_8$in
  – B 9in x $1^3/_{16}$in
  – C $7^3/_4$in x $1^3/_8$in
  Spacers (D & E) $1/_2$in x 1in, 2 off
  Fanlight bar $3/_8$in x 3in
- Base render board $1/_8$in
  x $1^1/_2$in x 12in

FASCIA

- Obeche pieces as follows:
  Front $1/_8$in x $9^1/_4$in x $1^1/_8$in
  End caps $1/_8$in x 1in x $1^5/_{16}$in, 2 off
- Architectural moulding $1/_4$in x $9^1/_4$in

FLOORING

- 0.6mm plywood, $9^3/_4$in x 14in

DOOR

- Obeche pieces as follows:
  A $1/_4$in x $1/_2$in x $2^1/_8$in
  B $1/_4$in x $5/_8$in x $2^1/_8$in
  C $1/_4$in x $1/_2$in x $2^1/_8$in
  D $1/_4$in x $3/_8$in x $6^1/_8$in, 2 off
  E $1/_8$in x $1^3/_8$in x $2^1/_8$in
  F $3/_{32}$in x $1^3/_4$in x $1^1/_8$in
  G $3/_{32}$in x 1in x $2^1/_8$in, 2 off
  H $3/_{32}$in x $1/_4$in, 4 off
  Door lining $1/_{16}$in square x 16in
- Door frame moulding A $1/_4$in x 40in
- Door frame moulding B $3/_{16}$in x 6in
- Door glazing 0.7mm acetate
  x $3^3/_{16}$in x $2^3/_8$in

STEPS

- Softwood pieces as follows:
  $5/_8$in x $1^1/_2$in x $3^1/_2$in
  $5/_8$in x $3/_4$in x $3^1/_2$in
- Obeche pieces as follows:
  Tread A $1/_8$in x $7/_8$in x $3^1/_2$in
  Tread B $1/_8$in x $1^5/_8$in x $3^1/_2$in

WINDOW

- Obeche pieces as follows:
  Uprights (A & B) $3/_{32}$in x $3/_{16}$in x 11in
  Upright bars $3/_{32}$in x $3/_{32}$in x 40in
  Cross bars $3/_{32}$in x $3/_{32}$in x 40in
  Framing $1/_{16}$in x $3/_{32}$in x 20in

- Window-sill moulding 11½in
  (see text page 55)
- Grille (GRD1), 1 piece (North Eastern
  – see Suppliers)
- Decorative brackets (BRC 1), 4 off
  (North Eastern – see Suppliers)
- Acetate glazing 0.7mm
  x 5⁷/₁₆in x 7¼in
- Acetate glazing 0.7mm x ⁵/₁₆in
  x ³/₄in, 2 off

ROOF AND ROOFING
- 9mm MDF pieces as follows:
  Back 3³/₄in x 14in
  Side 3³/₄in x 7¹/₂in, 2 off
  Top 5¹/₁₆in x 14in
- 6mm MDF front 5¹/₂in x 14in
- 6-sheet card, 1 sheet

MISCELLANEOUS
- Fanlight lining, obeche ¹/₁₆in
  square x 8in
- Front top trim (GBD 1A), 1 piece 18in
  (North Eastern – see Suppliers)
- 12 volt light fitting, double lamp
  chandelier
- Aluminium oxide abrasive paper
  (P180, grey)
- Plastic railings strips 6in

WORKING NOTES
Where 'glue' is referred to it means a PVA
adhesive unless otherwise stated.
Measurements in the book are imperial,
however, as MDF is only sold in the UK
in metric sizes, these thicknesses are
given with approximate imperial equivalents, e.g. 6mm (¹/₄in), 9mm (³/₈in).
A selection of commercial paints were
used for this project so an exact match
can be made. You could, of course,
choose your own colours from other
paint brands.

CUTTING OUT THE CARCASS

Cut and prepare the two sides to the dimensions shown in Fig 1, checking that the edges and corners are square. Mark up the 6mm (¹/₄in) rebate for the back on both pieces. Use a set square to mark out the two 9mm (³/₈in) wide rebates for the top and floor – these are set at identical distances of 1¹/₈in from the top and bottom edges. Cut out the three rebates on each piece using the appropriate sized router cutter and check that they are all the correct size by using MDF offcuts, adjusting if necessary. Note that each side should be a mirror image of the other when the inner surfaces are placed together. When the back is glued into the housed rebate later it will give the building strength and resist twisting.

Cut out the top (ceiling) and the floor, each 14⁵/₈in x 9³/₄in, checking they are square and the same size. Drill a ³/₃₂in diameter hole dead centre of the ceiling for lighting wires. Use a tenon saw or sharp craft knife to cut a ³/₃₂in wide x ³/₃₂in deep groove from this hole to the back on the top or outer face of the roof for the lighting wires.

FIG 1

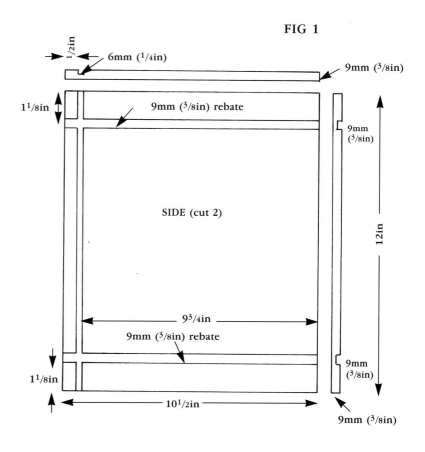

½in — 6mm (¹/₄in)

9mm (³/₈in)

1¹/₈in — 9mm (³/₈in) rebate

9mm (³/₈in)

SIDE (cut 2)

12in

9³/₄in

9mm (³/₈in) rebate

9mm (³/₈in)

1¹/₈in

10¹/₂in

9mm (³/₈in)

Cut the back from 6mm MDF 12in x 14 5/8in with all sides finished at dead right angles to each other or the carcass will not sit squarely. Use a set square to check this.

Dry fit all these parts together, without using adhesives, to ensure that the carcass will assemble correctly (see Fig 2).

FIG 2

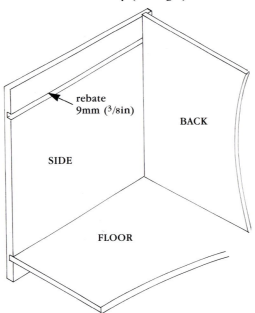

rebate
9mm (3/8in)

BACK

SIDE

FLOOR

The toy shop ready to be stocked with the front already attached

Cut the skirt to fit under the front of the floor and against the two sides. It is not fitted into a rebate but is a simple butt fitting.

Lines should now be drawn on the outer surface of each of the sides to mark the location of the floor, roof and back rebates. Drill two 1/8in diameter holes 4in from each end through the floor and roof rebates and counter-sink these on the outer face to take 3/4in long No.6 wood screws. Do not drill though the rebate for the back as 6mm is too thin to take a screw fitting well, simply gluing should be sufficient. Dry fit each of the sides to the floor and ceiling rebates and mark and drill 1/4in deep pilot holes into each of the sides, two-thirds of the depth of the screws.

CUTTING OUT THE ROOF

The small mansard-type roof sits directly on the top floor (ceiling), with just enough clearance on either side for it to be slid on and off.

From a 9mm thick MDF strip 3³/₄in high, cut the back 14in long and the two sides each 7¹/₂in long. Cut an angle of 55 degrees on both of the sides to reduce the top edges to 4⁷/₈in each. The top is also cut from 9mm MDF 14in long x 5¹/₁₆in wide with the front edge planed to 55 degrees so that it matches the slope on each of the sides (see Fig 3).

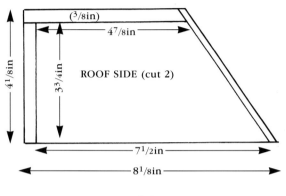

FIG 3

The sloping portion of the roof is a piece of 6mm MDF 14in x 6¹/₄in. Plane both the top and bottom edges to a matching 55 degrees in parallel as this will allow the bottom to sit flush with the top of the shop, and the other edge flush with the top of the roof. It is a good idea here to plane the bottom edge first and then plane down the top edge to fit flush with the roof top once it is assembled.

CUTTING OUT THE FRONTAGE

From a 15in x 12in piece of 9mm MDF cut out the dimensions given in Fig 4, checking with a try square to make sure that all sides are at right angles to each other. This is essential if you are using a powered router with a guide on the side to cut out the apertures. Route out the main window aperture 7in x 6in and the doorway 7¹/₂in x 3in, cleaning up the edges and squaring off the rounded corners left by the router cutter.

Cut three window formers A, B and C from 6mm MDF to the measure-

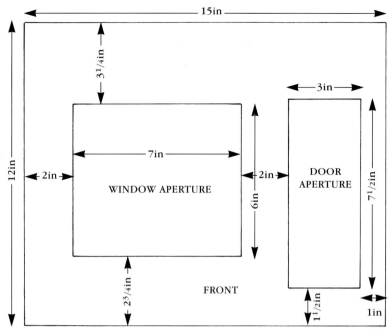

FIG 4

ments given in Fig 5 below. Note that A and B are wide enough so that they can be notched and sit inside the window aperture, overlapping at the front (see Fig 6 overleaf). Former C fits directly onto the frontage and does not need to be notched but is planed to give a 10 degree angle at the front edge in order to point the fascia board down toward the viewer in the 'street'.

Cut two spacers D and E for either end of the window fascia from a 6mm MDF offcut,

FIG 5

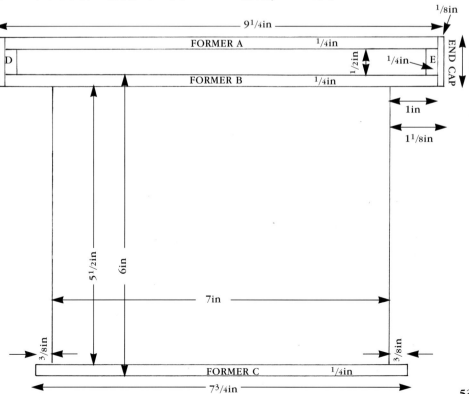

Collections of old miniature, or toy, shops that are found in America often reflect a German influence in design because many American toys were imported from Europe. Not all though, as a catalogue of American toys printed in 1893 shows a hand-painted lithographed wooden Post Office. With a glass front and fifty-six letter boxes it cost just US$8.50, for a dozen!

FIG 6

FORMER A & B

9in

1³/8in

1in

³/8in

³/8in x ³/8in

FORMER C

1³/8in

7³/4in

³/8in

to separate window formers A and B equally (see Fig 5 and Fig 7). Cut two end caps from ¹/8in thick obeche 1in x 1⁵/16in, reducing to 1in (see Fig 7).

The fascia board is made from ¹/8in thick obeche x 1¹/8in wide and can be trimmed to the angles required on site using a sharp block plane. The ¹/4in x ³/8in fanlight bar is produced from an offcut of 9mm MDF.

The cutting and assembly of all the window bars is best done 'on site' and after the gluing up of the main window former components, as measurements on your model may vary slightly from the drawing and a good fit is essential. Place all the timber cut for the components to one side until the main carcass assembly is complete (see below).

CARCASS ASSEMBLY

Commence the assembly by holding the floor firmly in a suitable bench vice or 'workmate' with one side part uppermost. Cover all the surfaces of the matching rebate of one of the sides with PVA glue and assemble this onto the floor, checking that it is flush at the front. Tap the side into place using a small hammer shielded from the surface by an offcut of MDF, until it fits snugly along the length of the rebate. Use two 1in long counter-sunk No.6 screws to fix them together.

Repeat the above method for the ceiling

using the same side piece, and check that both the floor and the ceiling are at right angles to the side. At this stage it is a good idea to fit and glue the back into its rebate so that all three parts are assembled to one of the sides. Remember to coat the back edges of the floor and ceiling with glue and

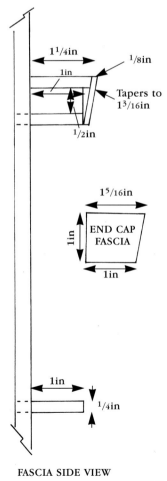

1¹/4in

¹/8in

1in

Tapers to 1³/16in

¹/2in

1⁵/16in

END CAP FASCIA

1in

1in

1in

¹/4in

FASCIA SIDE VIEW

FIG 7

use ⁵/₈in long panel pins to fix the back to them.

An alternative method would be to slide the back down into its rebates once the second side has been assembled, but if the back is a very tight fit this may prove difficult and result in the assembly being distorted and glued joints being broken.

Once the first side has been assembled to form the carcass, turn it over to fix the second side using glue and screws as before. Before the glue has set, check that all the components are at right angles to each other and that the floor and ceiling fit snugly into their rebates.

Finish off the carcass by adding the skirt under the floor, butting it against the two sides and fixing by pinning and gluing. It should not be necessary to screw the skirt into place though you may do so if you wish.

Drill a ³/₃₂in diameter hole through the back, flush with the surface of the top and aligned with the groove to allow the wiring for the centre light to pass through.

FRONTAGE ASSEMBLY

After cutting out the apertures and cleaning up any rough edges the window formers can be added. Fix the bottom former C into position first by gluing and pinning, checking that it sits at right angles to the frontage. Now fit the longer former B at the top of the window aperture, again using a try square to check that it sits at 90 degrees to the frontage. Allow the glue on both these parts to set hard before proceeding.

Using PVA glue, fix the support blocks, one at each end on top of former B and add former A, with the angled face to the front, to form the basic fascia box. Glue on the two end caps and when these are firmly in place add the ¹/₈in thick fascia board. If this is cut with the height slightly oversize it can be planed on site to match the angle of fit against formers A and B (see Fig 8). To finish off add ¹/₄in moulding along the top edge of the fascia board.

The moulding forming the window-sill on the bottom window former C is basically a D-shape but with a more pronounced downward slope to its profile (see Fig 9). This special moulding is manufactured for the leading edge of a model aeroplane wing and can be purchased from a hobby-craft shop. Cut both of the corners to 45 degrees using a mitre box and glue into place after cutting and fitting all the window bars. Note that the moulding is wider than the window former and sits flush at the top, overhanging below.

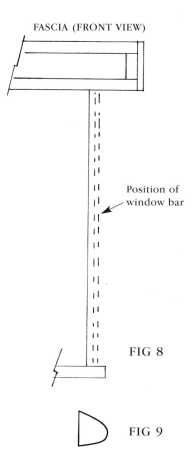

FASCIA (FRONT VIEW)

Position of window bar

FIG 8

FIG 9

Cut the base render board from ¹/₈in obeche 1¹/₂in x 12in, with one long top edge planed off to a bevel of 45 degrees. This piece stretches along the bottom edge of the frontage but is cut to allow the steps to be positioned. Fix this into place using a spirit-based adhesive.

Doorway and Door

Cut a fanlight bar from 6mm MDF, ³/₈in x 3in, and fit it into the door aperture 1in from the top (see Fig 10 overleaf). Line the finished aperture with ¹/₃₂in square obeche

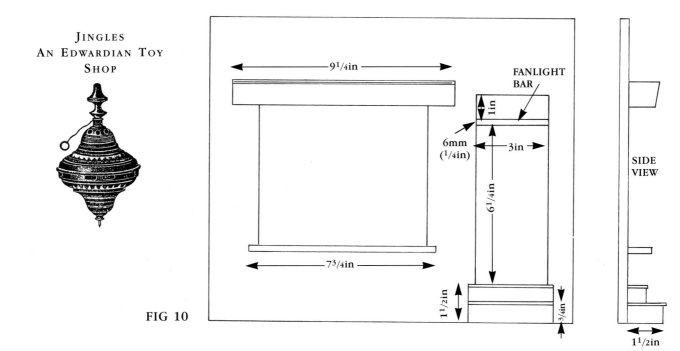

FANLIGHT
BAR

9¹⁄₄in

1in

6mm
(¹⁄₄in)

3in

6¹⁄₄in

SIDE
VIEW

7³⁄₄in

1¹⁄₂in

³⁄₄in

1¹⁄₂in

FIG 10

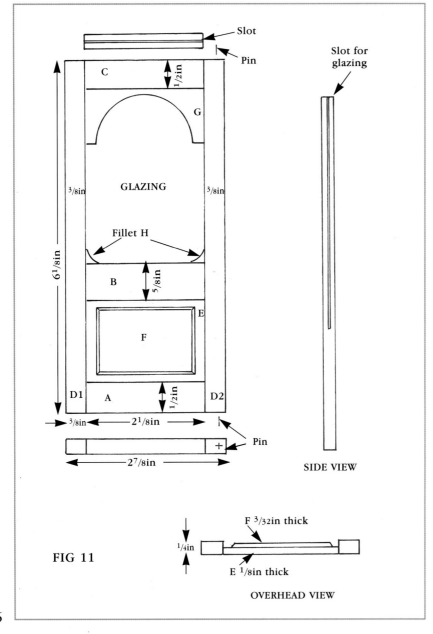

Slot

Pin

Slot for
glazing

C

¹⁄₂in

G

³⁄₈in   GLAZING   ³⁄₈in

6¹⁄₈in

Fillet H

B   5⁄₈in

E

F

D1   A   D2

¹⁄₂in

³⁄₈in   2¹⁄₈in

Pin

2⁷⁄₈in

SIDE VIEW

F ³⁄₃₂in thick

¹⁄₄in

E ¹⁄₈in thick

FIG 11   OVERHEAD VIEW

strip, notching the top inside corner to allow the pin-hinged door to swing open.

The door framework (see Fig 11) is made up from ¹⁄₈in, ³⁄₃₂in and ¹⁄₄in thick obeche. The two upright stiles, centre and top rails have been machined with a ³⁄₆₄in x ¹⁄₁₆in deep slot on the inner surfaces to take the acetate glazing sheet.

Following the dimensions given in the Materials list on page 50, all the stiles and rails A–D2 should be cut and machined first, followed by the ¹⁄₈in thick centre panel E and the ³⁄₃₂in panel F that lies on top. Use a small block plane or abrasive paper to produce a ¹⁄₁₆in wide bevel along all four edges of panel F and glue this centrally onto E.

Use a bench jig or clamps to assemble and fit parts A through to D2 but not C. Although the top rail C can be used to keep the assembly square until the glue has set, it is added *after* the glazing is in place.

Use a fine-bladed fretsaw and bench plate to fret out and shape the decorative top shape G, cutting two from ³⁄₃₂in thick obeche. Cut four corner fillets H from ³⁄₃₂in obeche. Parts C, G and H are painted and added after the glazing is slotted into place.

Door Steps

The steps are made up from machined ⁵⁄₈in thick softwood blocks to which have been added ^{1}/$_8$in thick obeche treads. Cut the bottom block 1^1/$_2$in deep x 3^1/$_2$in wide and the upper ^{3}/$_4$in x 3^1/$_2$in wide. Cut two obeche treads to the same width measurements but 1^5/$_8$in deep and ^{7}/$_8$in deep respectively. Glue these on to the steps (see Fig 10). Glue the two assembled treads together to form the completed steps. We suggest that they are added after the main window bars are assembled as it will be easier to work this way.

FLOORING

Cut the flooring from one sheet of 0.6mm thick model plywood 9^3/$_4$in x 14in and lightly sand smooth. Mark the floorboards out across the width into ^{1}/$_2$in wide strips using a steel ruler and a 0.1mm felt-tipped marker pen. Then mark artificial joins at right angles on a staggered basis, keeping them in line with imaginary joists below. As a final touch mark the heads of two nails on either side of the joins using the same marker pen. The flooring is kept as one sheet and laid using a spirit-based contact adhesive after all the decorations are completed.

ROOF ASSEMBLY

Following the dimensions given in the Materials list on page 51, cut the back, sides and top from 9mm MDF (see Fig 12) and cut the front piece from 6mm MDF. Secure the back piece into a suitable bench vice in an upright position and glue and pin the top onto it so that it is flush with the outer back edge (see Fig 13). Remove from the vice and make sure these two parts are at right angles before pinning and gluing the two sides into place against the back and the top. Place to one side and allow the glue to set before adding the front. If you decided to plane the front after assembly do this only after the glue has set.

Roof Slates

Roof slates are added to the front surface of the roof only: the top is covered later with a material to mimic asphalt and the sides are painted.

The roof slates are cut from 6-sheet card obtainable from most good art shops. Any colour will do as the surface will be painted but it might be better to avoid anything too bright. Cut one long strip ^{3}/$_{16}$in wide and set it aside. Mark up the remainder of the sheet into ^{3}/$_4$in wide strips using a steel rule and a pencil. Turn the sheet around at right angles and mark up a second set of lines, again at ^{3}/$_4$in intervals (see Fig 14). Using a sharp scalpel and a steel rule cut the card into horizontal strips following the first set of lines, placing one or two strips to one side for use later. Take one of the strips and

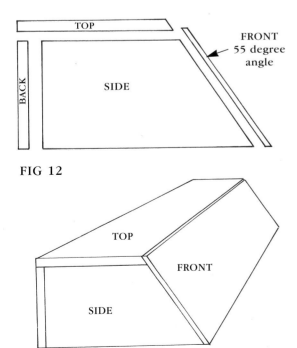

FIG 12

FIG 13

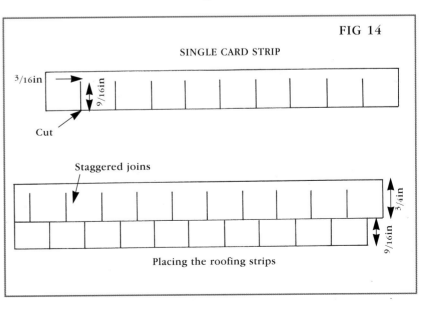

FIG 14

SINGLE CARD STRIP

^{3}/$_{16}$in

^{9}/$_{16}$in

Cut

Staggered joins

^{3}/$_4$in

^{9}/$_{16}$in

Placing the roofing strips

cut $9/16$in up each of the vertical lines to leave a series of 'slates' attached by $3/16$in at the top edge. Repeat this for as many strips as you require in order to cover the surface of the roof.

Guide lines for each row of slates can be drawn across the roof front so that they are evenly spaced and do not dip down at one end or give a wavy appearance. Draw the first line $3/4$in above the bottom edge and the second $3/8$in above that, but subsequent lines should be $3/4$in apart.

Use a spirit-based adhesive to fix the $3/16$in wide strip of card along the length of the bottom edge. The next step is to cover the roof with strips of card 'slates', the first strip being laid flush with the bottom edge and on top of the piece that is $3/16$in wide. This 'throws' the rain water off the edge and looks far more realistic than flush slating. It is important that the slates are evenly balanced at each end and it may prove necessary to trim this strip to give odd slate widths. Avoid leaving part slates of less than $3/8$in wide at the outer edges. Instead, replace these by cutting the strip back to the nearest second whole slate and replacing both the part and the first full width slate with a wide spare (cut from one of the uncut strips saved earlier). The second row of slates must be laid across and show staggered joins over the first, again adjusting the outer slates to provide a neat finish. Trim off the edges flush with the roof sides. See below for paint finishes.

The asphalt finish was cut from self-coloured grey P180 aluminium oxide abrasive paper and is applied after painting the entire roof and slated area. The paper in this model was applied in three strips, laid back to front, the front overlapping by $1/8$in and the back cut flush. To fold the abrasive paper more easily, lightly score the back of the sheet with a sharp craft knife, being careful *not* to cut all the way through. The two joins in the sheets are covered with $1/8$in square obeche strips, rounded off on the front edge and fixed in place with a spirit-based adhe-

sive. Paint them with a dark grey acrylic paint before applying.

FRONT WINDOW ASSEMBLY

This is a delicate assembly and it is a good idea to work on a flat, clean, uncluttered surface.

Cut two strips of $3/32$in thick obeche $3/16$in wide x $5 1/2$in long for the vertical front bars A and B. Cut seven lengths of $3/32$in square obeche to the same length measurement and trim all these pieces to fit between the upper and lower formers without bowing, C

through to J. (Uprights C and D are behind A and B and so are not shown on Fig 15 on page 60.)

Clamp the two $3/16$in wide pieces together and use a bench jig and razor saw or small circular saw, to cut five $3/32$in square notches in each, in order to support the cross beams K–N as shown in Fig 15 overleaf. Using these two strips as guides, mark up the positions of the middle three notches on three of the $3/32$in square strips E, F and G and cut halving joints at each mark (see Fig 16). The cen-

tre bar F is cut down at the top to allow the laser-cut panel to be glued in position. It is essential that each of these notches is cut in exactly the same place or the window will not assemble squarely.

Glue one of the un-notched $3/32$in square strips C behind the $3/16$in upright A and fit together to make an L-shaped moulding (see Fig 17). Repeat this with D for the second upright piece B. The notches should be evenly spaced top to bottom, but you might want to mark the tops of both the $3/16$in

The decorative display unit on the right is full of enchanting toys. And what child could not want to hold this delightful teddy bear?

59

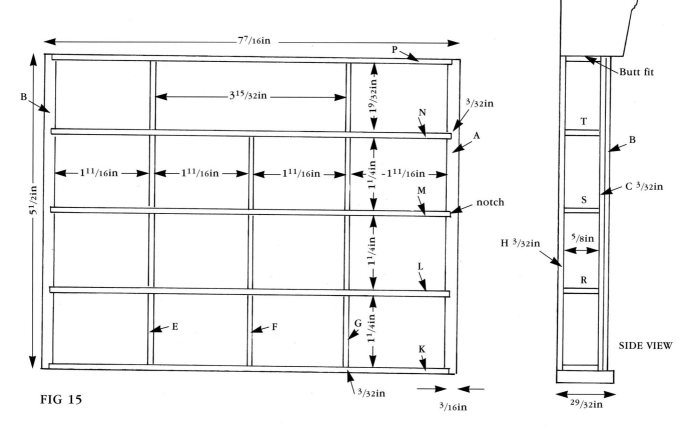

FIG 15

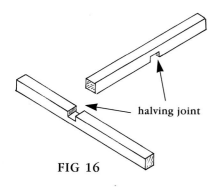

halving joint

FIG 16

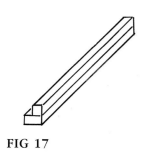

FIG 17

wide pieces A and B, remembering to glue the $^3/_{32}$in square strips at opposite outer edges.

Glue A and B to the front corner of the top and bottom window formers with the $^3/_{16}$in wide strip to the front and the notches and the strips in complete alignment.

Cut five $^3/_{32}$in square obeche horizontal bars K, L, M, N and P, each $7^7/_{16}$in wide but check this measurement with the distance between the outer limits of the notches in A and B and adjust if necessary. Place them together on a bench jig, marking off and cutting the three halving joints in all pieces.

Glue the horizontal bars K and P onto the top and bottom formers respectively, locating them into the notches of uprights A and B.

Lay the horizontal bars L, M and N face down on a flat surface and fit the uprights E, F, G and H into the halving joints. Check that all are square and glue the bars together. When this assembly is firm enough to handle, cut out the top portion of upright bar F and glue into the notches in the outer uprights A and B and horizontals K and P to complete the basic window. If you are not using the etched moulding and wish to keep this window as bars do not cut off the top of bar F.

Check the measurement between uprights C and H, and D and J is $^5/_8$in, adjusting if necessary. Cut horizontal side bars R, S, T, U, V and W and glue into position, parallel with those at the front to give a continuous line.

In order to make the window more attractive the delicate laser-etched panel grill moulding GRD 1 was added. The two side panels were carefully cut off and trimmed and the centre panel that remained was shortened to fit the opening using a sharp razor saw. In order to make the two side panels fit they were each framed with $^1/_{16}$in x $^3/_{32}$in obeche strip, having longer horizontal lengths cut to fit each corner. Other patterns are available from the importers or, alternatively, you could add a stained-glass panel.

Once the window is complete, the assembled steps can be glued on to the frontage.

GLAZING

This is added after the painting is completed. Glaze with 0.7mm thick, clear plastic sheet, cut to match the internal measurement of the main window. Lightly glue into place using a spirit-based adhesive. The two side panels are added after the front but in the same manner. This method has the advantage of using the side panels to hold the centre piece of glazing in place without additional bars.

Cut the fanlight glazing to fit the aperture and glue into place after fixing the front door.

FINISHING OFF THE FRONTAGE

Cut architectural moulding strips for outside the front doorway so that they reach to the top of the fanlight and slightly overlap the inner edges of the aperture. Cut a second and smaller moulding to span the bottom edge of the fanlight between the uprights and glue all the parts into place. Repeat this for the inside of the doorway but note that the mouldings must stop at the bottom of the doorway not the frontage, or it will not close.

The front door is pin-hinged into place on the right-hand side of the doorway when viewed from the front (Fig 11, page 56). Cut a dressmaking pin to about $^5/_8$in long, with the point, and insert this into the bottom edge of the door leaving at least $^3/_8$in proud.

Place the door against the doorway and mark the position of the pin, allowing a $^1/_{16}$in clearance between the edge of the door and the frame. Use a $^1/_{32}$in diameter drill bit with a pin drill to make a shallow hole into the bottom edge of the doorway and drop the door into the doorway with the pin located into the hole. With the door in an upright position, mark the positions for the top pin on the door and the frame. Remove the door and drill a $^1/_{32}$in diameter hole up through the door lintel and into the fanlight. Cut a second pin approximately $^3/_4$in long, this time leaving the pin head on. Replace the door into the doorway, checking that it is vertical and with the bottom pin in place, then push the second pin down through the lintel and into the door. Do not push the pin all the way down until you are sure the door will open and close easily. Leaving the head on the pin will give you something to grip should you need to make

any adjustments, and to paint the door before final assembly.

Railings

Cut four pieces of railings from a commercially produced plastic railing strip. Paint them to match the dominant colour of the woodwork and then glue to the steps.

Brackets

Add four wooden laser-cut brackets to the frontage (see photograph page 49). First paint these the same colour as the remainder of the paintwork and set to one side until thoroughly dry to the touch. Clean off the two right-angled sides of each bracket and assemble onto the front, placing one below each outer corner of the top fascia, with a second pair placed under the two outer edges of the window assembly. Use a clear adhesive for quick bonding.

EXTERIOR DECORATION

The sides of this building were given a rough pebble-dash appearance by gluing sheets of 40 grit aluminium oxide abrasive paper to either side with a PVA craft glue and priming this with white vinyl emulsion (matt or silk will be suitable). The model shown was finished off with two coats of Old English White by Farrow & Ball (see Suppliers), or you could use your own choice of paint. The top and frontage of the shop and the sides of the roof were also painted with two coats of the Old English White emulsion paint on top of a basic white emulsion primer undercoat.

A miniature dolls' house and toy fort make useful additions to stock

61

Paint the roof slates very roughly with matt white emulsion, leaving lots of gaps and unpainted areas. Dab on a little light or dark green to some areas, again not being too careful. Leave this to dry. Finish off with a coarse mixture of grey, white and black acrylic paints so as to leave traces of all three shades. Make sure that the entire area is covered and pay particular attention to the joins and crevices.

The wooden components in the model shown were painted with a silk finish colour called Caulke Green by Farrow & Ball as this gave a nice sheen to the woodwork and did not compete with the walls of the shop. The actual window bars and the delicate laser-cut panel were painted a soft off blue/white acrylic that was specially mixed in a palette to tone in with the remainder of the decorations, but you could use the green again if you wish.

The name for the shop, 'Jingles', was chosen because it is so jolly and would appeal to everyone. The lettering was purchased from a sign shop producing pre-cut vinyl letters and words. The front was measured off and the font and size of type carefully selected from those available to give a 'best fit'. The finished result is far more professional looking than the average person can sign write and the cost is minimal.

This type of lettering is supplied sandwiched between two sheets of paper, often cut roughly around the wording chosen. If possible trim this sandwich to give a regular shape, especially along the top edge. The lettering will be visible through the top layer and it should now be possible to lay it onto the fascia board and position it accurately and level. Once you have done this, secure the top edge of the lettering to the fascia using a piece of masking tape and you should now be able to lift it upward by the bottom edge, with the top acting as a hinge. Gently peel off the under layer of paper to expose the adhesive side of the lettering, making sure that the masking tape is maintaining the sheet in the correct position.

Lower the sheet onto the fascia and check it is correctly positioned before pressing down through the top sheet onto the letters. Run the edge of a piece of smooth-edged plastic (like a credit card), over the letters to make sure the adhesive comes firmly into contact with the fascia and then carefully remove the top layer of paper and the masking tape to expose the lettering. Once you have reached this stage it is virtually impossible to remove or re-position the lettering without damaging it. If for any reason you have to remove it, do so as soon as possible by lifting one edge of each letter with a scalpel and peeling it away, although it may break up as you do this. Lettering that has been in place for some time can be removed using a gentle heat, such as that from a hair dryer.

The delicate 'iron' moulding placed along the very top of the frontage breaks the hard line of the roof and is obtained as one long wooden strip. Paint the strip with a dark grey acrylic paint and when dry use your fingers to rub in a silver designer gouache to produce a 'cast iron' effect.

Mark the base of this strip 3in in from each end with a sharp awl and drill $1/32$in holes about $1/4$in deep. Cut two $1/2$in lengths of piano wire and glue these into the holes using a rapid epoxy cement. Allow this to dry and then align it over the top edge of the frontage, marking where the two pins should locate and drilling a $1/32$in hole for each. Glue and pin the strip into place to finish off.

INTERIOR DECORATION

Give the ceiling and the area below two coats of matt white emulsion being careful not to overlap the line, using masking tape to protect unpainted areas if your hand is not too steady. This small shop has a dropped ceiling line so as to allow us to glue on a coloured frieze that was taken from a single panel found in an old book of illustrations for children. It was scanned into a computer and from there it was duplicated using a desk top publishing programme,

made into a series of strips and then printed onto photo-quality glossy paper using an inkjet printer. The strips were trimmed so that the ends matched and then assembled around the walls at the predetermined level, in this case 1½in below the ceiling, and glued into place using PVA craft glue. Use a straight edge to measure the 1½in drop and mark with a light pencil line.

Alternatively, a frieze can be made by using a suitably patterned dolls' house wallpaper or gift wrapping paper. The paper is cut into strips, each strip being trimmed and the ends matched to create the impression of one long strip when laid together.

Paint the walls a nice warm colour to give the room a good ambience: a sandalwood coloured vinyl matt emulsion was used in

this model right up to the pencil line for the frieze. This colour was extended to the inside of the frontage to provide continuity.

LIGHTING

The central electric light can now be assembled. Remove any end plug from the fitting and thread the wires, from the inside, through the centre hole, across the roof level and out through the hole in the back ready for connection to a suitable transformer. Reconnect any plugs if required. Place the fitting against the ceiling and shorten the fitted chain if necessary. Use a spirit-based clear adhesive or silicone sealant to attach the light to the ceiling and support it until it is dry enough to support itself. Lay the wiring flat into the groove and glue into place.

With lots of toys displayed at child height, this shop becomes a real adventure to visit

Making up more than one flower box with different flowers will allow you to change the seasons whenever you want to.

The flower box is made up separately from the fascia and could be used to enhance other shop fronts

FINISHING OFF

Lay the thin plywood sheet flooring into place and fix down to the base with a spirit-based clear adhesive and place a large weight onto this to provide good adhesion.

To attach the frontage to the rest of the shop, first measure off the height of the left-hand side (12in) and cut a length of piano hinge ensuring that the screw holes are more or less evenly balanced top and bottom. Lay the hinge against the inside of the frontage and mark off the positions of the top and bottom screw. Pre-drill the holes slightly undersize in diameter and depth and attach the hinge. Line the hinge up with the side and again mark the positions of the top and bottom screw holes. Pre-drill the holes as you did for the front and support the front whilst you attach the hinge to the side. When you are happy with the alignment of the hinge and the front, pre-drill the remainder of the pilot holes and insert the screws. Your toy shop is now ready for its accessories.

FLOWER BOX

This is a free-standing item that is not fixed to the structure but placed into position when everything else is completed.

MATERIALS
- 1/8in obeche pieces as follows:
  Sides 8 1/4in x 3/4in, 2 off
  Ends 3/4in x 3/4in, 2 off
  Dividers 3/4in x 5/8in, 3 off
  Base 8in x 3/4in
- Wire-based greenery
- Flowerheads
- Modelling clay

Lay the base piece onto a flat surface and glue on the two sides and the ends to form a box. Fix two dividers 1 1/2in from each end and the third dead centre. Leave the glue to dry. Once dry, paint the flower box green to match the frontage woodwork.

Fill each of the divisions with air-drying modelling clay to within 1/8in of the top edge. (You could use polymer clay instead but this will not harden unless removed and baked.) Whilst the clay is still damp cut the stems of ivy or other greenery to various lengths, each about 3in, to allow them to trail outside the box. Push these into place and arrange in a pleasing pattern so that it trails down but does not obscure the window too much. When the surface of the clay has dried hard, paint this with a brown acrylic.

The flowerheads can be made with a round or patterned punch using coloured paper, adding a centre with a coloured felt-tipped pen or pencil. Flowers can also be purchased commercially from specialists. Use a spirit-based adhesive to fix the flowerheads onto the greenery, taking care to add just enough flowers to make it look natural and realistic – too much will spoil the effect.

SHOP DOOR BLIND

A blind makes a nice finishing touch to the door, adding to the attractive frontage and suggesting a little mystery.

MATERIALS
- Cream coarse cotton, 6in x 2 1/2in
- Batten 3/32in obeche 2 3/4in x 5/32in
- Dowel 1/8in x 2 3/4in
- Brass eyelets 1/8in diameter, 2 off
- Cream cotton thread

Insert the two eyelets on the inside of the door onto the top stile so that the wooden dowel rod will be held centrally. Trim the cotton fabric to size and seal the edges with glue if necessary to prevent fraying.

Drill a 1/32in diameter hole through the centre of the batten – on the 3/32in edge not the 5/32in. Pass a length of thread through

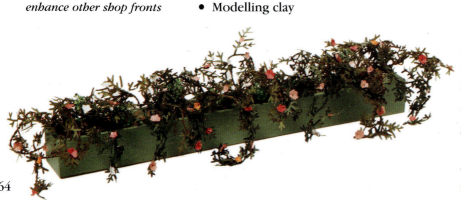

the hole, gluing one end in place and threading a fine needle on the other. Fold one end of the cotton strip around the batten and pass the needle and thread through it, then glue the strip around the batten. Ideally, use a PVA craft glue that will dry clear. If a spirit-based glue is used it should be done so very sparingly.

Wind the other end of the strip around the dowel and glue into place when an appropriate amount of 'drop' remains. Avoid too much cloth or it will not fit snugly to the door.

To make the tassel, wind a length of the cotton thread eight or nine times around a piece of card about $1/4$in wide, to form a hank. Gently pull the hank off and tie a spare piece of thread securely around the top third. Snip through the bottom two-thirds of the hank and arrange neatly to form the tassel. Pass the piece of thread attached to the batten, with the needle attached, through the top of the hank and tie off about $1/2$in below the batten.

Fit the dowel to the eyelets to finish this off, making sure that the blind is the right way round and hangs straight.

INTERIOR SHELVING
The shelves on the back wall of the shop are a useful addition as they will allow for a tempting display of toys.

MATERIALS
- $1/8$in obeche pieces as follows:
  $1^1/4$in wide x $8^1/2$in long, 3 off
  Bracket strip A $1/4$in x 1in, 6 off
  Bracket strip B $1/4$in x $3/4$in, 6 off
- Bracket strip C $1/4$in wide slice
  from $3/8$in x $1/2$in cornice moulding,
  6 off

Trim one edge of each of the strips A and B to 45 degrees. Glue bracket C to the underside of part B to form a stepped assembly. Glue part A on to the top of this assembly to form a wide bracket with a decorative base (see photograph on page 59).

Fix the brackets to the underside of the shelves 2in from either end and set aside for the adhesive to dry thoroughly.

Finish off by painting all the surfaces with a cream vinyl emulsion as a primer and undercoat and allow this to dry. Using a nearly dry brush, pick up a little sandalwood coloured vinyl matt emulsion and coat the top surfaces of the shelves. Before the paint has dried use a coarse cloth to pull off most of the paint to give a dragged effect. Repeat for the undersides to match.

Glue the shelves to the back wall with a clear, fast-grab adhesive, supporting them as necessary.

DISPLAY CABINETS
The instructions for making up the two decorative display cabinets on either side of the shop can be found in the Resource Section on page 38, however the paint finish was designed especially for this shop and can be followed if you are intending to match those in the model shown.

Seal off all of the surfaces with a good quality sanding sealer and carefully rub down any rough spots. Coat all the visible surfaces with a base coat of cream satin finish paint (a Farrow & Ball paint was used in our model – see Suppliers), applying a second coat if required to achieve a solid colour. A similarly coloured and dragged effect to the shelves, described above, was achieved by again coating with sandalwood emulsion applied with a nearly dry brush and then wiping off most of the colour before it is dry.

Instructions for making the glass-topped counter can be found in the Resource Section on page 26. The small wooden chests and shelves were taken from our own collection but were repainted in matching colours for this model.

Finally, to bring Jingles toy shop to life, fill all the shelves and cabinets, not forgetting inside the window, with lots of toys in keeping with the period and add one small and preferably well-behaved child.

A selection of small toys can easily be made to help stock your toy shop. For example, square wooden beads make excellent building blocks and can be placed into trays or used to make up puzzles. Glass beads placed inside a small, clear jar will look just like marbles. Toy train sets can be made from white metal kits and painted in a suitable livery. Miniature wheels for $1/12$ scale toys can be made with press studs and thin wire for axles.

LUSCOMBES
A VICTORIAN IRONMONGERS

Luscombes has been designed to represent a shop that would have been owned and run by an ironmonger and hardware merchant during the late nineteenth century. The building is a typical development of that period – many of these shops were often converted from houses. A hardware store of this period would be stocked with just about every nail and screw then available. The owner could find a washer for a hot water bottle made ten years earlier, and tell in an instant that a customer was holding a screw from a front door lock. A profusion of stock, from broom heads to balls of string, would be on display with many more of the smaller items stacked away inside boxes and drawers, many without identification marks. Somehow the owner would know exactly where anything was, even though there was no system or logic behind the location of anything. Often chaos reigned in the shop – candles would be here, brass knobs over there, 1/2in wire staples in the hessian sack on the floor and 3in brass hinges in the top cupboard.

The industrial expertise and new mass production techniques introduced at the start of the nineteenth century, gave everyone access to the many thousands of items seemingly required to improve everyday life, although powered tools were generally unknown. Home appliances were still very rare and wash day usually meant a tub and washboard more often than not in houses that still lacked a hot water supply.

Any DIY skills around the home were learnt then from books and magazines and the merchant with his great fund of knowledge was king – customers unfamiliar with rudimentary technical terms entered with trepidation and bowed to his superior knowledge. There was no such thing as self-service, you asked the owner, or his assistant, for what you wanted and it was found for you.

Collections of similar tools stacked together give a much more realistic appearance to displays on the shop floor

HARDWARE
IRONMONGERY

TINSMITH
FOUNDRY

ALL METAL WORK
CARRIED OUT ON
PREMISES

PLUMBING
SUPPLIES
FIREPLACES AND
FIREBRICKS
TRADE WORK
Established 1879

IRONMONGERS   LUSCOMBE & SON   HARDWARE

TINSMITHS   IRONMONGERY   HARDWARE

*Home appliances were
almost unknown at the
turn of the century and
most menial work was
still carried out by
women. Water for
washing clothes was
heated in a copper kept in
an outside wash house
and water for baths and
cooking was obtained
from a kitchen range. A
bucket for transporting
this was an essential part
of household equipment.*

*A selection of brushes
and dusters*

The decorations for this type of shop were normally basic and functional. Bare floorboards lasted longer than linoleum and brown or green paintwork did not show scuffs or dirty finger-marks easily. Walls would be a uniform cream colour, and ceilings may well have started as off white but would soon be aged by poor ventilation and tradesmen smoking. Lighting too would have been very plain and of a low level – a lot of tradesmen had yet to install electricity and gas fittings would have still been seen in some shops.

There is almost no limit to the amount and variety of stock that can be stocked in a miniature hardware and ironmongers – anything from seeds to baths and from paint to timber. Just remember not to include anything that had yet to be invented or in common use. With such a large amount of stock and the need to catch the customers' attention it is small wonder that so much was hung on the outside too.

MATERIALS

CARCASS

- 9mm MDF pieces as follows:
  Sides 22in x 11³/4in, 2 off
  Pediment 16³/4in x 2in
  Back base support 16³/4in x 1³/4in
  Pavement 16³/4in x 4in
- 6mm MDF pieces as follows:
  Back 22in x 16¹/4in
  Floors 11¹/2in x 16¹/4in, 3 off
- Pediment mouldings in obeche as follows:
  ³/32in x ¹/4in x 16³/4in
  ¹/8in x ¹/8in x 16³/4in
- Stone course ¹/8in obeche x ¹/2in x 16³/4in
- Brick-effect fibre-glass sheet, approx. 280sq in

FRONT

- Front 9mm MDF x 19⁷/8in x 16⁵/8in
- Main window support 6mm MDF pieces as follows:
  Display shelf 9¹/4in x 3in

Display shelf supports 2in x 12in
Support wall 2in x 9¹/4in
- Front support wall moulding ¹/32in obeche x 1¹/16in x 36in
- Fascia boarding as follows:
  Top A 6mm MDF x 1¹³/16in x 16³/4in
  Bottom B 6mm MDF x 1¹³/16in x 16³/4in
  Front C ¹/8in obeche x 1³/4in x 16³/4in
  End caps 6mm MDF x 1¹/4in x 1¹³/16in, 2 off
  Blocks softwood offcuts 1¹/4in x 1¹/4in x 1¹³/16in, 3 off
- Columns 6mm MDF x ³/4in x 9¹/4in, 3 off
- Column feet 6mm MDF x ³/4in x 1in, 3 off
- Column tops ¹/8in obeche x 1¹/4in x ³/4in, 3 off
- Architrave moulding ¹/4in x ³/4in, 3 off
- Plaster corbels, 3 off (see Suppliers)
- Decorative brackets BRC 1 (North Eastern – see Suppliers), 4 off
- Fascia trim strip BNB 1 (North Eastern – see Suppliers)

STAIRCASE

- Staircase kit (No. 7000 Houseworks – see Suppliers)
- Upper floor balusters x 10 (Houseworks 7009 – see Suppliers)
- Newel posts, 4 off
- ¹/8in obeche pieces as follows:
  A ⁷/16in x 7in
  B ⁷/16in x 3¹/4in
  C ¹/4in x 7in
  D ¹/4in x 3¹/4in
- Stair landing 3¹/8in x 4¹/4in
- Landing support A 4¹/4in x 1³/16in
- Landing support B 2⁷/8in x 1³/16in

MAIN WINDOW

- ¹/8in obeche pieces as follows:
  Uprights ¹/4in x 6in, 2 off
  Side frames ³/8in x 6in, 2 off
  Sill A ⁵/16in x 15in
  Sill B ³/16in x 15in
- ¹/8in square obeche x 80in (see page 78)

TOP WINDOWS

- Obeche pieces as follows:
  Lower rails $1/8$in x $1/4$in x $2^1/2$in, 2 off
  $1/8$in x $1/8$in x 36in (cut as instructions)
- Small window-sills 9mm MDF x $3/8$in x $3^1/4$in, 2 off
- A4 sheet 120gms card (lintels)

SHOP DOOR

- $3/16$in obeche pieces as follows:
  Stiles A & B $6^1/4$in x $1/2$in, 2 off
  Rails C, D & E $1/2$in x 2in, 3 off
- Centre panel $1/16$in obeche x $2^1/8$in x $2^1/4$in
- Fanlight lining $1/8$in square obeche x 9in
- Door surround architrave $5/16$in x 18in
- Door stop $1/32$in obeche x $3/32$in x 13in
- Door step 9mm MDF x $3^5/8$in x $1^3/8$in
- Fanlight bar 9mm MDF $3/8$in x 3in
- Door knobs, 2 off

TOILET ENCLOSURE

- 6mm MDF pieces as follows:
  A $9^5/8$in x 4in
  B $9^5/8$in x $3/4$in
  C $2^9/16$in x $3^1/4$in
- Door step $1/8$in obeche x $2^9/16$in x $3/8$in
- Architrave $1/4$in x 18in (total)
- Toilet bowl, high-level cistern and fittings

TOILET DOOR

- $1/8$in obeche pieces as follows:
  Stiles A & B $3/8$in wide x $6^1/8$in, 2 off
  Rails C & D $5/8$in x $1^3/4$in, 2 off
  Rail E $3/8$in x $1^3/4$in
  Stile F $3/8$in x $1^3/4$in
  Stile G $3/8$in x $2^3/4$in
  Panels H & J $1^{11}/16$in x $1^3/4$in, 2 off
  Panels K & L $11/16$in x $2^3/4$in, 2 off
- Brass door knobs $3/32$in diameter, 2 off

FLOORING

- 650in of $1/2$in wide ready-glued floorboard veneer
- Plain skirting $3/32$in x $1/2$in x 72in
- Card 120gms,12in x 18in

LIGHTING

- Lantern lamp 12 volt
- Globe lamp 12 volt
- 12 volt light fittings, 2 off
- Roof bars $1/8$in obeche x $3/16$in x $11^1/2$in, 3 off

MISCELLANEOUS

- 0.7mm acetate glazing 12in x 10in sheet (sufficient for whole project)
- Advertising board $1/8$in obeche x $2^3/4$in x 8in
- Legs $1/8$in square obeche x 5in, 2 off
- 2in brass cabinet hinges, 2 off

WORKING NOTES

Where 'glue' is referred to it means a PVA adhesive unless otherwise stated. You will also need panel pins, dressmaking pins and short lengths of piano wire. Measurements in the book are imperial, however, as MDF is only sold in the UK in metric sizes, these thicknesses are given, where appropriate, with approximate imperial equivalents, e.g. 6mm ($1/4$in), 9mm ($3/8$in).

A selection of commercial paints were used for this project but you may prefer to choose your own colours from other paint brands.

CUTTING OUT THE CARCASS

Cut two sides from 9mm MDF 22in high x $11^3/4$in wide. Square off all edges, checking that all the sides are machined or planed at right angles to each other. Lay both pieces side by side, with the inner surfaces uppermost and the two longest sides together. Following Fig 1 overleaf, mark out the positions of all the rebates starting with those along the long edge(s) that will hold the back in position. Starting with the right-hand side, draw a line 6mm ($1/4$in) in from the left edge, top to bottom and continue this line along the bottom edge. These two rebates should appear L-shaped when completed. Repeat the procedure for the left-

hand side starting with the right-hand or inner edge. When both sides are marked out you should have mirror images.

Mark up the 6mm (1/4in) wide rebates for the first floor level on both side pieces 9 3/4in above the bottom rebate (10in from the bottom edge) and repeat this for the top floor rebates, spaced at 9 3/4in above the first. Cut out all the rebates you have marked 6mm (1/4in) wide x 1/4in deep.

Cut out the back from 6mm MDF 22in high x 16 1/4in wide. Check that all the edges are square and at right angles to each other as this piece will determine that your structure both assembles and stands correctly.

Cut out three floors from 6mm MDF, each 11 1/2in deep x 16 1/4in wide. Check that all are exactly the same size and that the widths match that of the back piece exactly. Select one piece as the centre floor and mark out the stair opening as shown in Fig 2 and cut this out using a fine tenon saw or a pad saw. Clean up using a piece of fine abrasive

paper wrapped around a block or a small file. Drill a 3/32in diameter hole in the middle floor for the lighting wiring and cut a shallow groove from this point to the side wall so that the wiring can be run along the joint with the wall and out through the back.

Repeat this procedure for the top floor but this time cut the groove from the centre hole in a straight line to the back wall. When the shop is assembled it will be necessary to drill a 1/16in diameter hole through the back wall where the wiring slot terminates.

From 9mm MDF, cut the top pediment, back base support and pavement using the measurements given in the Materials list on page 68. From the pavement remove 3/8in from the two front corners, cut at 45 degrees, and use a small block plane to round these off (see Fig 3). There is no need to be absolutely accurate with this as it is intended to look as natural as possible. Finally, check that the floors fit snugly in the rebates and that the back does not protrude beyond the outer edges of the sides.

CUTTING OUT THE FRONTAGE

Cut the front from 9mm MDF 19 7/8in high x 16 5/8in wide, cleaning all edges and checking that they are all at right angles. Lay the blank front against the shop carcass and check that there is a clearance allowance of

FIG 1

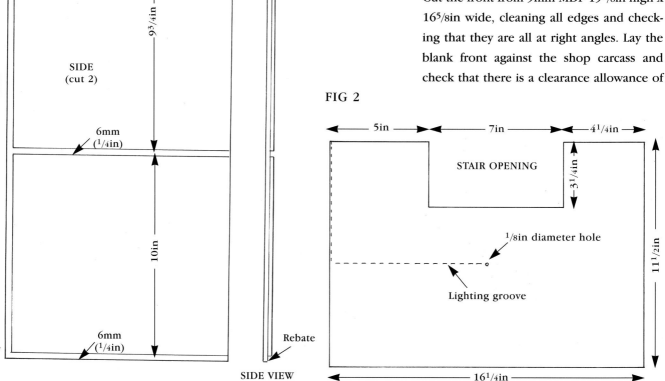

FIG 2

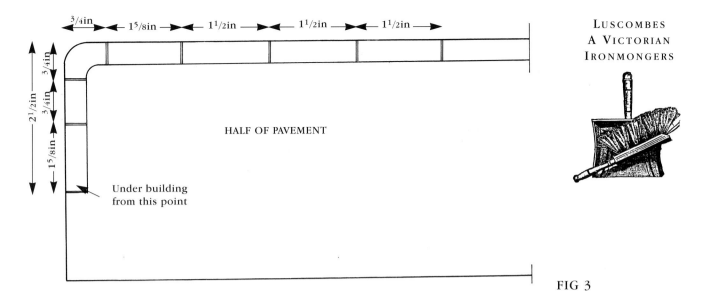

^{3}/4in ← 1^5/8in → ← 1^1/2in → ← 1^1/2in → ← 1^1/2in →

^{3}/4in

2^1/2in

^{3}/4in

1^5/8in

HALF OF PAVEMENT

Under building
from this point

FIG 3

^{1}/16in between it and the pavement and a further ^{1}/16in between it and the pediment.

Lay the front face down onto a flat working surface and following the measurements in Fig 4, mark out the upper windows, main display window and door apertures. The doorway is cut out complete with the space for the upper fanlight, as a bar is added later to divide the area. Cut out all the apertures with a powered router or use a drill and pad saw, and clean up the edges with fine abrasive paper wrapped around a suitable block.

Draw a continuous line along the front and two sides of the pavement ^{3}/8in from the edge and divide this into 1^1/2in lengths with the two corners measuring approximately ^{3}/4in each. Use a sharp knife to inscribe and cut out a 'V' cut along these lines to indicate the kerb stones.

CARCASS ASSEMBLY

Lay the two sides on a work bench with the rebates underneath and use a T-square and a pencil to draw a line along the centre line of all the rebate cuts, to provide locations for accurate pinning through to the floors and roof. Mark two points on each line 4in from each end on all the rebates and use a sharp awl to make starter holes for the panel pins.

Hold the centre floor (the one with the stairwell cut out) vertically in a bench vice and glue and pin one side to this, checking that the stairwell is to the back and that the

rebate on this side, that takes the back, is in the correct position. Carefully remove and set to one side while you fix the upper floor into the vice. Now pin and glue the same side onto this as well.

Turn the partial assembly over so that the first side is now flat on the work surface and

FIG 4

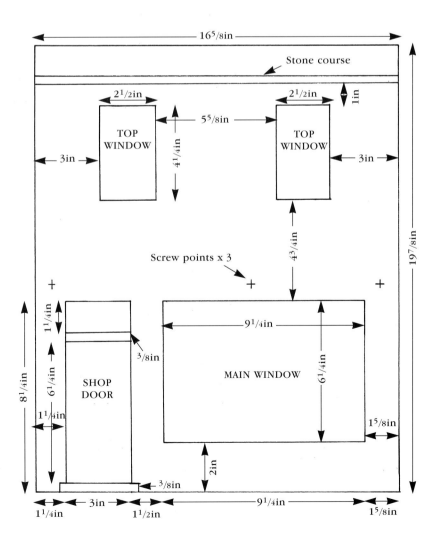

attach the second side to the two floors by pinning and gluing as before. Check that the two back rebates are aligned before proceeding and then turn the assembly over onto its top so that you can glue and pin the bottom floor into the bottom rebates. Before attaching the back check that the assembly is assembled correctly and that the walls are at right angles to the floors. Pin and glue the back into position and leave overnight for the glue to set hard.

Punch down any nail heads and check the walls and floors are square before cleaning up any rough edges with abrasive paper and a small plane. Check the inside for any nails that may have turned into the carcass and remove them. The pediment can now be glued and pinned into place.

Add the two pediment moulding strips starting with the 1³/₃₂in x ¹/₄in obeche and gluing on the ¹/₄in x ¹/₈in strip, both pieces level with the top of the pediment (see photograph on page 67). Turn the assembly over and attach the back support to the underside, flush to the back, and add the pavement to the front, leaving it protruding 2¹/₂in. The inner partitions for the toilet are dealt with later.

The Industrial Revolution in Britain and America led to the migration of hundreds of thousands of people into the towns and cities which in turn led to a demand for goods and supplies never known before. Entrepreneurs opened shops and stores to cater for the boom. The growth in manufacturing techniques led to a rapid increase in the quantity and variety of goods available and as Britain was still primarily an agriculturally based economy, the variety and quality of foodstuffs increased too. All this growth channelled itself through the market place. Boot makers, bakers, taverns, coal merchants and butchers soon gathered round a town centre if there was sufficient trade.

The ironmongers, showing the way the staircase is made to turn. It is now ready for the addition of the front

STAIRCASE

Instructions for making a staircase are given in Meadows grocer's shop (page 159) should you wish to make your own. However, for this shop a Houseworks model 7000 staircase kit was used, as, after a few modifications, it provided exactly what was wanted. One extra newel post was required for the bottom portion, see below.

Hold the staircase in a secure position and use a fine tenon saw to cut off the bottom two treads, cutting through on a parallel line to the second. Use a try square to draw a vertical line from the top tread with a second at right angles to this to provide a $1/4$in square location for the staircase against the upper floor. Alternatively follow this second cut through and add a triangular fillet afterwards to achieve the same effect. Cut the top end of the bottom two-tread piece with a vertical line so that it will fit against the stair landing assembly (see Fig 5).

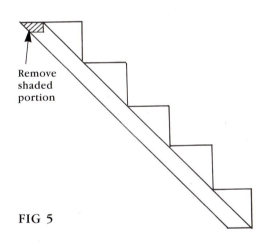

Remove shaded portion

FIG 5

Stair Landing

From 6mm MDF cut a stair landing $3^1/8$in x $4^1/4$in, and two landing supports – A $4^1/4$in x $1^3/16$in and B $2^7/8$in x $1^{13}/16$in. Holding landing support A firmly in a soft-jawed vice, pin and glue the stair landing piece to it so that it is flush at either end. Remove this and hold piece B in the vice and glue and pin this to the landing and piece A to complete the assembly (see Fig 6). When the glue has set hard clean up all edges, ensuring that they are flush.

Place the landing into position, without fixing, and lay the larger part of the staircase onto this whilst locating the upper end into the floor well. Hold this firmly in this position and mark the underside of the staircase against the back wall and the position of two treads on the top side. These marks are used as guides to drill holes through from the back and fix the staircase into position with screws (allowing its removal in order to

A well-stocked ironmongers with extra space for small items in this useful set of small drawers – see the Shopkeeper's Resource, page 40

FIG 6

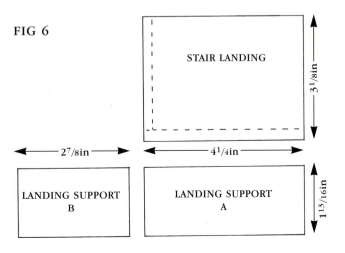

STAIR LANDING

$3^1/8$in

$2^7/8$in $4^1/4$in

$1^{13}/16$in

LANDING SUPPORT B   LANDING SUPPORT A

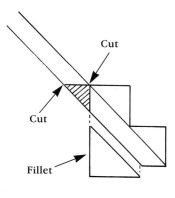

FIG 7

decorate the interior). Cut a small support wall, a fillet, from a 6mm MDF offcut $^{15}/_{16}$in x $^{15}/_{16}$in as shown in Fig 7 and glue into place under the two treads.

The staircase is supplied with treads, balusters, newel posts and handrail but because we have cut off two treads there are some modifications to make to the other components. Stain all the staircase components with a warm-coloured wood-stain diluted with 25 percent white spirit to make a paler colour and allow to dry. Do not smoke or work near naked flames when using white spirit or spirit-based stains and paints.

Glue the tread plates into place on each of the main parts of the staircase taking care that the overhang to the side is on the left-hand side as you look up the stairs, as the right-hand side is screwed to the wall. The top plate is trimmed off level with the edge to allow it to pass through the stairwell aperture. Add the balusters and bottom newel post and add the handrail trimmed to length. Glue the two-tread plates on to the bottom portion and add two balusters and one newel post. Cut a small portion of handrail to complete the link to the bottom newel post of the main staircase. Fix the main staircase onto position, and then add

the handrail but do not fix the top newel post until the flooring is laid.

Upper Balusters and Rails

Prepare the 12in strip of $^{1}/_{8}$in thick x $^{7}/_{16}$in wide obeche and cut into two lengths, A 7in long and B 3$^{1}/_{4}$in long. Mark each end of part A the position of the newel posts that sit on top of it (see Fig 8). From one of the marks measure off $^{3}/_{4}$in intervals and drill $^{3}/_{16}$in diameter holes dead centre, to take the bottom end of the wooden balusters. On part B measure off $^{3}/_{4}$in intervals from one end and repeat the drilling of $^{3}/_{16}$in holes.

Prepare parts C and D from $^{1}/_{8}$in thick obeche x $^{1}/_{4}$in wide, cut to the lengths shown in Fig 8. Bevel off the two top edges. Lay part C face down on a flat surface and place part A directly over it and, leaving an equal space at either end, mark through the drilled holes for the positions of the tops of the balusters. Remove and drill $^{1}/_{8}$in diameter holes $^{1}/_{16}$in deep. Repeat for the short lengths B and D.

Stain all the parts with the same 25/75 percent spirit wood stain mixture used on the main staircase and allow to dry.

Start the assembly by gluing in all the balusters on part A and then add the top rail B. Finish off with a newel post at either end.

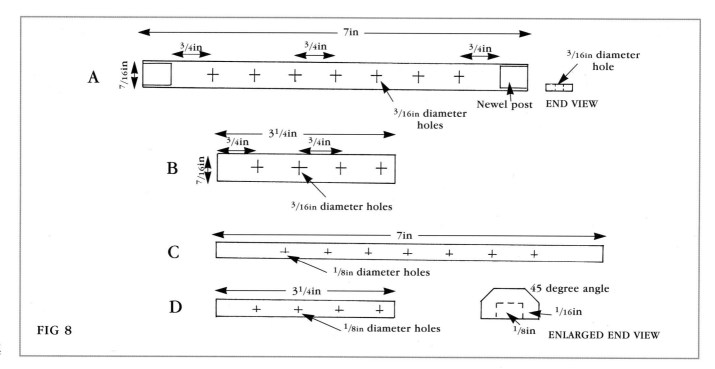

FIG 8

Repeat for parts C and D without newel posts ensuring that balusters are in an upright position. When both assemblies are set, glue them to the floor around the stairwell cut-out and before laying the flooring.

MAIN WINDOW SUPPORT ASSEMBLY

In order to make the window project beyond the body of the building, a lower support wall and window display area is built from 6mm MDF and fitted on to the front with the glazing connecting it to the upper fascia and signage boards.

Cut a display shelf 3in x 9¼in. From the 2in x 12in strip cut one piece 9¼in to match the width of the shelf, and two pieces 1¼in long. Place the longer piece into a bench vice and pin and glue the shelf on top, flush to the front edge. Check that this is at right angles and add the two pieces 1¼in wide, one at each end, to make up the support wall assembly (see Figs 9 and 10). Clean up any edges and plane matching edges flush. Slide the finished assembly into the main window aperture and glue and pin into place flush to the frontage.

Make the moulded panels from thin obeche sheet just ¹/₃₂in thick, cut ³/₃₂in wide, about 36in. Cut six pieces 2³/₄in long each with a 45 degree mitre at both ends. Cut six more 1¼in long, also with mitres at both ends. Assemble and glue onto the front wall to form three box shapes, equally spaced, ³/₈in below the sill (see Fig 10).

FASCIA BOARD ASSEMBLY

Cut out the pieces for this assembly following the dimensions in the Materials list on page 68. Make up the assembly for the top fascia board as a long open box by pinning and gluing the two longer pieces, A and B, onto the 1¼in wide end caps (see Fig 11). Glue the 1¼in square softwood blocks inside the assembly, one at either end and one dead centre.

Lay this assembly into position on the

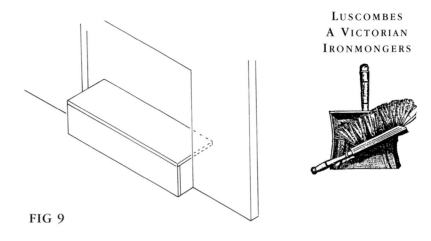

LUSCOMBES
A VICTORIAN
IRONMONGERS

FIG 9

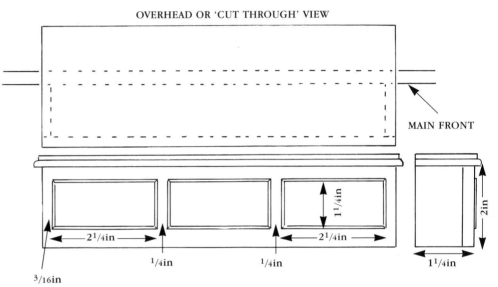

OVERHEAD OR 'CUT THROUGH' VIEW

MAIN FRONT

2¼in   1¼in   2¼in

¼in   ¼in

³/₁₆in

2in   1¼in

FIG 10

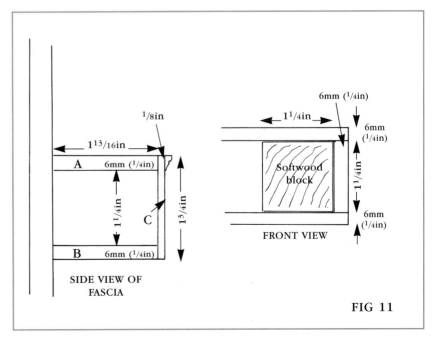

1/8in

1¹³/₁₆in

A   6mm (¹/₄in)

1¼in   C

B   6mm (¹/₄in)

1³/₄in

SIDE VIEW OF FASCIA

6mm (¹/₄in)

1¼in

6mm (¹/₄in)

Softwood block

1¼in

6mm (¹/₄in)

FRONT VIEW

FIG 11

frontage, flush with the top of the main window and mark the position of the three blocks. Drill three $1/8$in diameter holes through the frontage dead centre of each of the block positions (see Fig 4, page 71). Counter-sink these on the inside of the front to take $3/4$in No.6 counter-sunk wood screws.

Offer the fascia assembly to the frontage and, provided that all fits properly, run a bead of PVA glue along the back edges and fix into place, fixing with the three No.6 screws from the back.

Cut the signboard (Front C) for the fascia from $1/8$in thick obeche and glue it into place on the fascia box. Smooth off with fine abrasive paper and add one length of $1/4$in architrave moulding along the top edge to finish it off neatly.

MAIN WINDOW ASSEMBLY

The main window forms a square bay and fits between the lower supporting wall and the fascia boarding. The side frames are cut and made up on site first, leaving out the upper window bar until later. The main window is made up on the bench and offered up as a completed assembly. The measurements given are based on the main window being cut out accurately according to the dimensions given in the Materials list on page 68 and you should make any adjustments before commencing should yours not be quite the same in all respects.

This assembly takes at least 80in of $1/8$in square obeche and if you are not purchasing this from a commercial source it is recommended that you cut it all at the same time using the same circular saw setting in order to achieve identical sizes. We also recommend that you make a clear drawing of the main window assembly (copy Fig 12 provided on page 78) on a clean sheet of paper and pin this to a suitable flat working surface. Lightly grease the paper with petroleum jelly, to prevent the assembly sticking to the paper, and glue and pin the work to it as you progress.

Paint tins can be made from $3/16$in diameter plastic styrene tubing cut into $5/8$in lengths. Fill with modelling clay and cap with card. Paste on a wrap-around label cut from a catalogue.

Small spiral flue brushes for hardware stores can be made from the tooth brushes used for brushing in tiny gaps.

(Picture, left) *Stock and dried goods are piled everywhere and give a sense of ordered chaos. See the Shopkeeper's Resource, page 46, for how to make some of the small items*

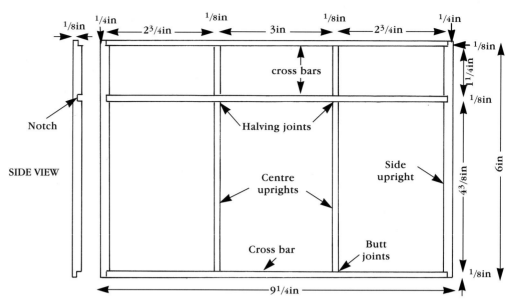

FIG 12

Side Frames

There are two sides frames, each supporting the main window assembly. Check that they are square and dead upright on fitting into the frontage or the main frame will not sit perfectly.

Cut two strips of 1/8in x 3/8in x 6in obeche for uprights and fix one to each side of the main window aperture, flush with the outer edge of the column. Cut six pieces 1/8in square x 1in long and glue one at the bottom of each of the uprights, projecting outward along the top of the support wall and flush with its edge. Glue two more pieces at the top, parallel with the ones at the bottom, and then add the front upright, cut 6in long from 1/8in square obeche, to each side to complete the basic frame. Check that the total width between the two side frames matches that of the main frame, top and bottom. Place the remaining two pieces of 1/8in square x 1in to one side and glue into position after the main window has been assembled onto the side frames.

Main Frame

Prepare two strips of 1/8in x 1/4in obeche for uprights, each 6in long and cut a 1/8in notch at each end into one edge to take the top and bottom horizontal cross bars. Place these together so that the notches match exactly and measure 11/4in from one end

and cut matching 1/8in wide x 1/8in deep notches in each piece to take the 'upper' bar (see Fig 12).

From 1/8in square timber cut three strips 9in long for the cross bars. Pin one upright into position on the work surface with the notches facing inward and glue in the bottom cross bar. Fit the second upright into position and add the top cross bar. Pin this into position also and check that everything is at right angles before leaving the adhesive to set hard.

Cut two centre uprights 1/8in x 1/8in x 53/4in – they should fit snugly inside the main window assembly – and lay them against one of the uprights. Mark the position of the notch for the upper bar on each of them and cut 1/8in wide halving joints in this position (see Fig 16, page 60).

Lay the 'upper' cross bar onto a flat surface, mark two positions 27/8in from each end and then cut 1/8in wide halving joints. Dividing the bar in this way will leave the centre portion of the window 1/8in wider that the outer ones. We felt that this gave a more natural look but purists may wish to divide the window into exactly equal portions, in which case the measurement between bars should be 2.79in, approximately 2 25/32in!

Glue the upper bar into the window assembly with the uprights and leave it until it can be handled without distortion.

Offer up the main window frame to the two side frames and glue so that they are flush together. The top should fit snugly under the fascia board and along the front of the top of the support wall. Secure them together lightly using masking tape and allow the glue to set.

Finally, add the two side 'upper' bars so that they line up with the main bar to complete the window frames. The window is glazed later, after painting.

Main Window-sill

This sill is built up from two pieces of obeche to make a step moulding (see Fig 13): these both require lengths of approximately 15in. The first, A, is ^{1}/8in thick x ^{5}/16in wide and is cut with 45 degree mitres at each end to fit around the window support wall, level with the top surface. The second, B, is ^{3}/16in wide and one edge is planed off at 45 degrees and gently rounded over with fine abrasive paper. This second bar is added so that it is flush to the bottom of the first and, again, is fitted to the side pieces with 45 degree mitres.

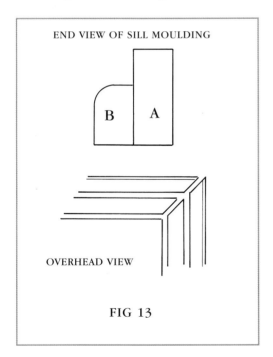

END VIEW OF SILL MOULDING

B   A

OVERHEAD VIEW

FIG 13

COLUMNS

Prepare from 6mm MDF three strips each ^{3}/4in wide x 9^1/4in long. Check that they extend from a point immediately under the

fascia to the bottom of the frontage and cut 1in off one end of each for the feet (see Fig 14). Set up a small circular saw with a ^{1}/32in depth of cut and cut four equally spaced reeded slots along the length of all three. The reeding can also be achieved using a small cutter fitted into a hobby drill that has been mounted on a stand, or by very carefully cutting with a fine saw.

Prepare the three feet from 6mm MDF, ^{3}/4in x 1in, cutting the tops at 45 degrees (see Fig 14 side view) and gluing these to the bottom of the columns.

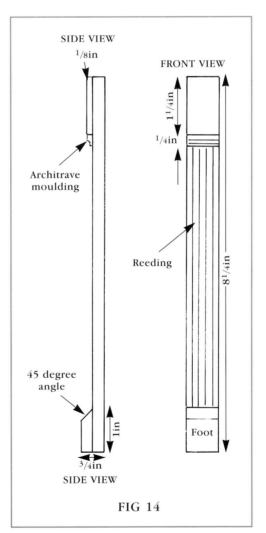

SIDE VIEW
^{1}/8in

FRONT VIEW

1^1/4in

^{1}/4in

Architrave moulding

Reeding

8^1/4in

45 degree angle

1in

Foot

^{3}/4in

SIDE VIEW

FIG 14

The three column tops are each made from ^{1}/8in thick obeche and cut 1^1/4in long x ^{3}/4in wide and glued flush to the top end of each of the columns. A ^{3}/4in long x ^{1}/4in wide piece of wooden architrave moulding is added under each of the tops to complete the column assembly.

Glue the columns into place, one flush with

An ironmonger's best advertisement was his shop window and pavement, so put as much stock as you can on display at the front. Also, you can't have too many signs and notices for an ironmongers shop. Advertising from large manufacturers was becoming very prevalent and coloured posters and hoardings were everywhere. Many signs were made by gluing metal or china letters to windows. You can achieve this with press-on lettering applied to the front of acetate windows.

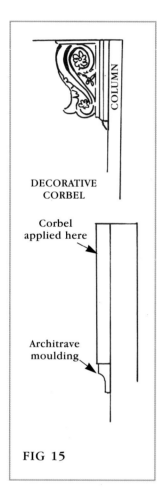

DECORATIVE
CORBEL

Corbel
applied here

Architrave
moulding

COLUMN

FIG 15

the left-hand edge, and with the second and third placed either side of the main window. Glue the three plaster corbels to the top faces of each of the columns so that the top of each one supports the fascia (see Fig 15).

TOP WINDOWS

Buildings of this period were fitted with the boxed sash windows that originated in the late Georgian period, the only difference being that the manufacture of large sheets of 'float' glass allowed larger panes. Here, each window has two, arranged as an upper and a lower sash, with the top sash lying over the bottom to prevent water driving inwards. You will notice that the bottom rail on a sash window is always deeper that those of the sides or top.

Start work from the back of the frontage. Cut two lower rails from $1/4$in obeche x $1/4$in wide x $21/2$in and glue each of them into the window recesses at the bottom and $1/8$in from the back edge (see Fig 16). Cut two uprights per window from $1/8$in square obeche, all $23/8$in long and use a sharp craft knife to trim one end at 30 degrees for the 'horn'. Glue these into place above the bottom rail, keeping them also $1/8$in from the

back edge. Cut the centre cross rail from $1/8$in square obeche x $21/4$in wide and fit this dead centre of the window aperture, $21/16$in from top and bottom.

Turn the frontage round so that you are now working from the front and cut two top rails from $1/8$in square obeche, $21/2$in long and glue them into place $1/8$in from the front edge in each aperture. Cut the vertical bars $23/8$in long, trim the ends for the horns as before and glue into place. Complete the assembly by cutting and fitting the centre rails as before, lining them up level with those of the bottom section of the window. These windows are glazed later, after painting.

Cut two window-sills from 9mm MDF x $3/8$in x $31/4$in long and glue both to the frontage immediately below and flush to the bottom of the window apertures.

Lintels

In our model, projecting lintels were added over both of the top windows but as we did not want to make this a dominant feature both were made from thin but good quality card. Cut two pieces of card $31/4$in long x $3/4$in wide and trim both ends of each at 60 degrees so that the bottom measures $21/2$in, the same as the window apertures (see Fig 17). Using the back of a scalpel blade score lines, also at 60 degrees, to mimic brick joints, spaced at $1/4$in apart. Cut the two keystones from the same card, $11/8$in tapering to $3/8$in, and glue these to the centre of the header strip. Glue both strips over the window using a spirit-based adhesive.

STONE COURSE

To mimic a stone course, glue a strip of $1/8$in obeche x $1/2$in wide x $163/4$in long across the width of the frontage, $11/8$in below the top.

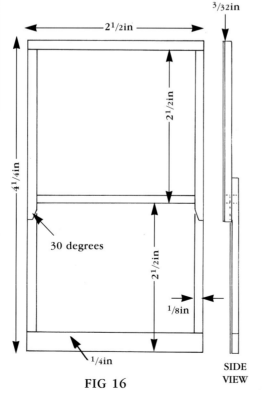

$21/2$in

$3/32$in

$41/4$in

$21/2$in

30 degrees

$21/2$in

$1/8$in

$1/4$in

FIG 16

SIDE
VIEW

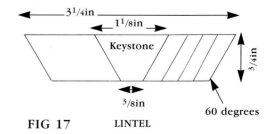

$31/4$in

$11/8$in

Keystone

$3/4$in

$3/8$in

60 degrees

FIG 17   LINTEL

SHOP DOOR

Cut the stiles and rails from $^3/_{16}$in thick obeche as detailed in the Materials list on page 69 (see also Fig 18). Machine the two upright stiles, and the bottom and top rails to give a $^1/_{32}$in wide x $^1/_{16}$in deep slot along one edge to take the panel or the glazing. You may find it easier to machine one complete length of $^3/_{16}$in thick obeche so that the saw setting for the slot remains constant. Take the centre rail and cut the second slot.

Cut the centre panel from $^1/_{16}$in thick obeche, $2^1/_8$in x $2^1/_4$in and machine away to $^1/_{32}$in wide all around one edge, leaving $^1/_{32}$in thickness. Using a flat surface and bench jig, assemble and glue the two sides and the bottom and centre stiles around the centre panel and allow to set.

Measure and cut a piece of acetate to fit the door and place it to one side for the moment. Paint the assembled door the same brown as the frontage, leaving the top stile separate, putting this in place after the final coat of colour, along with the acetate glazing.

Door Architrave and Fanlight Lintel

Cut enough $^5/_{16}$in architrave moulding to fit around the front of the door opening, gluing the moulding flush to the inner edge.

For the fanlight lintel above the door, cut a piece of 9mm MDF, $^3/_8$in x 3in and insert into the doorway $1^3/_8$in below the top of the door, cut out to leave $6^1/_4$in for the door (see Fig 4, page 71). Prepare a strip of $^1/_8$in square obeche and from this cut two 3in and two $1^1/_8$in strips and use these to line the inside of the fanlight $^1/_4$in in from the front (and $^1/_4$in from the back).

Door Step

The step is made up from a piece of 9mm MDF $3^5/_8$in wide x $1^3/_8$in deep. Round off the two front corners with a sharp chisel and finish off with abrasive paper. Fix into a bench vice and cut two $^3/_8$in x $^5/_{16}$in notches on the back corners so that it will fit into the doorway (see Fig 19). Check this

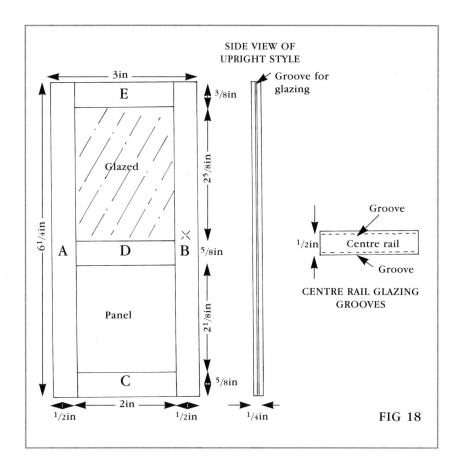

FIG 18

measurement on site to ensure a snug fit then glue into place.

Prepare two strips of $^1/_{32}$in x $^1/_{16}$in obeche for a door stop moulding and glue these $^1/_8$in inside the doorway on each side.

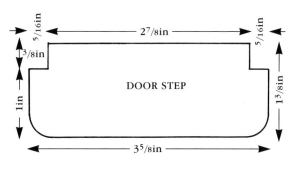

FIG 19

Hinging the Door

The door is pin-hinged with two ends of a dressmaking pin to avoid working with hinges that are never quite small enough. When the door is finally painted and assembled drill a hole into the fanlight lintel, the same diameter as the pin being used ($^1/_{32}$in diameter) $^1/_8$in inside the doorway and repeat this through the step below. Cut the sharp end of the pin to about $^1/_2$in in length and push it into the top of the door, $^1/_8$in from the left-hand edge of the door stile. Offer the door into the doorway aperture and push the end of the pin into the hole specially drilled for it. Straighten up the door and push the headed end of the pin

The upstairs part of the shop doubles as a stock room and staff room, complete with toilet enclosure

through the bottom of the pavement and into the door stile. Check that the door is straight and will open, adjusting as necessary.

LIGHTING

Lighting should be installed after the final coat of paint to the ceilings and walls (this decoration is done later) but before finishing off the roof or laying the floors. Drill 1/16in diameter holes through the back wall where each of the two lighting slots on the floors terminate at floor level. Shorten the lamp chain on the lantern for the ground floor shop area so that it hangs 6in above the floor and remove the plug at the end by pulling out the push fit pins. Thread the wires through the ceiling hole and then lay a thin line of spirit-based adhesive along the groove cut earlier and lay the wire into this. It should lay flat immediately, providing that you have taken all the kinks out of the wire, if not cover with a piece of masking tape until set. Thread the wire out through the hole in the back wall and re-assemble the plug. Repeat this procedure for the second lamp on the upper floor, laying the wire

across the roof and through the second hole.

Cut three roof bars from 1/8in obeche, each 3/16in x 11 1/2in long. Glue them down with the centre one covering the wire, setting the others at equal distances apart from the centre.

TOILET

Before proceeding with the assembly of this enclosure it is worth noting that this is intended to appear as an *addition* to the building, not something that was designed and built into the carcass at the outset. You will notice that the walls abut the upper floor baluster and rails, fit around the skirting boards and sit on top of the flooring. The thickness of your flooring may vary from our model so we suggest that you check the height to the ceiling, allowing for the thickness of the floorboards to be laid later, and reduce this amount by 1/16in to allow it to slide into place.

Cut and prepare a piece of 6mm MDF for wall A, 9 5/8in x 4in, ensuring that all edges are square. Cut a 3/32in wide x 1/2in high slot in the bottom left corner to accommodate

the back skirting (see Fig 20). Cut out wall B from 6mm MDF, $9^5/8$in x $3/4$in, and again cut a slot in the bottom corner for the right-hand skirting. Finally, cut piece C $2^9/16$in x $3^1/4$in and drill a $1/32$in diameter hole for the pin hinge as shown in Fig 20. Glue and clamp A, B and C together to form a doorway, with C above the doorway (see photograph page 82). Now is a good time to test fit the toilet wall assembly and make any necessary adjustments.

Whilst in real life this door would use hinges, we used a simple pin hinge and for this reason we needed a door step. This is cut from $1/8$in thick obeche x $3/8$in x $2^9/16$in and glued into place. Finish off the doorway with a $1/4$in architrave all round the outer side allowing it to overlap the aperture by just $1/32$in to act as a doorstop.

Toilet Door

Prepare all the main parts for the door from $1/8$in obeche and the four panels from $1/16$in thick obeche (see Materials list on page 69). Glue and clamp together in a suitable bench vice, laying the panels to give a flat surface at the back (see Fig 21).

Paint the doorway and door separately with pale brown matt emulsion and when you are happy with the finish check that the door will still fit the doorway, adjusting as necessary. In order for the door to swing in the aperture it will be necessary to remove a fine bevel along the length of the 'hinged' edge of the stile. Don't over-do this though and if anything take off small amounts of material each time until you achieve the fit you want. Repaint any bare areas and add a small $3/32$in diameter door knob on the right-hand stile.

Cut a dressmaking pin into two parts and insert the sharp end into the top of the door, $1/8$in from the left-hand end. Place the door, with the pin in place, into the doorway until it is upright. Hold it firmly in place and insert the headed portion of the pin through the step and into the door. Check that it swings correctly, adjusting if necessary.

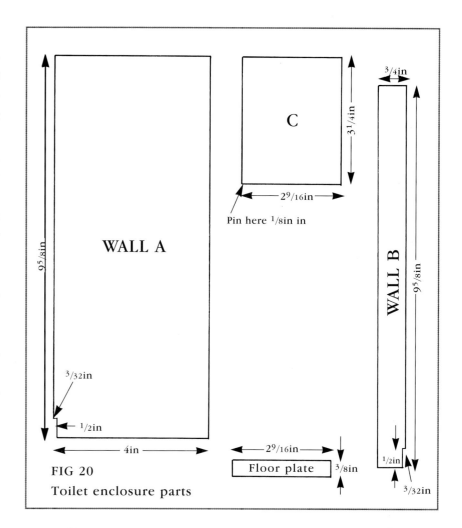

FIG 20
Toilet enclosure parts

EXTERIOR DECORATION
Decorative Fascia Strip

To add the decorative strip to the fascia, cut the BNB 1 strip to fit directly over the main window, taking care to trim it from both ends so that the pattern matches. Drill two $1/32$in holes into the base of the strip 2in from either end, taking care that the drill does not break through into the pattern as it may shatter. Use a rapid-set epoxy glue to fix two short pieces of piano wire into the holes allowing about $3/8$in to protrude. Place the strip onto the fascia and mark the position of the two pins, then drill matching $1/32$in diameter holes ready for assembly.

Paint the strip with an off-white sealing coat of emulsion. The strip on our model was finished off by rubbing on a gold paste and buffing it up with a dry cloth to give a dull sheen. Place to one side until the assembly and painting of the shop is complete.

Painting the Exterior

Check that all nail heads are punched down below the surface and use a proprietary

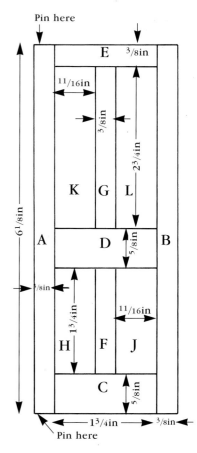

FIG 21

83

plaster or wood filler to fill all the holes and gaps around the building. When this has dried use abrasive paper wrapped around a sanding block to smooth off all the surfaces. Check that there are no splinters or snags hanging off mouldings and carefully rub down any of the fine window bars to remove fibres. Painting methods will vary according to the tools you have available: most people use a standard bristle brush, however on this model a combination of mini foam-rubber paint rollers and a good quality 3/8in wide artist's bristle brush was used to apply emulsion paints to the surfaces of the larger areas. The brown colour used on the lower half of the model shown is a satin finish, oil-based paint from Dulux 80YR 19/177. The upper part of the building is painted with a cream emulsion.

Cover the inside and outside surfaces of the frontage with a light coloured emulsion paint primer, including the upper window parts and all of the lower main window assembly. Paint a top coat to the inside of the frontage wall using the pale brown emulsion that was applied to the interior but avoid all window assemblies. Using the paint roller, apply a top coat of pale stone silk finish emulsion to the exterior of the frontage down to the level of the fascia.

The upper window assemblies are finished with a flat colour using a white acrylic paint – an artist's bristle brush is best for this.

Painting the Fascia

This includes all of the main window assembly, the front door and the fascia board above the window including the inner surfaces of the window and the window shelf. Apply two coats of brown satin finish paint (Dulux 80YR 19/177). This should be sufficient but more coats can be added if required.

Pavement

The pavement is attached to the main body of the building and should be finished at this stage. Paint the surface with a grey acrylic or emulsion to provide a base colour. The best

finish for this surface will need to be mixed from a variety of colours. Use a palette to mix up brown, black and white acrylics, taking care that the mix is not too thorough. Apply roughly all over the surface.

Roof

As this is an entirely self-contained area it can be finished off after the lighting has been installed on the upper ceiling and the wiring covered by a roofing bar. However it can also be painted before, providing that the centre bar is painted with the same mixture and placed to one side until required, then simply glued into place.

In this period flat roofs would have been covered with weathered asphalt or possibly lead. You can achieve this effect by using a mixture of acrylics, sealing off the surface first using a thin application of a grey artists' acrylic paint.

Sides and Pediment

The upper part of the sides of the building and pediment are painted, whilst the lower half of the walls are covered with brick-effect fibre-glass sheet. Measure off the halfway mark on both walls and avoid painting below that line if at all possible, using masking tape if necessary to achieve a straight division between brick and paint. Use a suitable brush or roller to apply a thin sealing coat of pale stone-coloured vinyl silk emulsion paint and allow this to dry. Apply two more coats, preferably with a mini paint roller as this will give a better textured effect than a brush.

To decorate the walls with brick-effect sheet, two pieces of matching fibre-glass brick sheet need to be added to each side, from the ground level to that of the first floor level, 10¼in high x 11¾in wide. In this case a standard English bond pattern was used but the finish could be varied according to the bond prevalent in your part of the world. Cut the sheets so that there is a good clean front edge to the building: in this case it's wrapped around the front wall, but you could add a separate matching strip if you think that would be easier. If you follow our method around the front, lightly score a line down the first ³⁄₈in to enable a sharp fold. Remember when cutting the second sheet that it is a mirror image of the first – the front becomes the back and the back the front. Make sure the paint finish is completed before gluing on the sheets or there may be some paint splashes and over-run. Apply a white PVA glue brushed or spread evenly over the surface of the wall and lay on the sheet paying attention to the wrap-around sections and the edges.

INTERIOR DECORATION
Painting the Interior

Paint all the surfaces with a thin sealing coat by adding 10 percent water to some matt finish emulsion – white on the ceilings, light cream on the walls – paying special attention to crevices and allowing this to dry thoroughly. Although any colour can be used for this it is a good idea to use the same colour as you intend to use for the top-coat in order to avoid darker colours 'grinning' through.

Finish off both ceilings with a second coat of matt white emulsion, being careful not to get any paint on the walls as these will be a different colour. Paint all the internal walls with a pale brown silk vinyl emulsion.

Toilet

Paint the entire assembly, inside and out to match the walls, with the pale brown emulsion used for the remainder of the interior. Note that the toilet bowl and cistern are added later after all the decoration is complete (see page 87).

FLOORING

Cut one piece of good quality card, over 120gsm, to fit both of the floors exactly, remembering to cut around the stairwell and bottom landing. Try for a good snug fit and if necessary tape two pieces of card together to achieve this. Measure off and draw pencil lines showing the positions of imaginary floor joists so the joins in the boards can be indicated to add realism.

The flooring veneer strip is coated on the back with heat sensitive adhesive and is activated with an ordinary domestic iron set to a medium temperature. Miniature boards usually look best when laid from left to right as most joists in houses run from front to back.

Lay the card onto a flat surface with the front furthest away from you and lay the first board into position flush with the front edge. Press the warm iron down firmly until the glue melts, being careful not to move the board out of position. The second board can be laid almost immediately, taking care to lay it against the first with no gap. Proceed in this manner until all the boards are laid on the card, working around the stairway and other cut-outs. Cut some of the boards at the position of the joists and simply rejoin to indicate a board joint.

When all the boards are laid, turn the completed sheet over and cut off any ends of veneer flush with the card and check that the sheet fits the floor space exactly and lays around any obstacles. Remove onto a flat surface and smooth off the sheet with abrasive paper wrapped around a block. Press a sharp pencil point into the board at the joints to indicate nail heads. The floor may be varnished or waxed if you prefer: we decided that as this was a practical and working shop, we would leave ours as they were.

Glue the flooring sheets into position using a rapid-drying contact adhesive: it would be advisable to seal the floor before gluing to prevent dry timber absorbing the glue before it can take effect. Water-based adhesives such as PVA are not recommended on this job, as the card may warp when taking up the moisture present in these glues. Add the skirting boards after laying the floors to make the edges look neat.

Rolls of asphalt and fence wire displayed in a dustbin from shop stock

85

At one time Brighton, in
southern England,
boasted a 'cork shop', not
actually made of cork but
one that only sold items
made from this natural
material. Bungs, liners,
potmenders, and clutch
pads for motor cars were
all openly displayed.

Skirting Boards

It should be remembered that this is a very plain shop not a dwelling and that any skirting boards would be there simply to make the ends of the walls and floors look neat, consequently they would be very plain. Machine off sufficient $1/2$in wide boards from $3/32$in thick obeche and cut to fit, remembering to mitre all the corners. Paint all of these the same colour and shade of brown as for all other woodwork (brown satin finish oil-based Dulux 80YR 19/177) and fit after laying the flooring. Note that they are glued into position *before* inserting the toilet walls as this is meant to be an addition built around existing fixtures.

Once the flooring and skirting is completed, glue the stair landing into place and add the bottom two flights, then screw the main staircase into position.

GLAZING

Cut acetate or Perspex sheet 0.7mm thick to fit the main window, fanlight and top windows. Glue the pieces into place using a spirit-based adhesive. This glue can 'string' leaving traces across the acetate but it can be removed, once dry, using a cotton bud soaked in methylated or denatured alcohol.

SIGNAGE
Advertising Board

In the model shown this board was placed onto the frontage of the building in order to facilitate the photography and achieve a balance, however it would be more correct to place it on legs on the roof.

Cut the main board from $1/8$in thick obeche and square off all edges. Paint brown to match the other wooden paintwork and then add the laser-cut lettering. See below for the application of the lettering.

If standing the board on the roof, prepare two legs from $1/8$in thick obeche x $1/4$in wide x 5in long and glue these onto the back of the board $1/8$in from each outer edge (see Fig 22).

Poster

The advertising poster in the centre of the main wall and the two strips on the outer edges of the fascia were designed on a computer using a desk top publishing package and printed off onto photo quality paper. Any number of effects, colours and typefaces can be achieved in this way.

Lettering

The advertising board on the top frontage of the building (Hardware – Ironmongery) and the sign on the shop fascia (Luscombe & Son), were made using wooden laser-cut letters to give a striking three-dimensional effect (see Suppliers). These are really excellent and quite robust, although care must be taken with really thin sections, such as the letter V. Each letter is painted and placed on separately so great care must be taken to avoid crooked letters and spelling errors! Check that you have the correct letters and lay them along the fascia to find out the best arrangement, making a note of the centre, start and finish points and checking that the spacing is correct. Make a note of all these measurements and then remove the letters.

To paint them, first fix a piece of masking tape to a flat board with the adhesive side uppermost. Press each of the letters onto the tape to keep them in place and paint on a sealing coat. We recommend using car spray enamel to do this as it is less likely to drip and gives even coverage. Those letters

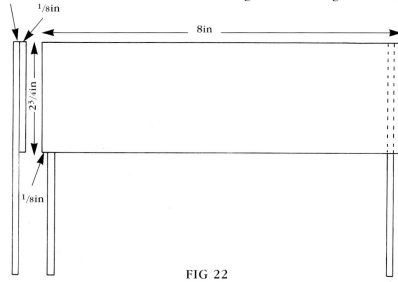

$1/8$in
$1/8$in
8in
$2^3/4$in
$1/8$in

86

FIG 22

used for the signboard were then painted a cream colour, again using car spray enamel of a suitable colour. Avoid overspraying and building up too many coats of paint as it will show at the edge of the letters when removed from the tape. If you need more than two coats we suggest that you carefully remove the letters from the masking tape after they are dry and then repeat the above method using a second piece of tape. The letters for the fascia of Luscombes were first painted a cream colour then had gold paste rubbed over to give an aged appearance.

To apply the lettering, first lay the finished lettering out onto a flat surface to check the spelling and the spacing. Find the centre of the word, not the middle letter, and locate the centre of the fascia. Use a straight edge (a steel ruler will do) and practise building up the word along the fascia. It may be necessary to remove the straight edge if some of the letters have tails that fall below the base line. When you are confident that you can do this with adhesive on the letters proceed by applying a very thin coat of clear spirit-based adhesive to the back of the first letter and pressing it into position. Build up the wording slowly and carefully checking by eye and ruler as you go.

Window Signs

The instructions for making up these three signs from lettered beads are given in the Shopkeeper's Resource section on page 47. The wires at each end were simply inserted into the ceiling of the inner part of the window, flush with the glazing.

SHELVING

The five narrow shelves fitted to the shop interior are useful for displaying various items, such as the tins of paint, bowls and saucepans shown in the photograph on page 82.

MATERIALS

- $3/32$in thick obeche x $3/4$in x 42in
- Strip of $5/8$in x $3/8$in cornice

From the obeche cut five shelves each 6in long and add $1/4$in wide wooden brackets cut from a strip of $5/8$in x $3/8$in cornice. Glue two brackets onto each shelf $1^1/2$in from the outer edge and colour with a diluted mixture of oak wood stain. (It's best to stain all parts before gluing up to avoid leaving 'spots'.) Fix to the wall with a clear spirit-based adhesive.

COAT RACK

This useful and very easily made item could be constructed for any of the shops featured in the book.

MATERIALS

- Obeche $3/32$in thick x $3/8$in x $2^1/2$in
- Coat hooks, 4 off

Smooth off the edges of the obeche strip and stain a light oak colour if required. Add the four hooks equally spaced and glue into position outside the toilet.

FINISHING OFF

Complete the toilet enclosure by adding a toilet bowl and high-level cistern, sliding the wall assembly in afterwards.

Add two 2in cabinet hinges to attach the frontage to the main building, positioning them centrally on the lower and upper right-hand walls (a piano hinge can be used if you prefer).

Push in a series of small, thin, brass nails just under the fascia, bending them upward to form hooks for hanging stock outside. A series of shop signs can be printed off from a computer using a very small type face of 6pt and mounted on thin card.

The instructions for making the special counters and wall-mounted sets of drawers can be found in the Shopkeeper's Resource chapter on pages 22, 24 and 40.

The amount of stock you have in your shop and the placement of it is a personal matter but various examples of the stock found in Luscombes is shown in the photographs accompanying this chapter.

Many branded goods available at the turn of the last century are still available today but remember that many of the packaging designs will have changed.

THE CLARENCE
AN ART DECO TEA ROOM

The taking of tea in elegant surroundings probably had its origins in the coffee houses of the seventeenth and eighteenth centuries – a place to meet, discuss the day's business and talk about an acquaintance or two. The main difference between coffee houses and tea rooms or shops is that the former are thought to have catered almost exclusively for gentlemen. The Lyons Corner Houses everywhere became famous in their own right as tea rooms and many people will be familiar with the sight of a 'Nippy' or waitress fitted out in a snug black dress, shoes and stockings, complete with a white apron and head-dress. Completing the ensemble were an order pad and pencil, suspended from the waistband on a thin cord.

The range of tea rooms is probably larger than at first thought and yours could be any one of several. Typical might be an English 'Copper Kettle' establishment, usually located in a small country town and tucked inside a Tudor-style building. It would be full of heavy oak furniture, hung with brass ornaments and have a house speciality, such as rock cakes. Not so typical are the shiny chrome, glass and tiled 'cafés', doubling up as milk bars during the day and coffee houses at night, probably situated in a large industrial town or the outskirts of London, especially prevalent during the mid 1950s. A tea room could even be a 'greasy spoon', with oil cloth-covered tables and a proprietor who leans on the counter, dropping cigarette ash into the cups as he selects a curled-up cheese sandwich for a weary traveller. It might also be a special room within a large hotel with comfortable chairs, pewter-coloured teapots and lashings of hot water, perhaps with a snoozing retired colonel tucked into one corner.

THE CLARENCE AN ART DECO TEA ROOM

The tea room with all the decorations completed

Our tea room is set in the period between the two great wars, years famous for so many things, including the 'roaring twenties', flappers, jazz, cubism and a design concept that swept the world called Art Deco. This radical design was characterised by strong geometric patterns contained within simple lines and extreme streamlining.

Charles Rennie Mackintosh, a notable Scottish designer, was one of a number of artists who produced work that predated and strongly influenced the concept of Art Deco. The Willow Tea Rooms in Glasgow are a typical example of his work and although these are somewhat different to our project they include the strong geometric design elements so prevalent in Art Deco.

Architects in this period gave Art Deco treatments to both the interior and exterior of buildings, even skyscrapers and railway stations. Cinemas also embraced the design, leading to the famous 'Odeon' look. Interior decoration varied enormously. Muted oranges and yellows combined with gold were dominant, but design classics with striking geometric patterns in black and silver provided a dramatic look. Lighting was usually indirect with the use of 'uplighters' and wall light fittings or illuminations concealed behind a decorative pelmet or frieze.

We had several options when selecting furniture for The Clarence tea room. We decided to use the bentwood table and chair designs of the Thonet Company but alternatives could be the basket-work chairs and tables of Pierre Chareau or the tubular metal tables and bar-stools seen in dining rooms of some of the ocean-going liners.

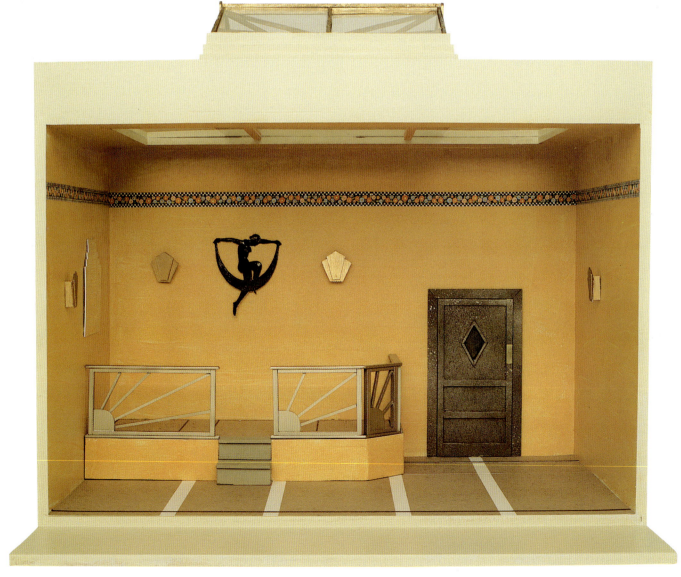

MATERIALS

CARCASS

- 9mm MDF pieces as follows:
  Side 12$^1/_4$in x 15in, 2 off
  Roof beams A & B 19$^5/_8$in x 2in, 2 off
  Roof beams C & D 8$^1/_4$in x 2in, 2 off
  Pavement 20in x 5$^1/_2$in
  Floor 19$^5/_8$in x 12in
  Pediment 19$^1/_4$in x 1$^5/_8$in
- Back 6mm MDF x 15in x 19$^5/_8$in
- Roof glazing support bars $^1/_8$in
  obeche x $^1/_4$in x 8$^1/_4$in, 2 off
- A4 sheet of thin card, 120gsm

FRONTAGE

- 9mm MDF pieces as follows:
  Main front 19$^1/_4$in x 12$^1/_4$in
  Top 20in x 3$^1/_2$in
  Base 20in x 4in
  Side 3in x 12$^1/_4$in, 2 off
  Fanlight bar $^3/_8$in x 3in
  Fascia pediment 2$^5/_8$in x 19$^1/_4$in
  Fascia under-pediment 1$^7/_8$in
  x 19$^1/_4$in
  Block supports 1$^1/_2$in x 2$^1/_2$in
  Window formers A 2$^3/_8$in x 7$^1/_8$in, 2 off
  B 2$^3/_4$in x 7$^1/_8$in, 4 off
- $^1/_8$in obeche pieces as follows:
  Frontage base A 5$^3/_4$in x 1$^3/_4$in, 2 off
  Frontage base B 2$^3/_4$in x 1$^3/_4$in, 2 off
  Step $^3/_4$in x 3in
  Motif over doorway A 4$^1/_4$in x $^3/_4$in
  B 4in x $^1/_2$in
  Plaque support $^1/_4$in x 2$^1/_2$in (total)
- Fanlight moulding $^1/_{16}$in obeche x
  $^1/_{16}$in x 10in total
- Window-sill bar $^1/_8$in x $^1/_8$in square
  obeche x 20in
- Window frame $^3/_{32}$in obeche x $^1/_4$in x
  8$^1/_4$in, 8 off
- Window bars $^3/_{32}$in square obeche x 76in
- Door architrave $^1/_{16}$in obeche
  x $^3/_8$in x 36in

EXTERNAL DOOR

- $^3/_{16}$in thick Perspex x 6$^3/_8$in x 3in
- Brass bar $^1/_{16}$in x $^1/_{16}$in x 6in

INTERNAL DOOR

- Obeche pieces as follows:
  $^1/_8$in x 6$^1/_4$in x 3in
  $^1/_{16}$in x $^1/_4$in x 6$^1/_4$in, 2 off
  $^1/_{16}$in x $^1/_4$in x 2$^1/_2$in, 3 off
  $^1/_{16}$in x $^1/_2$in x 2$^1/_2$in
  $^1/_{32}$in x $^3/_{32}$in x 6in (total for
  'diamond' surround)
- Finger-plate $^1/_{32}$in thick brass strip
  $^1/_4$in x $^3/_4$in

WALL LIGHT FITTINGS

- $^1/_{16}$in styrene (plasticard) sheet:
  4sq in per light
  $^3/_8$in diameter tube x $^1/_4$in x 2in
- Grain of wheat light bulbs, 2 off

PLATFORM

- Top 6mm MDF x 5$^1/_2$in x 12in
- 9mm MDF pieces as follows:
  Floor support A 1$^1/_4$in x 5in
  Floor support B 1$^1/_4$in x 3$^1/_2$in
  Floor support C 1$^1/_4$in x 2in
  Floor support D 1$^1/_4$in x 4in
  Floor support E 1$^1/_4$in x 11$^3/_4$in
- Platform steps in softwood as follows:
  1$^1/_2$in x $^5/_8$in x 2in
  $^3/_4$in x $^5/_8$in x 2in
- Tread nosing $^1/_8$in obeche as follows:
  1$^5/_8$in x 2in
  $^7/_8$in x 2in
- Platform balustrade in styrene
  (plasticard) as follows:
  $^3/_{16}$in sq tubing 3 pieces x 48in (total)
  $^3/_{32}$in sq bar 4 pieces x 10in
  $^5/_{16}$in wide x $^3/_{32}$in deep 'U'
  channel, 3 pieces x 20in
  $^1/_{16}$in x 6sq in (total for quadrants)
- Liquid polystyrene cement

GLAZING

- 1mm thick acetate for windows:
  8$^1/_4$in x 5$^3/_4$in, 2 off
  8$^1/_4$in x 2$^3/_4$in, 2 off
- 0.7mm thick acetate as follows:
  Roof 8$^1/_4$in x 15$^7/_8$in
  Skylight 3$^7/_8$in x 4in, 4 off
  3$^1/_4$in x 1$^1/_2$in, 4 off

Many striking and memorable motifs were incorporated into Art Deco designs. Dominant amongst these were the elegant greyhound, or borzoi, the stylised leaping gazelle and Diana the huntress complete with bow, all produced as lamps, sculptures and wall silhouettes. Tables in public dining rooms and tea rooms were often left without covers but white cloths were seen everywhere, although it was not unknown for establishments to use coloured cloths printed with Art Deco designs. A number of notable designers of this period concentrated on pottery and in particular tea services. Pre-eminent amongst these was Clarice Cliff and the use of her patterns on the tables would provide a strong focal point for any project.

WORKING NOTES

Where 'glue' is referred to it means a PVA adhesive unless otherwise stated. You will also need 12mm panel pins, No.6 ³/₄in counter-sunk screws, dressmaking pins and flooring papers (readily available from dolls' house shops).

Measurements in the book are imperial, however, as MDF is only sold in the UK in metric sizes, these thicknesses are given, where appropriate, with approximate imperial equivalents, e.g. 6mm (¹/₄in), 9mm (³/₈in).

A selection of commercial paints were used for this project but you may prefer to choose your own colours from other paint brands.

CUTTING OUT
THE CARCASS

Prepare two sides from 9mm MDF, 15in high x 12¹/₄in wide, checking that all the sides are square to each other. Mark out all the 6mm

(¹/₄in) rebates for the back as in Fig 1. Lay both sides onto a flat surface so that the marked rebates for the back are touching in the centre and then mark out the two 9mm (³/₈in) rebates for the floor and base on each piece. The bottom rebates are in fact marked one thickness of timber (9mm) above the bottom edge and this is best set with an offcut and not measured. The top rebates are set 1⁵/₈in from the top edges.

When both sides are marked up they should be mirror images of each other and you should check that the rebates on each side line up to each other. Machine out the three rebates on each piece using a powered bench saw or router, ensuring that they are parallel with the edges of the timber. Check that the rebates match by placing the two sides together with the backs flush on a work surface: the two 9mm rebates must line up perfectly or the floor will twist the carcass and it will not sit square.

Cut the back from 6mm MDF 19⁵/₈in x 15in high, and use a try square to check that all sides are square to each other. Offer the back up to the two sides and check that it sits within the two rebates and matches the sides for height. Cut the floor from 9mm MDF, 19³/₈in x 12in.

Cut and prepare the four roof beams A, B, C and D from 9mm MDF 2in wide by the lengths given in the Materials list on page 91. Machine out the ¹/₈in x ¹/₈in rebate to take the glazing sheet along one edge of each beam (see Fig 2). Note that the beams are assembled with this edge towards the centre and uppermost, not inside the rebates cut into the sides.

Cut the base pavement from 9mm MDF, 20in x 5¹/₂in – it takes up the full width of the building. In order to place this under the main floor a notch is cut on each of the two back corners (see Fig 3).

Cut the pediment from 9mm MDF 19¹/₄in x 1⁵/₈in (although it might be advisable to machine this part *after* the carcass is assembled to ensure an exact fit between the sides).

FIG 1

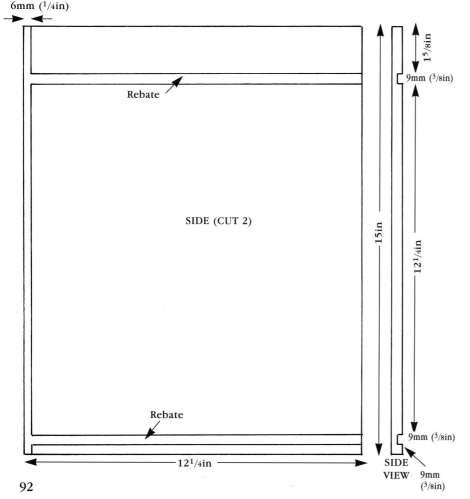

6mm (¹/₄in)

Rebate

SIDE (CUT 2)

Rebate

15in

1⁵/₈in

9mm (³/₈in)

12¹/₄in

9mm (³/₈in)

SIDE
VIEW

9mm (³/₈in)

12¹/₄in

FIG 2

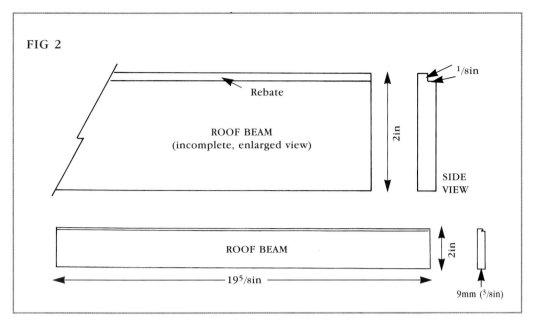

ROOF BEAM
(incomplete, enlarged view)

Rebate

2in

SIDE
VIEW

$^1/_8$in

ROOF BEAM

2in

19$^5/_8$in

9mm ($^3/_8$in)

CUTTING OUT THE FRONTAGE

The main part of the frontage is prepared from one sheet of 9mm MDF, 19$^1/_4$in x 12$^1/_4$in, and this is then marked as shown in Fig 4. Ensuring that all the edges are square and that the two sides are parallel will ensure accurate machining and cutting of this shape especially if a powered router is used with fitted guides. Cut out the three main apertures from the blank sheet, smoothing off all the edges and checking that they are parallel to the top and bottom.

Cut and prepare two sides from 9mm

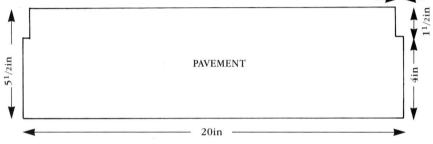

PAVEMENT

5$^1/_2$in

9mm($^3/_8$in)

1$^1/_2$in

4in

20in

FIG 3

MDF, each 3in x 12$^1/_4$in, checking that they are exactly the same and that they match the frontage for height.

From 9mm MDF cut out the base 4in x 20in and the top 3$^1/_2$in x 20in, noting that the top is $^1/_2$in wider than the sides. Cut the

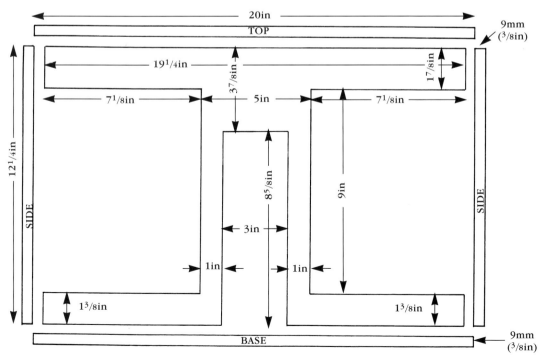

20in
TOP
9mm ($^3/_8$in)

19$^1/_4$in
3$^7/_8$in
1$^7/_8$in

7$^1/_8$in
5in
7$^1/_8$in

12$^1/_4$in

SIDE

8$^5/_8$in

9in

SIDE

3in

1in
1in

1$^3/_8$in
1$^3/_8$in

BASE
9mm ($^3/_8$in)

FIG 4

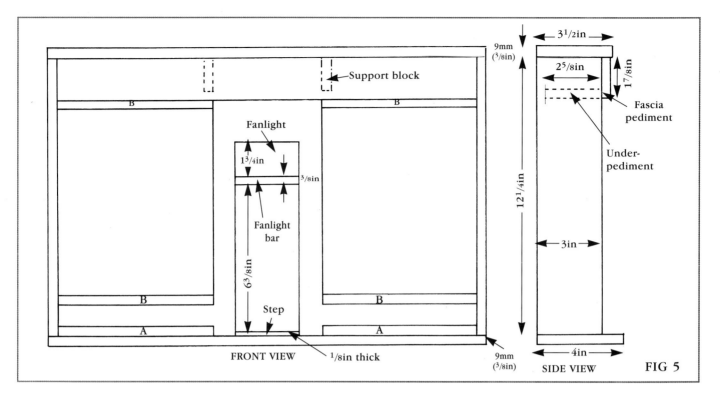

Support block

B

B

Fanlight

1³/4in

³/8in

Fanlight bar

6³/8in

B

B

A

A

Step

FRONT VIEW

¹/8in thick

9mm (³/8in)

9mm (³/8in)

3¹/2in

9mm (³/8in)

2⁵/8in

1⁷/8in

Fascia pediment

Under-pediment

12¹/4in

3in

4in

SIDE VIEW

FIG 5

fanlight bar from a piece of 9mm MDF offcut machined or planed to 3in x ³/8in.

Prepare both the under-pediment and the fascia pediment from 9mm MDF to the dimensions given in the Materials list on page 91. The under-pediment is added below the top to support the front pediment or fascia board (see Fig 5). Prepare two blocks of 9mm offcuts, 1¹/2in x 2¹/2in, to act as supports for both these parts.

The double window arrangement is built around six window formers (three per side) assembled with two at the bottom and one at the top on each side. It is important that the 60 degree angles are cut accurately and that all the parts match or subsequent assemblies will not fit correctly. Cut out the window formers following the dimensions given in Fig 6 noting that formers B are deeper than A and are trimmed on assembly.

The obeche parts for the frontage window bases (A and B), step, over-door motif and window frame and bars are best machined and cut on assembly once the window formers are in place – follow the dimensions given in the Materials list on page 91. The internal platform assemblies, false internal door and skylight are dealt with later.

CARCASS ASSEMBLY

The use of sash clamps will prove extremely useful for this stage. Fit the floor piece and the roof beams into their respective rebates before gluing to ensure that they will assemble in the correct way without undue pressure being necessary – smooth down and correct if necessary.

Draw pencil lines from front to back on the outer surface of each of the sides to indicate the dead centre of the bottom 9mm (³/8in) rebates and place a small mark 3in in from either end. Drill a ¹/8in diameter hole through at each of the marks and countersink each of them on the outer surface to take a No.6 wood screw. Mark up and drill holes for the top rebates in the same manner, adjusting the measurements to ¹/2in and 4in from each end on each side.

When assembling the roof beams check

FIG 6

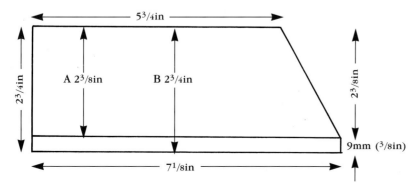

5³/4in

2³/4in

A 2³/8in

B 2³/4in

2³/8in

9mm (³/8in)

7¹/8in

that all the glazing rebates are uppermost and point toward the centre (see Fig 7).

Hold the floor in a secure bench vice so that one end is uppermost. Apply a layer of PVA wood glue along the length and assemble the side onto this, ensuring that it fits right down to the bottom of the rebate. Check that the floor is flush with the outer edge of the side and that it does not foul the rebate for the back. Use a sharp awl to mark though the drilled holes into the side and then drill 3/32in diameter starter holes into the sides of the floor edge to avoid splitting the timber. Insert No.6 counter-sunk wood screws to fix the side securely to the floor. Remove the part-assembly from the vice and place to one side whilst inserting one of the longer roof beams A into the vice with the short side uppermost and the rebate pointing to the centre. Coat the end with PVA glue and lay the part-assembled side onto the beam so that it fits into the rebate, flush with the front, and assemble with a No.6 screw after pre-drilling with 3/32in diameter holes as for the floor above. Repeat to fix the second long roof beam B in the same way.

Remove the part-assembly from the vice, turn it over onto a flat surface and fit, glue and screw the second side into place ensuring all the outer edges are flush, repeating the methods described above.

The two centre roof beams C and D can now be added, fitting them snugly between the front and the back beams, adjusting if necessary. Before the glue has set on the assembly completed so far, glue and pin the back into its rebates. Check with a try square to ensure that the carcass sides are at right angles to the floor, make any adjustments necessary then set aside to allow to set hard.

Fit the pavement at this point, gluing it to the underside of the floor. This part is decorated with painted card later.

FRONTAGE ASSEMBLY

The main part of the frontage is actually at the back of this assembly, with sides and top positioned to the front. Hold the shaped

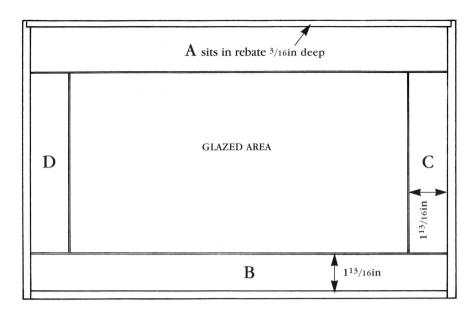

FIG 7 Top view

front securely in a bench vice so that one side edge is uppermost and glue and pin on one side so that it extends to the front, checking that it is flush top, bottom and back before proceeding. Remove this from the vice and turn it over, coat this side too with PVA glue and pin on the second side, checking as before.

Turn the assembly over so that the bottom is uppermost and glue and pin the base onto the front and the bottom of each of the two sides. Turn again and repeat for the top. It should resemble a shallow box with holes.

Glue the two support blocks into position on the front so that they fit under the top, over each side of the doorway. Add the fascia under-pediment, pinning it with 3/4in long panel pins from the sides and back. Add the front fascia pediment. Punch down any nail heads and fill all holes and counter-sunk screw heads with a suitable wood or plaster filler and smooth off when dry.

WINDOWS

Refer to Fig 8 overleaf for the main window assembly. Glue and pin the two window formers A onto the base, one each side, with the angled portion pointing at and leading to the doorway. Clamp these together to ensure a flush fit. Formers B lie inside the window aperture, one each top and bottom of each side, flush with the back of the frontage and should be trimmed at the narrowest

If you wish you can lightly abrade the surface of acetate with fine abrasive paper to produce a frosted glass effect. The edges of Perspex can be polished using a cloth and a liquid metal polish.

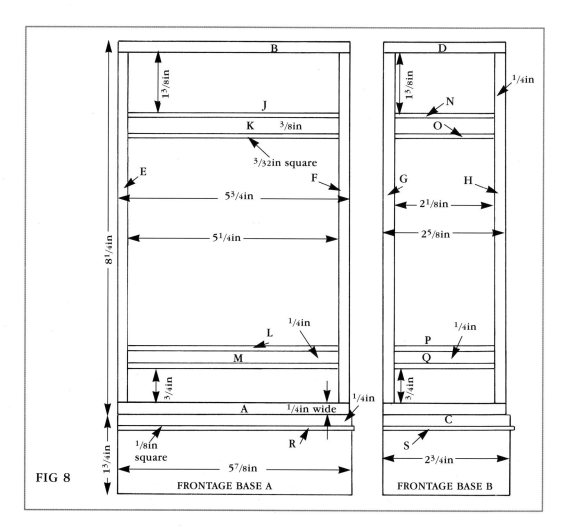

FIG 8

FRONTAGE BASE A

FRONTAGE BASE B

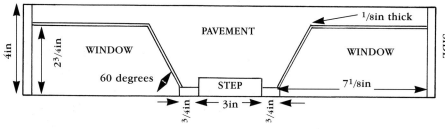

FIG 9

PAVEMENT

WINDOW

WINDOW

SIDE

4in

2³/4in

60 degrees

1/8in thick

STEP

7¹/8in

3/4in   3in   3/4in

FIG 10

FIG 11

A and B window base

R   S

CUT-AWAY VIEW OF BASE
OF WINDOW

Vertical
bars

CUT-AWAY VIEW OF
WINDOW UPRIGHTS

point to provide a snug fit (see Fig 9). Check that all three formers will line up at the front by 'dry' fitting both the parts labelled B, then pin and fix into place with a PVA wood glue both of the two formers at the top of the aperture, flush with the under-pediment board. Finish this part of the assembly with

those inside the bottom of each aperture, pinning through into the edge of the aperture. Check that all parts line up and are square before setting aside to allow the glue to harden.

Measure off the parts for the frontage window bases A in 1/8in thick obeche trimming one end of each piece to 60 degrees. Cut out parts B noting that this time both ends are shaped in parallel to 60 degrees, in other words the angled cuts should not converge to form a part pyramid but point in the same direction (see Figs 10 and 11). Dry fit and when perfect fix both parts B into place using a rapid-setting clear spirit-based adhesive. Add parts A to finish off under the windows on both sides, smoothing off the joins in A and B with fine abrasive paper to provide a perfectly angled corner.

Cutting the Window Bars

Preparing all the different widths of 3/32in thick obeche strip in one session will eliminate any possibility of dimensions varying, but if this is not possible and ready-cut timbers are used, check those in the batch all have identical dimensions.

Making up spacers for measuring and keeping constant the spaces between the decorative window bars in advance will prove very useful. To do this cut at least one each of the following widths from 9mm MDF offcuts: 1 3/8in, 3/4in, 1/4in and 3/8in (6mm and 9mm offcuts can be used in lieu of cutting 1/4in and 3/8in pieces without affecting the overall result).

We have started with the largest part of the left-hand window but there is no reason why the right-hand cannot be started first. A clear spirit-based adhesive was used to fix all window bars and components.

Assembling the Framework

In the event that the window assembly is even slightly under or oversized to the plan (see Fig 8) it is recommended that these bars are not prepared in advance but are cut to fit. Cut two of the thicker horizontal window bars (A and B) 1/4in wide x 3/32in. Trim one end of each bar at 60 degrees and then assemble A onto the bottom window former 1/8in from the outer edge of the window base, (flush with the edge of the top window former not the window base part). B is glued to the top of the aperture under the edge of the window former.

Cut two horizontal bars C and D, trim both ends with parallel cuts at 60 degrees and glue into position, butting onto parts A at the bottom and B at the top.

Cut four upright window frame bars E, F, G and H to fit between the ones at the top and bottom.

Glue upright E so that it fits flush with the left-hand side wall and sits on top of A and under B. Upright part H abuts the frontage. Fix upright bars F and G into position lining them up with horizontal bars A and B, and C and D respectively.

Fix upright frame bar F in alignment with G so that it is in line with horizontal bars

and forms an angled fit with G. When the adhesive has set and the whole assembly is firm to the touch, horizontal bars J to Q can be cut and fitted.

The following sequence will avoid accidentally moving bars where the adhesive has not set, however it is better to allow each bar to set in place thoroughly before using a spacing bar or touching it in any way.

Cut the 3/32in square bars J and N, fitting them by using the 1 3/8in spacer to set the distance between them and the top. Follow this by fitting bars M and Q at the bottom using the 3/4in spacer. Use the 3/8in spacer to distance and fit bars K and O and the 1/4in spacer to fix bars L and P.

The 1/8in square bars R and S that are fixed to the window bases are cut in the same manner as the bases – first cut S with both ends trimmed with parallel 60 degree ends and then add R with one end cut at 60 degrees (see Fig 10). Smooth off the ends with fine abrasive paper wrapped around a suitable flat-faced block to provide a flush fit.

EXTERNAL DOOR

Glue the fanlight bar 1 3/4in from the top of the doorway aperture (see Fig 5, page 94). Line the fanlight and the doorway with 1/16in square obeche 1/8in in from the front and fix into position with a clear spirit-based adhesive. The 1/8in thick obeche piece for the step is rounded at the front leading edge and is also glued into position (see Fig 9).

Cut the 1/16in x 3/16in door architrave from obeche so that it can be glued into position flush with the doorway. Mitre the top corners, left and right, with matching mitres on the centre piece. Cut a second set of architrave from the same material but this time glue it into position so that it is 1/16in away from the outer edge of the first layer and overlaps the inner edge of the doorway by the same 1/16in. The joints should again be mitred for a neat finish.

The decorative motif over the door is made up from two pieces of 1/8in thick obeche with the ends trimmed to 60

White metal and plastic tea sets can be painted with a variety of patterns and in many different styles. Art Deco patterns are usually geometric and very bright.

Menus and signs would be small and probably hand-written in small tea rooms. They rarely varied and would include both Indian and China Teas.

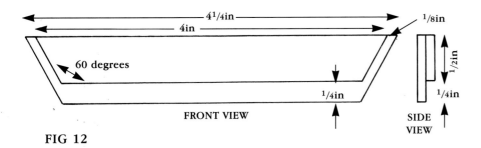

FRONT VIEW

SIDE VIEW

FIG 12

or hinged edge of the door to allow it to open within the doorway (see Fig 13).

Cut two lengths of $1/16$in square section brass bar and bend to shape (see Fig 13A). Drill a $1/32$in diameter pin-sized hole for the hinge, $1/4$in in from the left-hand edge, top and bottom of the door and a hole to match through the fanlight bar above and through the base and step, from the bottom. Drill four holes $1/16$in in diameter to match the two angled bars in the positions shown and glue the ends of the bars into position using rapid-set epoxy adhesive or 'super glue'. Leave this to set hard before proceeding.

Insert the top and bottom pins to fit the door and check that it has sufficient clearance to open cleanly. The top pin is inserted through the fanlight, the one at the bottom through the pavement and the step.

degrees. The upper piece B is 4in x $1/2$in and the lower piece A is $41/4$in x $3/4$in. B is glued on top of A leaving $1/8$in clearance at either end but flush at the top edge (see Fig 12). Glue the assembly centrally over the doorway.

The door itself is cut from $3/16$in thick Perspex to mimic a solid glass door, with brass handles placed at an angle. Cut and shape the Perspex to fit the aperture and smooth off the edges using fine abrasive paper and a fine-cut file. Round off the inner

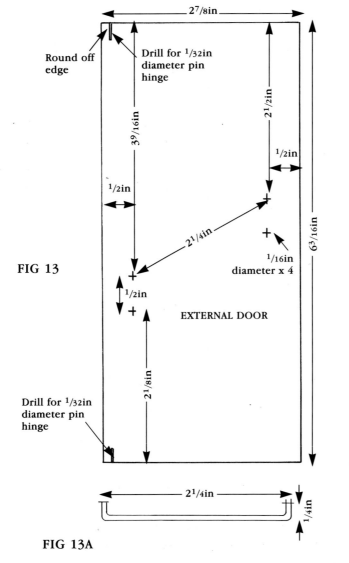

FIG 13

EXTERNAL DOOR

FIG 13A

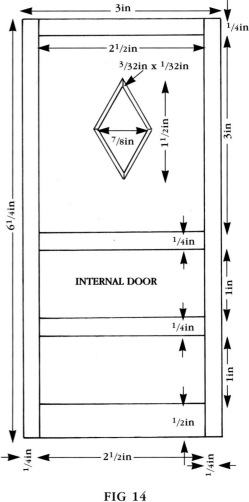

INTERNAL DOOR

FIG 14

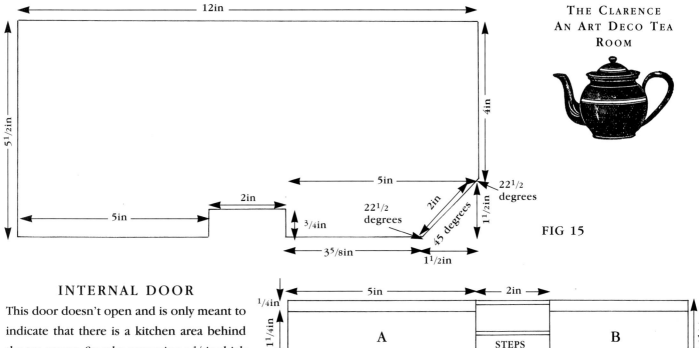

FIG 15

FIG 16

FRONT VIEW

INTERNAL DOOR

This door doesn't open and is only meant to indicate that there is a kitchen area behind the tea rooms. Start by preparing a 1/8in thick piece of obeche 6¼in x 3in, and mark up the diamond-shaped window aperture (see Fig 14). Cut out using a fretsaw with a fine blade and smooth off the edges using fine abrasive paper wrapped around an offcut.

Prepare a 24in length of 1/16in thick obeche and cut two pieces 1/4in wide x 6¼in long for the outer stiles. Glue these to the outer edges of the door blank. Cut the three horizontal rails and glue them on as shown in Fig 14. Cut one piece of 1/16in obeche x 1/2in and fit as the bottom rail.

Fit the door window surround using 1/32in x 3/32in obeche, mitring the corners at 60 degrees. Prepare an 18in length of 1/8in obeche 3/8in wide for the door architrave. Cut to fit round the door itself with 45 degree mitred joints at the two top corners.

Seal all the surfaces with sanding sealer and leave this to dry, then finish off with fine abrasive paper before painting.

RAISED PLATFORM

This platform is a separate assembly that sits on the main floor in the back left-hand corner of the room. Cut the top from 6mm MDF 5½in wide x 12in long. The front right-hand corner is cut at 45 degrees or 1½in x 1½in (see Fig 15). To reach the platform a small set of steps is inset into the front by

cutting a gap 3/4in deep x 2in wide positioned 5in from the left-hand side (see Fig 16).

Cut the floor supports A, B, C and D from 9mm MDF each 1¼in high to give a total platform height of 1½in (see dimensions in Materials list on page 91). Note that parts B and D have their inner edges cut at 22½ degrees. Part C has both edges cut at 22½ degrees to match. Part E is cut 11¾in long to butt up against D (see Fig 17 overleaf).

Pin and glue the platform top to supports A to E, gluing the supports together at the same time. Note there is no support required for the left-hand side but one can be added if you wish. Punch down any nail heads visible and fill the holes with a suitable plaster or wood filler.

Platform Steps

Cut from a softwood block the bottom step 1½in long x 5/8in high x 2in wide and cut the upper 3/4in x 5/8in high x 2in long (see Fig 18 overleaf). Prepare two treads from 1/8in thick obeche, the first 1 5/8in x 2in and the second 7/8in x 2in. Round off the front edge of each and glue them on top of each step. Finish by gluing and clamping the two blocks together so that the backs are aligned.

Smoking in tea rooms wasn't frowned upon until recently, so put out ash trays if you want to. You could also leave one table with the remains of a meal and some dirty crockery for an authentic touch.

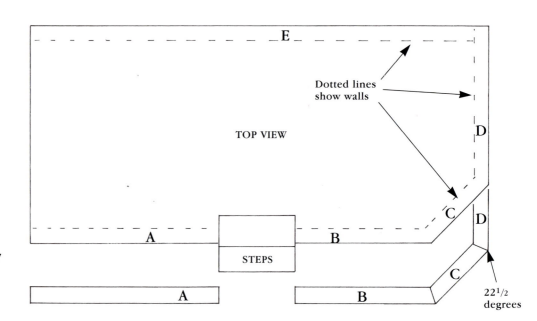

TOP VIEW

Dotted lines
show walls

E

D

C

D

C

A

B

A

B

$22^1/_2$
degrees

FIG 17

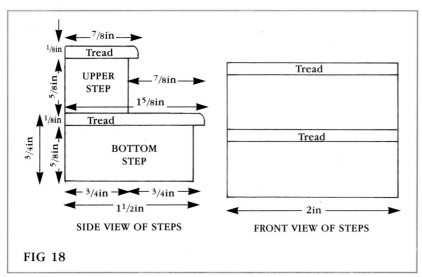

FIG 18

Tread

UPPER
STEP

$^7/_8$in

$^1/_8$in

$^5/_8$in

$^7/_8$in

$1^5/_8$in

Tread

$^1/_8$in

$^3/_4$in

$^5/_8$in

BOTTOM
STEP

$^3/_4$in $^3/_4$in

$1^1/_2$in

SIDE VIEW OF STEPS

Tread

Tread

2in

FRONT VIEW OF STEPS

*The three parts of the
decorative balustrade,
glued together and painted*

Platform Balustrade

The decorative balustrading around the platform can be replaced with other tracery if you prefer but it is very important that the Art Deco theme is maintained. Standard outdoor railings or stair bannisters would almost certainly be out of place here. The balustrade shown in this project combines several of the more obvious geometric elements, comprising square sections and straight lines combined with the popular 'sunburst' effect.

Everything can be made up on a standard work-table and no special tools are required except for the plastic weld adhesive necessary for joining styrene parts. Note that in order to work, styrene weld or styrene cement dissolves a layer of the plastic, so avoid contact with the fingers and the surface of the piece, or the surfaces will mark. Follow the manufacturer's instructions regarding personal safety at all times and always use away from naked flames.

Use a small sliding bevel and a protractor to measure off the $22^1/_2$ degree angles required to match two parts to the 45 degrees end of the platform.

Cut the parts as follows: cut eight lengths of $^3/_{16}$in square tubing $2^1/_2$in long for the uprights. From the same material cut the following horizontal bars for the sections listed: Section A $4^3/_8$in, 2 off; Section B $2^{15}/_{16}$in, 2 off; Section C $1^1/_4$in, 2 off; Section D $3^1/_4$in, 2 off.

Cut two lengths of 'U' channel for each of the sections noting the direction of the $22^1/_2$ degree angles. Each pair should match when the parts are placed together with the channel innermost: A 5in; B $3^5/_8$in (one end has angled cuts); C 2in (two converging

angles); D 4in (one end has angled cuts). The 3/32in square bar is cut to length with the assembly, see below.

To assemble the various balustrade parts follow Fig 19 – Sections A, B, C and D. Start with Section A and lay the lower piece of 'U' channel onto a flat surface and place the matching length of 4³/₈in x ³/₁₆in square tubing inside (see Fig 19 side view), positioning it equally distant from either end. Hold the parts together and use a small ¹/₄in paint-brush to apply a small amount of plastic weld adhesive to fix together. Repeat this for the matching upper piece of 'U' channel and when fixed securely, position and fix both the uprights. Check that the uprights are square to the horizontal bars and place to one side.

Repeat the procedure for section B noting

that the angled end is to the right and matches the angle on the platform itself. Section C has two angled ends so ensure that they all match and point inwards. Section D has the left-hand end angled but is assembled in the same manner.

Cut four one quarter circles from ¹/₁₆in thick styrene (plasticard), each with 1³/₄in radii and weld one of these into the bottom left-hand corner of each section at the front so that they are ¹/₁₆in in from the front edge of the ³/₁₆in square upright and bottom bars.

Turn each of the sections over so that they are face down on a flat surface and start with Section A. Cut a ³/₃₂in bar so that it is behind the quarter circle and touches the bottom left and the top right corner. Weld into position and hold until set. Repeat for Sections B,

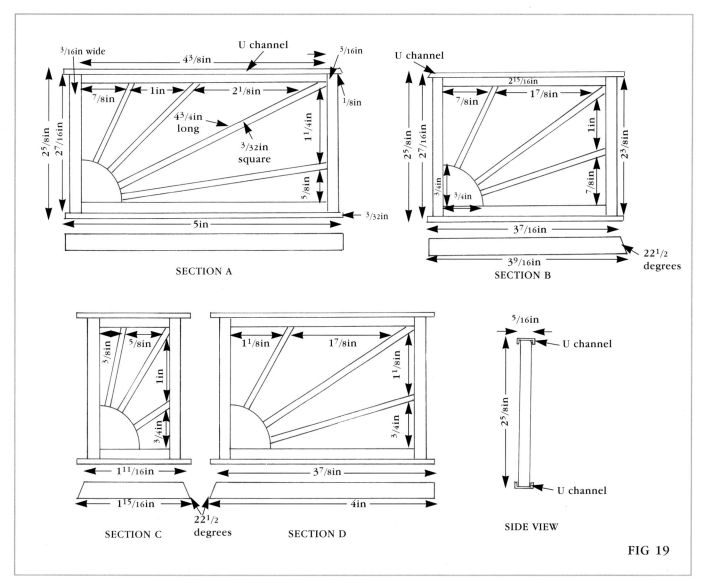

SECTION A

SECTION B

SECTION C   SECTION D   SIDE VIEW

FIG 19

The elegant lady waiting for her companion is enjoying the atmospheric lighting of the tea rooms

C and D. Using the same method cut and weld in all the other bars in the positions shown in Fig 19A–D, noting that section A has four bars whilst the others all have three each.

Use a car spray paint to cover all the surfaces with a primer coat of grey and when this is dry finish off with a gold spray paint. There are a number of these gold shades available, some with metallic finishes, and most will prove suitable for this purpose. Allow to dry and place to one side until final assembly.

NOTE: We recommend that any flooring be laid and glued into place before fixing the balustrade into position. We used flooring papers, readily available from good dolls'-house shops.

DECORATIVE
WALL LIGHTS

These simple but effective wall light units are made up from $1/16$in thick white styrene (plasticard), the separate parts for which are glued together using the liquid polystyrene cement or 'plastic weld' used for the

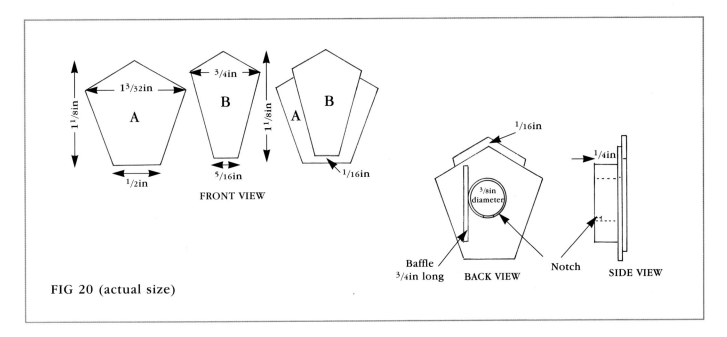

FRONT VIEW

FIG 20 (actual size)

Baffle
3/4in long   BACK VIEW   Notch   SIDE VIEW

balustrades. There are four lights altogether in the model shown, but only two of these are working items.

To make one light, trace the two main parts A and B from Fig 20 which has been provided actual size so you can copy the angles more easily. Cut out and shape both parts from white styrene using a sharp craft knife or scalpel and clean up any edges. Check the angles are correct and position them together with B overlaying A. Lightly clamp the two parts together and 'paint' on plastic weld with a soft brush – the adhesive will use capillary action to fuse the parts together. Be careful not to allow any of the liquid to touch your fingers or you may leave fingerprints on the smooth surfaces of the plastic parts.

Cut a 1/4in length of 3/8in diameter styrene tubing and cut a small notch to allow the lighting wire to pass through. Weld this onto the back of the lamp, dead centre. Cut a small 1 1/8in strip of white plasticard 1/4in wide as a baffle so that the tube cannot be seen. Position this on the side facing the front of the shop and weld on to the back of the lamp and the side of the tube. If you are not sure of the final position of the lamp make two baffles, one for each side. Finish off with a gold enamel paint, coating all visible surfaces. Make three more wall lights in this way.

SKYLIGHT

The decorative raised skylight, with a motif derived from the Art Deco sunburst, adds to overall design and stops the roof being another flat surface. It also reflects the Art Deco skyscraper theme, which a plain ceiling would not be able to do. The framework is made entirely from obeche stripwood and this is best cut using a sharp razor saw and assembled using a bench jig. Use either a clear spirit-based adhesive or PVA wood glue.

Cut parts A to D for the supporting platform first from obeche as follows (see Fig 21 overleaf and note that the parts overlap in a step formation to give an overall height of 2 1/4in):

A 3/32in x 2in x 1/8in, 4 off

B 3/32in x 7/8in x 3/32in, 4 off

C 1/8in x 3/4in x 1/8in, 4 off

D 3/32in x 2in wide x 1/8in, 4 off

E 3/16in square x 1/2in wide x 1/8in, 4 off

Start the assembly by gluing parts D 1–4 together, overlapping the ends, with one support post E at each corner. Check that all is square and the adhesive has set before adding parts C 1–4. C is flush at the bottom with D and so stands proud at the top to provide the location for the skylight frame to rest in.

Add the 3/32in thick parts B 1–4 allowing a 3/8in drop at the top from C. Finally, add the

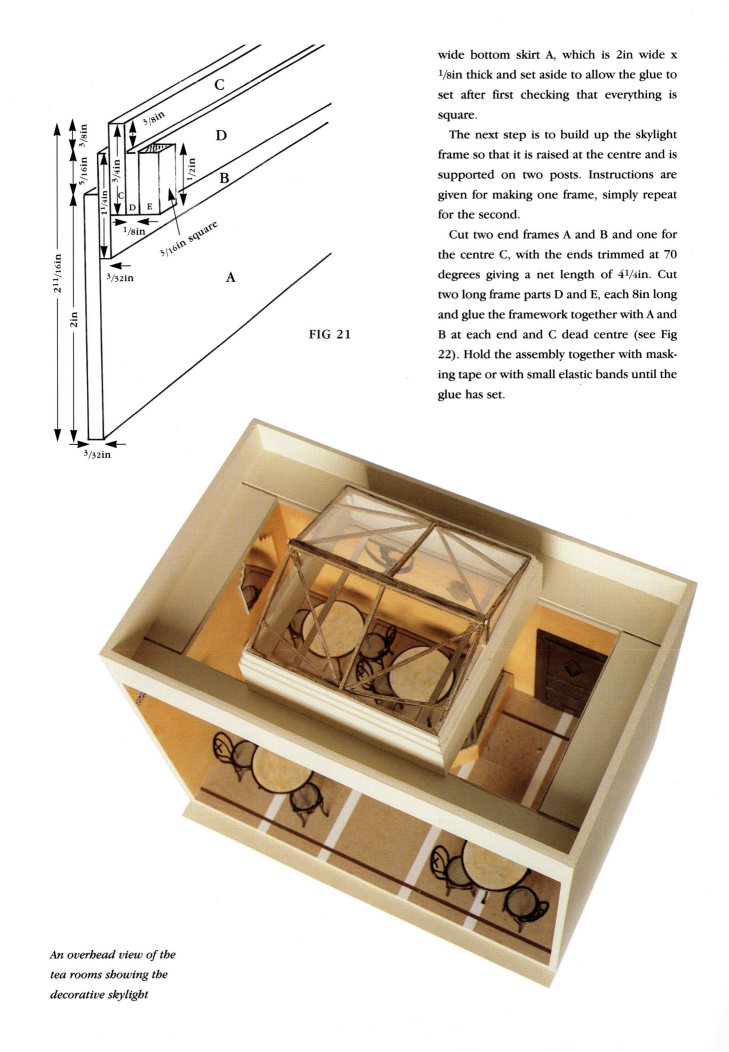

FIG 21

Dimensions shown in Fig 21:
- C, D, B, A (frame parts)
- 3/8in
- 3/8in
- 3/4in
- 5/16in
- 1/4in
- 1/2in
- 1¼in
- 1/8in
- 3/16in square
- 3/32in
- 2¹¹/16in
- 2in
- 3/32in
- C, D, E

wide bottom skirt A, which is 2in wide x ⅛in thick and set aside to allow the glue to set after first checking that everything is square.

The next step is to build up the skylight frame so that it is raised at the centre and is supported on two posts. Instructions are given for making one frame, simply repeat for the second.

Cut two end frames A and B and one for the centre C, with the ends trimmed at 70 degrees giving a net length of 4¼in. Cut two long frame parts D and E, each 8in long and glue the framework together with A and B at each end and C dead centre (see Fig 22). Hold the assembly together with masking tape or with small elastic bands until the glue has set.

An overhead view of the tea rooms showing the decorative skylight

The glazing bars F, G, H and J (two sets) are cut from a strip of $\frac{1}{8}$in square obeche and sit at the bottom of the framework, allowing the glazing to be placed on top of them. F and J are each $3\frac{3}{4}$in long, G and H are each $5\frac{1}{2}$in long. Trim both ends of bars G and H with a sharp craft knife to match the angles across the centre of each half of the framework and glue into place. Trim bars F and J so that they fit under the centre bar $\frac{3}{4}$in up from the bottom (see Fig 23).

Make another frame for the second side. When the two side frames are put together the angled long bars will pull the assembly into a peak (see Fig 23). Hold together and place into the platform to check for a good fit and make any adjustments necessary. Glue the two skylight frames together and place into the platform so that it sits as a good fit. Add the top bar, cut from $\frac{1}{8}$in thick obeche x $\frac{3}{8}$in x $8\frac{1}{2}$in long, to cover the join and finish off the top.

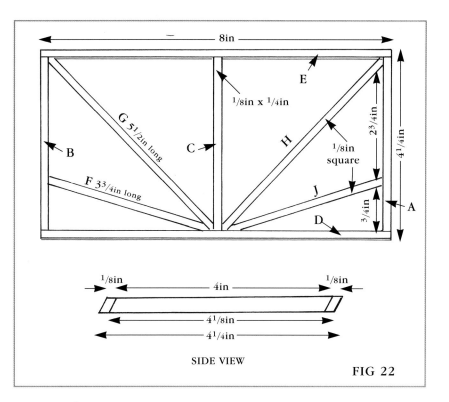

FIG 22

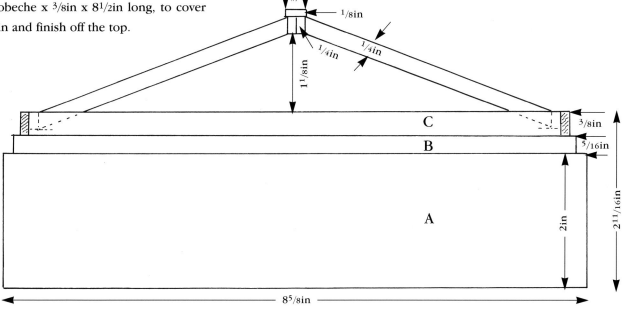

FIG 23

Make up two posts, each from two pieces of $\frac{3}{32}$in thick x $\frac{1}{4}$in wide obeche (see Fig 24). Part A, $1\frac{1}{4}$in long, sits on top of the inner framework of the platform. Part B is $1\frac{3}{4}$in long and is trimmed at the top with two 45 degree cuts to produce a point and is glued to A so that it locates on the outside of the platform framework. Glue the posts dead centre on one side of the platform. The top of the skylight framework sits on the inside of the posts.

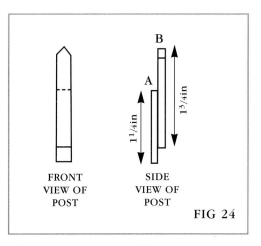

FIG 24

Coat all the bare timber surfaces with a single coat of sanding sealer as this will give the frame strength and allow paint to take more easily. Paint all the visible woodwork with a colour to match the body of the tea room (see Interior Decoration below) and finish off all the glazing bars with a gold colour enamel, ageing and weathering with a rough application of black or grey.

HANGING WINDOW PLAQUES

Two oval-shaped plaques (see photograph) hang in each of the main windows and make elegant invitations to Savouries and Pastries.

MATERIALS

- $^1/_{16}$in thick Perspex sheet, 6in x 2in approximately
- Fine gold-coloured jewellery finding chain 12in
- Fine copper wire
- Brass screw eyelets $^1/_8$in diameter, 4 off
- Transfer lettering in gold colour 24pt (6mm)

The two hanging signs are made from $^1/_{16}$in thick Perspex sheet cut into oval-shaped plaques $2^1/_2$in wide x $1^1/_2$in high. If you cannot cut oval shapes then rectangles can be substituted. Drill two $^1/_{16}$in holes 1in apart and equidistant from the centre along the

top edges of each piece. These take the chain by which they are suspended from the upper former after painting.

Select the lettering required for the plaque and draw this out to scale on a piece of plain white paper. Lay the plaque over the paper and secure into position with a small piece of masking tape so that the lettering is dead centre. Clean off the surface and, following the instructions for the transfer lettering, apply to the plaque. Lay a clean piece of paper over the finished lettering and press this down firmly to secure any loose edges. Remove from the paper and carefully place to one side.

Wrap fine copper wire around a $^1/_4$in diameter rod ten or so times to produce a coil and, using wire cutters, snip off the two ends. Push the two ends of the coil together tightly, remove from the rod and snip horizontally through the wire to produce a number of rings. Select eight rings and using two pairs of pliers bring the ends of each ring together to close up the ring.

Cut four lengths of fine chain $2^1/_2$in long. (Jewellery finding shops are a good source for fine brass chains with loops at one end.) Open two of the copper rings by holding each side with pliers and twisting gently sideways, then pass them into the holes drilled through the Perspex plaque (twisting the rings sideways will not distort their circular shape). Attach the end of one chain to each ring and close up the ring using two pairs of pliers as before, this time with the chain attached. Attach a ring to the other

end of each of the chains using the above method and repeat all this for the second plaque. Find the centre point of the under surface of the upper window former on each side and make starter holes for the brass eyelets at the same distance apart as the two holes in each of the plaques (1in). Open out each of the eyelets to form a hook so that they will take the top rings attached to the chains.

Cut and prepare two strips of $^{1}/_{8}$in thick obeche x $^{1}/_{4}$in wide x $1^{1}/_{4}$in long, to fit exactly between the back and front ceilings and spanning the roof opening. These will support the large Perspex sheet that forms the roof light. Paint the inner sides of these with the same colour scheme and technique as the body of the interior, and the exterior side to match that (see below). Fit these bars $4^{1}/_{2}$in in from each end, although this is not a critical measurement.

EXTERIOR DECORATION

The tea room was divided into two sections for painting, the interior and the exterior, all the glazing was cut to fit and completed last.

Painting the Exterior and Frontage

Paint the sides and roof area with a base of cream matt emulsion to provide a sealed surface. The frontage, which is all that piece containing the front windows, door and pavement edges, can also be painted with the same coloured sealing coat.

Rub down any rough spots and fill any holes with a suitable plaster or wood filler. Give all the exterior surfaces two coats of cream water-based eggshell paint (we used Farrow and Ball No. 44) leaving the window bars and sills with just a base coat.

Use a fine artist's paint-brush to apply a maroon gloss enamel (our model used Humbrol No. 20) to the surfaces of the window-sills and bars, being careful not to overlap the edges and spoil the lines. You may find that using adhesive paint masking tapes will assist you in keeping coloured lines of paint separate.

Once the painting is completed for this part you can attach the Perspex external door using dressmaking pins inserted through the fanlight and the pavement and into those pre-drilled into the door. Check that the door swings freely.

The remainder of the glazing to the frontage can also be added at this stage. Cut and fit the large panes of acetate first and lock these into place with the smaller side panes. A small strip of $^{3}/_{32}$in square obeche may be added behind the panes, top and bottom, to secure them in place if necessary. Use a clear spirit-based adhesive for additional support for the acetate sheets but be careful to avoid any 'stringing' of the adhesive over the surfaces. Glue residue can be cleaned off when dry using a cotton bud dipped in a little methylated or de-natured alcohol. Under no circumstances should you smoke or use any alcohol of this type near naked flames.

The brass eyelets for the hanging sign plaques can be re-inserted at this stage and the signs attached by means of the fitted chains.

Decorating the Pavement

Transfer the shape of the pavement (see Fig 9, page 96) to a piece of good quality thin card and check for a good fit around the

Cakes and sandwiches can be made up using any of the coloured polymer clays and resins and added to suitable plates and trays.

Cakes and pastries in The Clarence are freshly prepared, varied and delicious. They would be offered on a tiered stand and, once on the plate, were eaten with a specially designed fork.

doorway and its architrave. You will need to experiment with the colours in order to achieve the marbled effect shown on our model – we used a base of cream emulsion, roughly over-painting this with a deep orange poster paint and mixing in a yellow emulsion whilst the second coat was still wet. When the strip is dry, paint it over with a PVA glue to lock in the colours and produce a dull sheen similar to worn marble. Fix the sheet into place after the remainder of the paintwork is complete using a suitable white PVA glue.

Creating the Shop Sign

The vinyl lettering for the sign, The Clarence Tea Rooms, was purchased from a sign shop producing pre-cut vinyl letters and words. The cost of this was minimal and it produced a very professional finish, far better than hand lettering. The front was measured off to determine the best fit and composition and the font and size of type carefully selected from those available.

Vinyl lettering is supplied sandwiched between two sheets of paper, often cut roughly around the wording chosen. If possible trim this sandwich to give a regular shape, especially along the top edge. The lettering will be visible through the top layer and it should be possible to lay it onto the fascia board and position it accurately and level. Once you have done this, secure the top edge of the lettering sandwich to the fascia using a

piece of masking tape and you should be able to lift it upward by the bottom edge with the top edge acting as a hinge. Gently peel off the under layer of paper to expose the adhesive side of the lettering, making sure that the masking tape is maintaining the sheet in the correct position.

Lower the sheet onto the fascia and check it is correctly positioned before pressing down through the top sheet onto the letters. Run the edge of a piece smooth-edged plastic, (like a credit card), over the letters to make sure the adhesive comes firmly into contact with the fascia and then carefully remove the top layer of paper and the masking tape to expose the finished lettering.

With the decorative skylight removed, this unusual view shows the finished tea rooms

The taking of tea often took on a life of its own and became an occasion, a social event. Musicians might entertain on the piano or perform in three-piece ensembles, and large ballrooms might hold tea-dances. Dress was often quite formal in the classier establishments of London and Harrogate and a lady's wardrobe would contain a number of elegant day dresses bought especially for the occasion of taking tea

Once you have reached this stage it is virtually impossible to remove or re-position the lettering without damaging it. If for any reason you have to remove it, do so as soon as possible by lifting one edge of each letter with a scalpel and peeling it away, although it may break up as you do this. Lettering that has been in place for some time can be removed using a gentle heat, such as that from a hair dryer.

Place the completed frontage to one side now so that you can work on the interior of the building.

INTERIOR DECORATION

To achieve a similar paint finish to the one we used in our model, paint the entire room interior with a basic undercoat of cream vinyl silk emulsion, ensuring even and complete coverage and allowing it to dry thoroughly.

For the top coat we used a water-based eggshell finish paint from Farrow & Ball called Orangery. The trick is not to be too fussy about complete coverage as this allows the base coat to 'grin' through, giving a broken or mottled appearance. There is so little ceiling in this shop that it is a good idea to complete all the surfaces with the same colouring.

Paint the outer edge of the platform (not the steps) the same colour as you have used on the walls. Finish off the steps with a colour wash of drab grey. Alternatively you could colour the steps with a mahogany spirit-based wood stain and glue them into place when they are dry.

The 1/2in wide decorative frieze running all around the top of the walls was cut from a single sheet of Mini Graphics dolls' house wallpaper. Each strip was then carefully trimmed so that the ends matched – this was done in order to make it appear as one long piece when laid together. Glue the frieze into place 1 1/2in down from the top of the wall.

The dancing figure is simply a printed paper cut-out taken from a computer-scanned image, although this could have just as easily been photocopied.

Flooring Decoration

The unusual flooring papers for both the main area and the platform were taken from a box of designer photocopy letterheads obtained from one of the specialist mail order companies; three sheets of A4 size laid together and trimmed so that the lines matched covered both areas. This paper seemed to us to be a perfect foil for the colour of the room, adding just that touch of a geometric pattern and it proves that good effects can be achieved without using commercially made dolls' house papers.

Serving Door

The serving door was undercoated with a dark grey spray paint and then oversprayed with a russet brown car spray. This was allowed to dry thoroughly and then lightly over-sprayed again with a metallic gold colour so as to leave tiny spots of paint and give a 'spatter' effect. Finish the door off by inserting the acetate glazing and attach a small piece of black paper on the back of it to reflect the light. Glue on a piece of 1/32in thick brass strip 1/4in wide x 3/4in long as a finger-plate on the right-hand side.

The architrave is finished and painted in exactly the same way as the door. When this is dry the door may be glued to the back wall with the architrave around it, positioned 2in from the right-hand wall.

Installing the Lighting

Drill two 1/8in diameter holes on the back wall 5in below the ceiling and 7in apart to take the wires from the grain of wheat bulbs. Clean off the holes and insert the bulbs so that all the wiring is pushed through to the back and join these together to make a connection with suitable transformer. Glue the two light shades over the bulbs and add the second pair of light fittings (dummies without bulbs) 3in in from the right-hand side and 7in from the left.

> *Miniature cake doilies can be created from the larger ones used in the cake trade. Cut them out and trim the ends carefully so they remain symmetrical.*

FINISHING OFF

The tables and chairs used in this project are all available from a dolls' house shop (see Suppliers) and reflect the Thonet bentwood type. Remove the Perspex table insert tops and place to one side. Clean off any grease spots and give them all a base primer coat of grey car enamel and allow this to dry before over-spraying with a russet brown car enamel, taking care to cover all surfaces, visible or not. Please ensure that you use a proper face-mask before using spray paints and do this in a well ventilated area. Under no circumstances should you do this near naked flames or when smoking.

The table-tops should be supplied to you with a protective paper surface and we left this on so that we could over-paint with a marble effect. Paint only one surface with a cream emulsion as a base coat and allow this to dry. Using a nearly dry brush pick up a little of the Orangery coloured paint and drag this across the surface. Work in a very little grey acrylic, again with a nearly dry brush, keeping both colours in a wet state. Mix a little cream base colour if this will help and gradually build up a faint marbled effect. Try not to over-do this as too little is better than too much.

The wood and 'glass' display counter filled with a tempting array of cakes and pastries is made in the Shopkeeper's Resource section – see page 27.

Place the platform assembly into the back left-hand corner complete with its steps and add the balustrades. These may be glued into place but you will find it easier to dress this area if you add them after everything is in place. They should stand on their own bases without support.

Insert the large acetate roof sheet into place on top of the support bars and add the decorative skylight on top of this.

Connect the lamp wires to a suitable 12 volt DC transformer and check that the bulbs light correctly.

Lay out the tables and chairs and add any stock items to complete the model – see the list of Suppliers on page 174 for those pieces we used to dress out our tea rooms. Place the completed frontage onto the base pavement and you are ready for business!

THE CLARENCE
AN ART DECO TEA
ROOM

Apart from the ubiquitous tea, both coffee and chocolate would be on offer at The Clarence, probably at around one shilling (5p). Taking tea, in the leaf not bags, was then almost an art form and waitresses would ask customers if they preferred Indian, China or Earl Grey. It would be served in a heated pot with a separate jug of hot water supplied along with a strainer and slop bowl, milk jug and sugar bowl. Each waitress station would have sufficient cups and saucers, tea plates and teaspoons for each of the diners, with fresh plates for sandwiches and cakes.

A bentwood table and chairs evoke the style and elegance of the 1920s

111

PICKWICKS
A VICTORIAN BOOKSELLER

The first 'booksellers' dealt in parchment scrolls rather than books as we know them today and probably stored them in their house rather than in a shop. Until the fifteenth century all books had been copied and illuminated by hand, often by monks. The work was labour intensive and the production of even one book took years. However, once Caxton developed moveable type, printed books became more easily available, albeit expensive and still the exclusive properties of the educated and the very rich. Being valuable objects they were often kept under lock and key.

By the late eighteenth century, thanks to the printing presses and the establishment of publishers using regular coach routes for distribution, book shops could be found in most large villages, towns and cities. Authors, whose latest book could be readily purchased over the counter, soon became

popular and read widely throughout the country. Although books were by this time being printed in ever-increasing quantities they continued to remain out of the reach of the average person and so small, independent lending libraries, often within book shops, soon became established to service the growing numbers of those who could now read. That other printing phenomenon, the newspaper, was also found in eighteenth century book shops and soon spread the word about new authors and their latest works. Most libraries are now public institutions maintained by the ratepayer, but until as late as the 1950s Boots the Chemists operated lending libraries on the high street.

The nineteenth century saw book shops becoming more popular. In 1826 the novelist William Harrison Ainsworth talked about his new book shop in London's Old Bond Street as being, 'nearly ready, with lending library books removed, and new stock being transferred to the then vacant shelves, that are soon to be loaded with goodly tomes and the tables covered with magazines, new publications and newspapers'.

Book shops also became places in which a gentleman could read the latest newspaper or magazine (the only means then of readily disseminating news) and relax as if in a club.

In Britain, the concept of lending libraries started in privately owned book shops before local authorities operated them.

Many newspapers and single sheet publications in this period carried single episodes of novels written by the likes of Charles Dickens and Arthur Conan Doyle which were eventually gathered together and published as complete books. In 1852, one enterprising and successful twenty-one year old publisher, Samuel O. Beeton, published a 2d (1p) monthly magazine of thirty-two pages containing recipes and household advice. After his marriage to Isabella Mayson she joined with him in this work, contributing a great deal of her knowledge and experience. This magazine was soon to be a bestseller: by the second year the circulation was 25,000 and by 1860 it reached 50,000 – no mean achievement for the year 2000 let alone 1860! Isabella's now-famous work, *Beeton's Book of Household Management,* was a direct offspring of the magazine.

Publishing boomed and in 1895 London's famous emporium, Harrods, sold books by mail order, offering some from their catalogue at discounts of 25 percent. *Beeton's Book of Household Management* was then priced at 7s 6d (37$\frac{1}{2}$p) but was offered at 5s 7$\frac{1}{2}$d (29p). Dickens' *Pickwick Papers* was reduced from 4s (20p) to 3s (15p) and postage was charged at just 4d (2p) per pound, weight.

Not surprisingly booksellers who deal in old books, or incunabula, usually find that they are also drawn to other printed material – maps, diaries, receipt (cookery) books, posters and printed ephemera. The bookseller in this project is no different, with an array of varied printed stock about him. The time is set somewhere in the middle of the Victorian period and the books are housed within a cosy wooden-framed building of uncertain date but with definite Tudor origins. The owner is an imposing and knowledgeable sort who handles his stock with care, selling valuable books on the ground floor and prints and maps upstairs. His customer in this scene is a lady, looking perhaps for the latest romantic novel she has been told about by the squire's wife. . .

MATERIALS
BASE SECTION
CARCASS
- 9mm MDF pieces as follows:
  Side 10$\frac{3}{4}$in x 10$\frac{1}{4}$in, 2 off
  Floor 12$\frac{3}{4}$in x 10in
  Back 12$\frac{3}{8}$in x 10$\frac{3}{4}$in
  Pavement 4$\frac{3}{4}$in x 13in
- Flooring $\frac{1}{8}$in hardboard 10in x 12in
- Stair treads 18mm MDF x 2$\frac{1}{8}$in wide x 36in (makes 14 treads)
- Inner stair walls A & B $\frac{1}{8}$in hardboard 9 x 9in
- Stair stud beams oak $\frac{3}{16}$in x $\frac{3}{16}$in x 8in
- Hand rail oak $\frac{1}{8}$in x $\frac{3}{8}$in x 5$\frac{1}{2}$in
- External side beams $\frac{1}{8}$in thick obeche pieces as follows:
  $\frac{1}{2}$in x 100in (total)
  $\frac{3}{8}$in x 100in (total)

FRONTAGE
- 9mm MDF 13in x 9$\frac{3}{8}$in
- Outer beams $\frac{1}{8}$in thick obeche x $\frac{3}{8}$in x 100in (total)
- Coach lamp 12 volt

DOORWAY
- Door step 9mm MDF x 3$\frac{3}{4}$in x 1$\frac{1}{4}$in
- Tread $\frac{1}{8}$in hardboard 1$\frac{5}{8}$in x 4in
- Door surround $\frac{1}{8}$in thick oak pieces as follows:
  Uprights $\frac{3}{8}$in x 5$\frac{3}{4}$in, 2 off
  Caps $\frac{3}{8}$in x $\frac{1}{4}$in, 2 off
  Internal lintel 3$\frac{1}{2}$in x $\frac{3}{8}$in
- Exterior lintel $\frac{3}{16}$in oak x $\frac{7}{8}$in x 3$\frac{5}{8}$in

DOOR
- $\frac{1}{4}$in oak x 6$\frac{7}{16}$in x 3in
- $\frac{1}{16}$in obeche pieces as follows:
  Inside braces $\frac{3}{8}$in x 18in
  Outside weather strips $\frac{1}{32}$in x 36in
- Weather board $\frac{1}{8}$in obeche x $\frac{3}{8}$in x 3in
- Door handles, 2 off
- Short length plastic bar $\frac{1}{8}$in x $\frac{1}{8}$in
- Hinges 3in brass strip, 2 off
- Brass pins $\frac{3}{8}$in, 4 off
- Copper wire $\frac{1}{32}$in x 1$\frac{1}{2}$in

*The basic shop, fronts
removed ready for the
addition of shelves
and stock*

WINDOW

- 1/8in obeche pieces as follows:
  Surrounds A, B & C 1/4in x 24in (total)
  Surround D 3/16in x 7in
  Centre bar 1/4in x 43/4in
- Surrounds E, F, G & H 1/16in obeche x 3/32in x 24in (total)
- Bars 3/32in obeche x 3/32in x 48in (total)
- Sill 3/8in moulding x 7in
- 0.7mm acetate x 7in x 43/4in

WINDOW SHELVES

- 1/8in obeche pieces as follows:
  Inner shelf 13/8in x 7in
  Inner shelf support 3/8in x 7in
  Brackets 3/8in x 11/4in, 2 off
- Outer shelf 3/32in obeche x 11/4in x 7in
- 1/8in obeche pieces as follows:
  Support bar 1/8in x 7in
  Support prop arms 1/8in x 13/4in, 2 off

FIRST FLOOR SECTION

CARCASS

- 9mm MDF pieces as follows:
  Sides 123/8in x 81/4in, 2 off
  Back 131/8in x 77/8in
  Floor 131/8in x 121/8in
- Back retaining strip 1/8in obeche x 3/4in x 123/4in
- Inner beams under floor 1/2in oak x 1/2in x 80in (total)
- Stud wall 6mm MDF pieces as follows:
  Panels G & H 2in x 11/2in each
  Panel J 21/2in x 13/4in
- 3/16in x 3/16in oak pieces as follows:
  Vertical stud beams A, B and C 71/4in each
  Stud rails D & E 2in each
  Stud rail F 21/2in
- External beams 1/8in obeche pieces as follows:
  1/2in x 60in (total)
  3/8in x 90in (total)
  Curved beams 31/2in x 71/2in, 2 off

FRONTAGE

- 9mm MDF 14in x 63/4in
- External beams 1/8in obeche x 3/8in x 80in (total)
- Obeche pieces as follows (2 centre windows):
  A–D 1/8in x 3/8in x 24in (total)
  F–J 3/32in x 1/16in x 40in (total)
  Window-sills 3/16in x 3/16in x 6in
- Glazing (2 centre windows) 0.7mm acetate x 21/2in x 7in (approx.)

MISCELLANEOUS

- Ridge tiles 120gsm card, A3 sheet
- Iron bracket, 2in
- Brass pins 1/4in, 2 off
- Hanging sign 1/8in obeche x 2in x 2in
- Sign frame 1/16in obeche x 1/16in x 18in (total)
- 12 volt centre light with candle fitting
- 12 volt wall lights with candle fittings, 2 off
- 12 volt grain of wheat bulbs, 2 off
- Thin twin-wire flex 15in

TOP SECTION

CARCASS

- 9mm MDF pieces as follows:
  Base 141/2in x 131/2in
  Gable 93/4in x 141/2in, 2 off
- 6mm MDF pieces as follows:
  Roof A 141/2in x 131/2in
  Roof B 141/2in x 131/4in
- Beams under floor 1/2in oak x 1/2in x 110in (total)
- Gable external beams 1/8in obeche x 3/8in x 100in (total)
- Barge-board mouldings 5/8in x 18in, 2 off
- Barge-board support strip 1/8in obeche x 1/4in x 18in, 2 off

TOP WINDOW

- Framework 1/8in obeche x 1/4in x 10in (total)
- 1/32in obeche x 1/16in x 10in (total)
- Sill 1/4in obeche x 1/4in x 6in
- Glazing 0.7mm acetate x 21/2in x 21/2in

CHIMNEY STACK

- Softwood 1³/₈in x 1¹/₈in x 10in
- ¹/₈in obeche x 1⁵/₈in x 1¹/₄in, 2 off
- 6mm MDF x 2in x 1³/₈in offcut
- 2¹/₂in counter-sunk wood screw, 1 off
- Fibre-glass brick sheet 10in x 8in

MISCELLANEOUS

- Fibre-glass tile roofing sheets, 2 off (total approx. 420sq in)
- 12 volt grain of wheat bulbs, 2 off

WORKING NOTES

Where 'glue' is referred to, it means a PVA adhesive unless otherwise stated. You will also need No.6 and No.8 counter-sunk wood screws and ¹/₂in and 1in panel pins.

Measurements in the book are imperial, however, as MDF is only sold in the UK in metric sizes, these thicknesses are given with approximate imperial equivalents, e.g. 6mm (¹/₄in), 9mm (³/₈in).

A selection of commercial paints and stains were used for this project so an exact match can be made. You could, of course, choose your own colours from other paint brands.

This building is unusual in that it is made as three distinctive box-like parts – a base, a first floor and a roof section (see Fig 1). All three fit together ingeniously without the need for complicated fixing techniques, and they can each be readily disassembled should the need arise. The method of cutting and assembly is slightly different from the other projects, each stage being cut and built before proceeding on to the next, leaving the two lower frontages until last. This makes fitting the three sections together far easier and results in a better building. The base and first floor have no tops of their own as each uses the floor of the one above. Both of the removable frontages, base and first floor, are held in place by pressure from the floor above. No hinges were used for these but you could add them if you wish.

The amounts of material given for the outside beams is shown as slightly more than the total amount required – follow the drawings and cut accordingly.

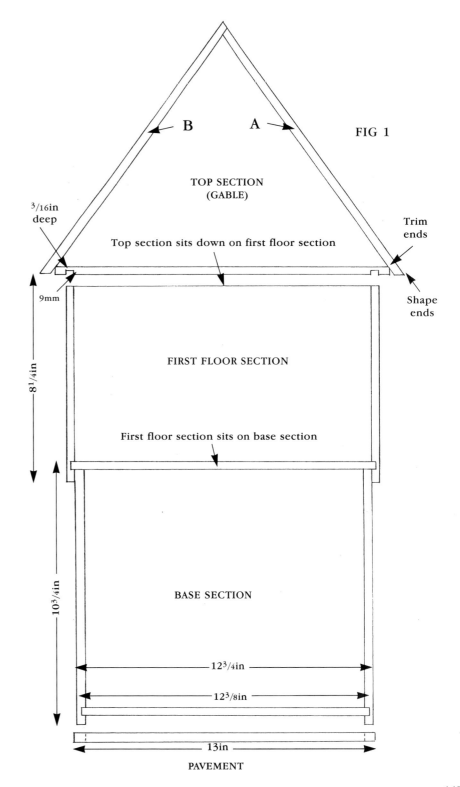

FIG 1

TOP SECTION (GABLE)

Top section sits down on first floor section

³/₁₆in deep

Trim ends

9mm

Shape ends

FIRST FLOOR SECTION

8¹/₄in

First floor section sits on base section

BASE SECTION

10³/₄in

12³/₄in

12³/₈in

13in

PAVEMENT

Base Section Carcass

CUTTING OUT THE BASE SECTION

Cut out two sides from 9mm MDF, each 10³/₄in high x 10¹/₄in wide and check that they are at right angles to each other. Lay the pieces face down side by side and mark out the two 9mm wide rebates for the floor and back so that the inner part of each of the rebates is ³/₄in from the outer edge(s) (see Fig 2). Machine out each of the rebates to a depth of ³/₁₆in using a powered router or circular saw and use an offcut of 9mm MDF to check that the fit is snug but not so tight that the parts will have to be forced together. When you have finished the two parts should be mirror images of each other.

Turn each of the pieces over and draw a line over the centre of each rebate, then use a sharp awl to make two marks on each line 3in from either end. Drill a ¹/₈in diameter hole through each mark and counter-sink to take a No.6 wood screw. Clean up the rebates using fine abrasive paper wrapped around a suitable block, being careful not to break the edges.

Cut the floor from 9mm MDF 12³/₄in wide x 10in and make sure that all four sides are dead square or this section will not assemble properly. Select and mark the front edge to make identification easier on assembly.

Cut the back from 9mm MDF 12³/₈in x 10³/₄in with the sides dead square to each other. Run a pencil line along the outer surface to mark where the floor butts against it.

Cut the pavement from 9mm MDF 13in long x 4³/₄in wide, with the parts cut out as shown in Fig 3. Smooth off the front edge with a small block plane and draw a line 3in from the front for the visible paving section – the remainder will sit under the building when it is assembled.

The flooring and the outer beams both need to fit their respective areas exactly and are cut and fitted after the stairs have been cut out and assembled – see below.

Cutting Out the Stairs

Prepare stair treads from a 36in length of 18mm thick MDF x 2¹/₈in wide, using a circular saw to maintain an even width. Select the best face and machine off a ¹/₈in wide strip from this to leave a ¹/₈in nosing along the top edge (see Fig 4). Turn the strip through 90 degrees and machine the separate treads each 2¹/₂in wide. Use a sharp craft knife to cut and gently distress the nosed edge of the stairs to indicate years of gradual wear. Finish off with a fine abrasive paper to smooth down any rough edges.

Cut the inner stair walls A and B from ¹/₈in thick hardboard sheet following the dimen-

FIG 2

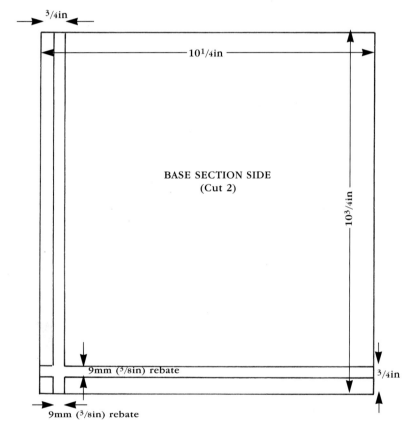

BASE SECTION SIDE
(Cut 2)

³/₄in

10¹/₄in

10³/₄in

9mm (³/₈in) rebate

³/₄in

9mm (³/₈in) rebate

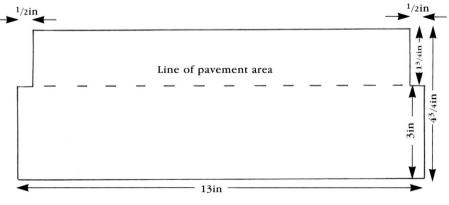

¹/₂in

¹/₂in

Line of pavement area

1³/₄in

3in

4³/₄in

13in

FIG 3

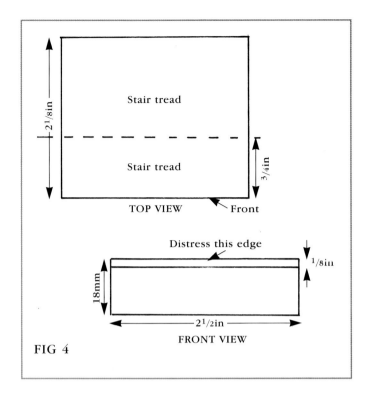

FIG 4

Stair tread

Stair tread

$2^{1}/_{8}$in

$^{3}/_{4}$in

TOP VIEW   Front

Distress this edge

$^{1}/_{8}$in

18mm

$2^{1}/_{2}$in

FRONT VIEW

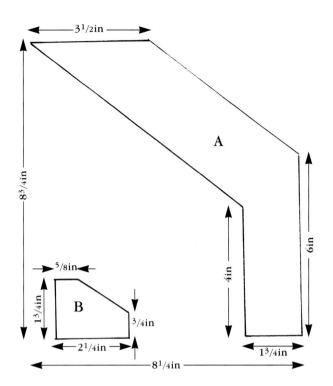

FIG 5

$3^{1}/_{2}$in

A

$8^{3}/_{4}$in

4in

6in

$1^{3}/_{4}$in

$^{5}/_{8}$in

B

$1^{3}/_{4}$in

$2^{1}/_{4}$in

$^{3}/_{4}$in

$8^{1}/_{4}$in

sions in Fig 5. Leaving the longer lower section $^{1}/_{4}$in longer on this piece will ensure a good fit between the floor and ceiling when the excess is trimmed off later. The two stud beams can be cut on assembly from an 8in length of $^{3}/_{16}$in x $^{3}/_{16}$in oak.

Prepare a $5^{1}/_{2}$in length of hand rail from $^{1}/_{8}$in thick oak x $^{3}/_{8}$in wide. Cut out the rebate on the back edge as shown in Fig 6.

ASSEMBLING THE BASE SECTION

Fix the floor into a suitable bench vice or 'workmate' with one long side edge uppermost. Place one of the sides onto this so that the floor fits into the rebate, flush at the front. Use a sharp awl to mark through the screw holes, remove the side and use a drill with a $^{1}/_{8}$in diameter bit to make starter

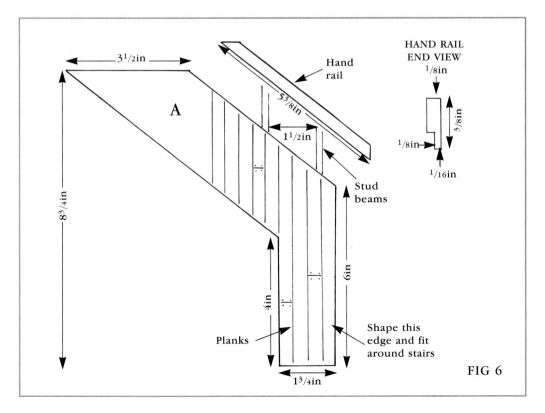

$3^{1}/_{2}$in

A

$8^{3}/_{4}$in

Hand rail

$5^{3}/_{8}$in

$1^{1}/_{2}$in

4in

6in

Planks

Stud beams

Shape this edge and fit around stairs

$1^{3}/_{4}$in

HAND RAIL END VIEW

$^{1}/_{8}$in

$^{3}/_{8}$in

$^{1}/_{8}$in

$^{1}/_{16}$in

FIG 6

holes half the depth of the screw being used. Remove the floor from the vice and turn it over so that the second edge is uppermost and repeat the above, this time using the second side.

Now fix the back into the vice, this time with one vertical edge uppermost, and place the correct side onto it so that the back fits into the rebate. Mark and drill starter holes as before. Remove the back, turn it over, secure in the vice again and repeat with holes in the second edge.

Hold the floor securely in a vice with one long side edge uppermost and coat this with PVA glue. Fit the matching side firmly into place ensuring that the floor is completely held in the rebate. Insert two No.6 wood screws to fix the parts together and then remove the part-assembly from the vice, checking that the parts sit at right angles to each other.

Lay the part-assembly down onto a flat working surface with the floor now uppermost and coat all the surfaces of the rebate for the back and the rear edge of the floor with glue. Push fit the back into the rebate so that it sits down to the bottom, using a mallet shielded from the work piece by an offcut of MDF to tap it down if necessary. Turn the assembly over so that the side is now on top and use two No.6 screws to make a firm fixing. Turn the assembly again so that the back is now uppermost and fix this to the floor using panel pins along the line you made earlier. Take the second side and apply glue to both rebates. Fit this onto the exposed edges of the floor and back pieces and secure by using No.6 screws. Before the glue sets make sure that the walls and back are sitting at right angles to the floor, correcting if necessary and then leave for the glue to set thoroughly.

Sit the base unit onto a flat surface and place the pavement against the front. Mark where the inner edges of the two sides touch the pavement (see Fig 1, page 117). Use a set square to extend the marks up to the 1³/₄in line made earlier when you cut

this part out. Use a sharp tenon saw to remove the waste pieces on either side and check that the pavement now sits under the building. Remove it and coat the under section with glue, including the edges, fit into place and secure with clamps placed along the length until the glue sets.

Flooring

Cut the piece of ¹/₈in thick hardboard to make an exact fit over the floor area, approximately 10in x 12in, ensuring that it is flush at the front. Draw out a pattern of flag stones (see photograph on page 115) using a sharp pencil and when you are happy with the design, lightly score along all the joint lines using a sharp scalpel or craft knife. Cut two lines parallel to each of the first but this time make them matching 'V' cuts and remove the waste. Finish off the cuts with a fine-grade abrasive paper but don't worry if the finish is uneven. The flooring can be glued and pinned into place at this stage or put aside for decorating later.

Stairs

The assembled staircase starts against the lower right-hand wall, seen from the front, and turns to the left through 90 degrees. Most of the treads are simply laid one on top of the other and only four actually turn. Cut away the upper portion of the top tread using a sharp tenon saw, as shown in Fig 7, to make it locate against the floor of the centre section. The bottom tread is reduced in thickness to give it the appearance of having sunk into the floor.

The stair treads should be coloured with a dark oak spirit-based wood stain and

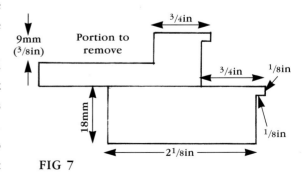

FIG 7

allowed to dry completely before assembly. You will need to lay the flooring into place before calculating the final height of the staircase.

Stack the treads one on top of each other, without adhesive, with the cut-away tread on top and place them against the back. The amount that they protrude above the back will need to be removed from the bottom of the first tread in the stack.

Mark up nine treads with a line across their width 3/4in from the front edge (see Fig 4, page 119). Each tread is laid along this line as they are assembled. Use PVA glue and clamps to assemble six of the treads together as a straight flight and add the top cut-away tread to finish this section. Glue two more treads together for the start of the staircase, adding the half tread to the bottom of these.

Make a pencil line across the top of the back wall 33/4in from the left-hand side – this is the point at which the front portion of the top tread will locate to the floor above. Use a large clamp to hold the top flight of seven stair treads in position against the back wall and place the bottom flight 43/4in from the front. The gap between the two flights can now be filled with the four spare treads, supporting and turning each one slightly to achieve the 90 degree turn. Mark the positions of each tread with a pencil line and glue together, adding them to the other sections to make one flight. You may find it necessary to trim the back edges of the treads that turn, to make them fit against the back and side walls.

Whilst the stairs are clamped to the back, mark the positions of two treads against the back wall. Remove the clamp and place the stairs to one side. Find the centre point of the two marks on the back wall and drill two 1/8in diameter holes through to the outside. Counter-sink these from the outside to take No.6 wood screws and use them to hold the stairs in place once the shop has been decorated.

Inner Walls A and B

Mark up the surface of wall A with vertical lines placed 3/8in apart to mimic planks, adding horizontal joins if you wish (see Fig 6). For a really good fit against all the stairs wait until the second floor is in place before cutting this part to length and fixing. Wall B can be cut from a hardboard offcut and fitted once the staircase is in place. Stain both parts with old English oak wood stain.

First Floor Section
Carcass

CUTTING OUT THE FIRST FLOOR SECTION

Cut the two sides from 9mm MDF, each 123/8in wide x 81/4in high and check that the sides are at right angles to each other. Lay the pieces side by side with the back edges touching and mark out the 9mm wide rebates for the floor and back, so that the inner part of each of the rebates is 3/4in from the outer edge(s) (see Fig 8 overleaf).

Machine out each of the rebates to a depth of 3/16in using a powered router or circular saw with a suitable cutter or blade, and use an offcut of 9mm MDF to check that the fit is snug but not so tight that the parts will need to be forced together. When you have finished, each part should be a mirror image of the other.

Turn each of the sides over and draw a line over the centre of each rebate and use a sharp awl to make two marks on each line 3in from the either end. Drill a 1/8in diameter hole through each mark and counter-sink to take a No.6 wood screw. Clean up the rebates using a piece of fine abrasive paper wrapped around a suitable block, being careful not to break the edges.

Mark the position of the two wall lamps (see Fig 8) and drill 1/16in diameter holes through from the inside. Use a set square and pencil to mark a straight horizontal line on the outside of each wall from the hole to the back. Lay the first side down onto a flat surface and using a sharp craft knife score

You might consider using the space upstairs as an extension of the main shop or for a secondary trade. In Luscombe's ironmongers the upstairs room has been left as one large space but used as an extension to the main shop. The over-spill of stock has been placed up there and at the same time it has been made into a staff rest room complete with a table and a toilet. Another idea is to use the room for an entirely different trade. In the beginning of the last century many upstairs rooms were let out to seamstresses or photographers. Pickwicks book shop has a slight variation on the trade carried on upstairs, in this case it is prints and maps – different from books but closely allied although the room has a different feel to it due to the paint finish.

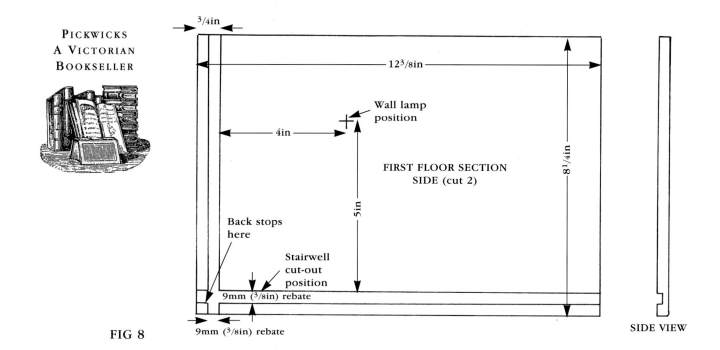

FIG 8

two lines 1/16in apart following the line.

Take a sharp miniature chisel (see Tools and Materials page 9) and gouge out the waste between the lines to a depth of 1/16in to take the wiring for the light. Repeat this procedure for the second side. Drill a 1/16in diameter hole 3/8in from the outside back edge of the wall, through the slot, to take the wiring through to the back.

Use a sharp pencil to run a line 1/8in from the bottom outer edge of both walls and with a sharp block plane, round off these

edges. Finish off with fine abrasive paper to produce a small, rounded profile.

Cut the floor from 9mm MDF 13 1/8in wide x 12 1/8in and make sure that all four sides are dead square or this section will not assemble properly. Select and mark the front edge. Use a large set square and a sharp pencil to mark up the cut-out for the stairwell 5 7/8in x 2 1/2in along the back edge (see Fig 9). Cut this out carefully using a sharp tenon saw. Use a craft knife and a steel straight edge or square to cut a 1/16in x 1/16in rebate across the underside of the right-hand end of the stairwell section for the wiring.

Cut the back from 9mm MDF 13 1/8in x 7 7/8in with the sides dead square to each other or this section will not sit correctly. The back for this section does not have a common measurement with the two sides, as is the case with the base section. When assembled the back is fixed flush at the top, short at the bottom.

ASSEMBLING THE FIRST FLOOR SECTION

Fix the floor into a suitable bench vice with one long edge uppermost. Place one of the sides onto this so that the floor fits into the rebate and is flush at the back and front. Use a sharp awl to mark through the screw

FIG 9

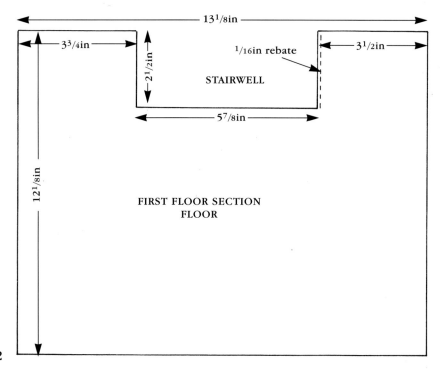

holes. Remove the side to make $^1/_8$in diameter starter holes half the depth of the screw being used. Remove the floor from the vice and turn it over so that the second edge is now uppermost and make a second series of starter holes, this time using the second side.

Now, fix the back into the vice, again with one edge uppermost, and place the correct side onto it so that the back fits into the rebate. Make sure that it is flush to the top not the bottom edge, then mark and drill starter holes as before. Remove the back, turn it over, secure in the vice again and repeat with holes in the second edge.

Dry fit, without adhesive, the two sides to the floor and fix together temporarily using screws. This should fit neatly over the base section with less than $^1/_{16}$in clearance each side. If it is too wide reduce the width of the floor by an appropriate amount. Once you have a correct fit, the parts can be separated.

Hold the floor securely in a vice with one long edge uppermost and coat this with PVA glue. Fit the matching side firmly into place ensuring that the floor is firmly held in the rebate. Insert two No.6 wood screws to fix the two parts together and remove the part-assembly from the vice after checking that the parts sit at right angles to each other.

Lay the assembly down onto a flat working surface with the floor uppermost and coat all the surfaces of the remaining rebate and the back edges of the floor either side of the cut-out, with glue. Push fit the back into the rebate so that it locates flush to the top, using a mallet shielded by an offcut of MDF to tap it down into the rebate if necessary. Turn the assembly over so that the side is now on top and use two No.6 screws to make a firm fixing. Turn the part-assembly again so that the back is now uppermost and fix this to the floor using panel pins.

Take the second side and apply glue to both the remaining rebates. Fit it onto the floor and back and screw down into place. Before the glue sets make sure that the walls and back are sitting at right angles to the floor, correcting if necessary. Leave for the adhesive to set thoroughly.

Cut a $^1/_{16}$in x $^1/_{16}$in notch into the bottom surface of the back where it butts against the

The upper floor of Pickwicks provides a quiet reading and print room

stairwell opening to match the rebate cut in the floor. Add an 1/8in thick piece of obeche as a retaining strip, 3/4in wide x 123/4in long, so that 3/8in of its width remains below the bottom edge of the back. When the glue has set hard, drill a 1/16in diameter hole through it for the lamp wiring to pass through.

Lay the flooring down into the base section and assemble the staircase, fixing it from the back with screws but do not add any adhesive at this stage. Place the first floor section onto the base and check that the staircase fits neatly into the cut-out for the stairwell and make any adjustments that may be required.

ADDING THE
INNER BEAMS

These beams are attached under the floor of the first floor section but appear, when assembled, to be on the ceiling of the base section. Turn the completed first floor section over to expose the underside of the floor and place it so·that the front is nearest to you. Then, cut and prepare a strip of 1/2in thick oak 1/2in x 80in for the beams, staining

each of the parts as they are cut with old English oak wood stain (before they are glued into place).

Start by cutting a 12in length beam, A (see Fig 10), and if you have a circular saw cut a 1/8in x 1/8in rebate down the entire length on one corner only. Alternatively, plane a 45 degree angle 1/32in wide. Cut a horizontal slot 1/32in x 1/32in across the width of the beam, dead centre on the same side as the rebate. The centre and hidden lamp wiring will be fed down the slot in the underside of the centre beam D. It is then fed through the horizontal slot in beam A and turns at right angles to follow the back rebate, feeding out to the back through the slot cut in the underside of the floor (see Fig 17, page 131).

Cut five beams B, C, D, E and F, each 91/8in long, and shape one end of each as shown in Fig 10A. Take beam D and machine or cut a 1/8in wide x 1/8in deep slot dead centre down 71/8in of the length, leaving 2in at the front uncut (see Fig 10B). Make a 1/8in wide by 1/8in deep saw slot across the centre slot and the surface of the beam 2in from the front edge to form a T-

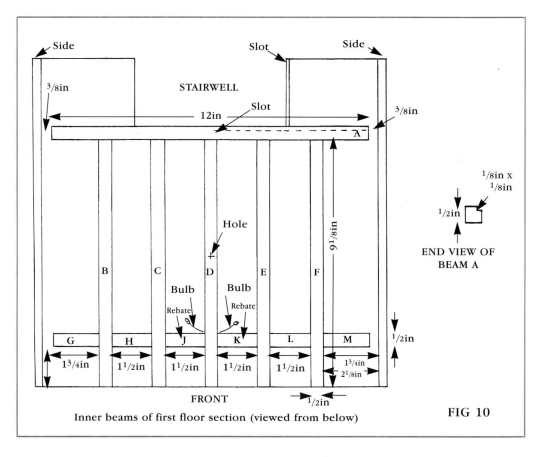

Inner beams of first floor section (viewed from below)

FIG 10

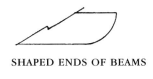

SHAPED ENDS OF BEAMS

FIG 10A

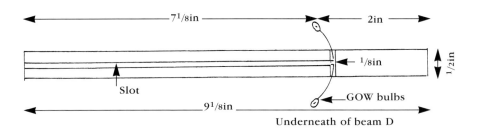

Slot

GOW bulbs

Underneath of beam D

FIG 10B

shaped slot. Be sure to do this on the side of the beam which has *not* been shaped and that will be glued to the underside of the floor. Drill a ¹/₁₆in diameter hole 5in from the front, through the beam and into the slot for the centre light wiring to pass through (see Fig 10B).

Mark with a pencil the position for the centre beam D on the upturned floor and lay this to one side. Use a clear, rapid-setting, spirit-based adhesive to fix the four outer beams B, C, E and F, spaced as shown in Fig 10.

Thread the wiring for the lamp up through the centre beam and glue the lamp into place using a rapid-setting adhesive or clear silicone sealant. Place this to one side and allow it to set hard. (The lamp used for this section should be painted matt black.)

From the ¹/₂in thick oak, cut the six short cross beams G, H, J, K, L and M to the lengths given in Fig 10. Cut ¹/₈in x ¹/₈in rebates into one long edge of J and K. Glue G, H, L and M into position as shown in Fig 10. (J and K are fixed either side of the centre beam D, with the rebates pointing into the shop and the hidden lamps will sit into these.) It can be seen from the photograph on page 115 that the top of the base section front butts under these cross beams.

Solder two 12 volt grain of wheat (GOW) bulbs to the ends of a 15in length of twin-wire flex and lay this flex down the centre slot of beam D, allowing the two lamps to turn out at right angles as shown in Fig 10B. The centre beam D can now be glued into position, followed by the two short beams J and K on either side. Push the two grain of wheat bulbs into the rebates of J and K and add a touch of adhesive to hold them in place. At this stage, the wiring for all three

lamps should trail out of the end of the centre beam.

Glue the back beam A down onto the surface with the rebate to the back and the wire passing directly through the centre slot. This beam should butt against the five beams running from front to back leaving ³/₈in either side of it for the top of the lower section to locate. When the glue has set, lay the wiring in the rebate of A, adding a little glue, and feed it at 90 degrees into the slot cut into the underside of the floor, and then pass it out to the rear through the hole in the retaining strip.

At this stage the first floor section can be assembled onto the base and left in place. If it is removed for any reason you must protect the hanging centre lamp by supporting the section on blocks or lay it on its back. Failure to do this will result in the lamp being crushed.

Assemble and fit the two wall lights by passing the wiring out through the pre-drilled holes and gluing them into place. Glue the wiring into the slots cut for the purpose and pass through the holes to the back, taping it down until it is needed for connection.

It should now be possible to fit the inner walls A and B into place in the base section and make any adjustments to ensure a tight fit. Check the measurement for the two vertical stud beams, locating the bottom of each onto a stair tread and the top to the upper edge of the floor above. Remove and slightly distress the surfaces with a sharp craft knife before gluing them into place on the back of wall A.

The small wall B can be cut and glued onto the side of the bottom treads after decorating.

Additional architectural elements placed onto the front of your shop can make it into something special and change it from a plain building into something quite elegant – this is especially true of kit shops. There are a number of plaster castings of columns and corbels available commercially and when used wisely they can add considerably to the appearance of the building. Luscombes ironmongers has decorative corbels placed either side of the doorway and the addition of laser-cut brackets and trim. Jingles toy shop has had part of the window bars cut away to allow us to inset a very pretty decorative laser-cut panel to great effect. All of these ideas can be incorporated into any standard shop front to give it a lift and make it different.

INTERNAL STUD WALL ASSEMBLY

Cut three $^3/_{16}$in x $^3/_{16}$in oak stud beams A, B and C, each $7^1/_4$in long and trim them so that they are an exact fit between the floor and the ceiling. Using a sharp craft knife or scalpel, distress the top 5in of each to provide a wavy edge to indicate that the beams have been recently exposed. Add a series of nail marks using a very fine felt-tipped pen and rub down with fine abrasive paper to make it all look natural. Cut three further lengths of the oak for rails – D and E each 2in long and F $2^1/_2$in long. Distress these in the same manner as the studs.

From a 6mm MDF offcut cut a strip $1^3/_4$in long and from this cut panels G and H each 2in long and J $2^1/_2$in long. Use a piece of abrasive paper wrapped around a block to round off one long edge of each. Lay all the parts onto a bench jig and glue and clamp the parts A, G, B and C together, gluing rails D and E into position at the same time (see Fig 11). When the assembly has set firmly, glue J and F to C at right angles.

Mix up plaster filler at normal strength and smooth a thin coat $^1/_{16}$in thick over panels G, H and J, avoiding the stud beams and rails as much as possible. Smooth down any rough surfaces with fine abrasive paper and paint the panels, back and front surfaces, with Farrow & Ball water-based emulsion paint Old White – this can be done at the same time as the remainder of the room is decorated. Carefully place the finished wall assembly into the centre section and position it over the stairwell with the studs placed between the ceiling beams. It may be

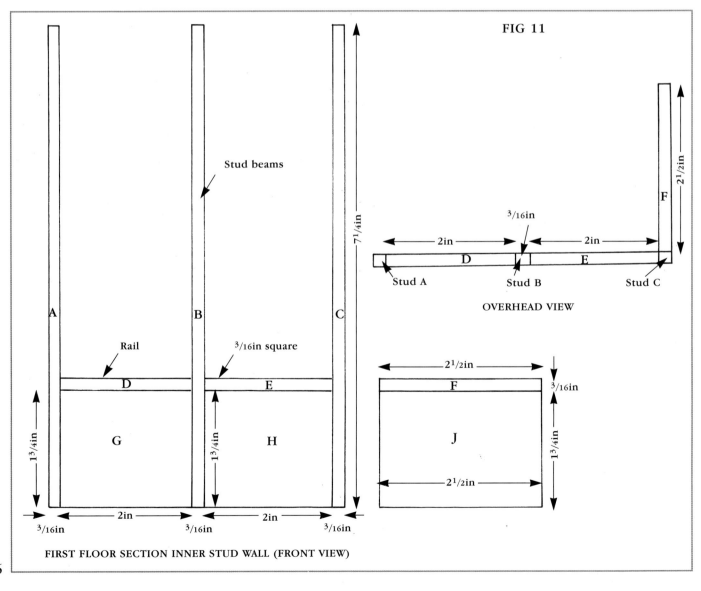

FIG 11

OVERHEAD VIEW

FIRST FLOOR SECTION INNER STUD WALL (FRONT VIEW)

necessary to tip the top section upwards in order to do this.

BASE AND FIRST FLOOR EXTERNAL SIDE BEAMS

All the external beams on this part of the shop are made from 1/8in thick obeche. These beams are placed onto the sides of the base section and the first floor section, creating a Tudor style for the building. Begin by punching down any nail heads and filling these, and any screw holes, with suitable plaster filler and smooth over. A clear, spirit-based adhesive with a fast grab action is used to apply all the beams directly to the surfaces of the sides.

Beams on the Base Section

Instructions are given for one side, the left, simply repeat for the right side. With reference to Fig 12, cut beams A and B from 1/8in obeche, 1/2in wide x 101/4in long and glue these into place first, noting that they fit flush to the back and the front and that A is placed 1/2in below the top. Cut beams C and D 1/2in wide x 93/4in long and glue them between A and B on the outer edges of the wall. Follow this by cutting the 1/8in x 3/8in vertical beams, V1–V5, so that they fit at top and bottom against A and B (the horizontal spacing is given in Fig 12). Cut the 1/2in wide beams J, K, L, M, N and P that fit between the verticals, locating them centrally between top and bottom and gluing them in position mid-way up the wall.

Beams on the First Floor Section

Instructions are given for one side, simply repeat for the second side but remember that the curved beam is always at the front.

With reference to Fig 13 overleaf, cut the horizontal beam A 3/8in wide x 123/8in long and glue this onto the side first, placing it 1/8in above the bottom and on top of the shaped edge. Now cut beams B and C each 1/2in wide x 75/8in long and glue these to the

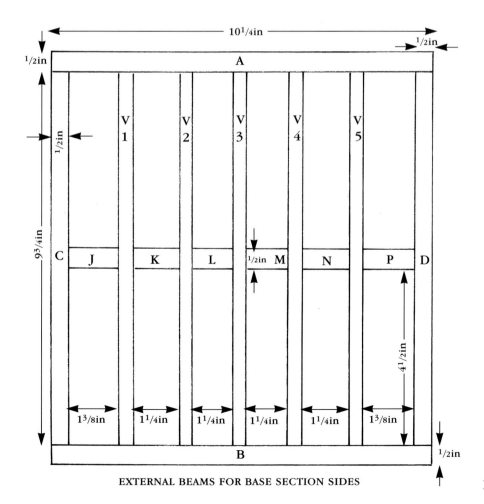

EXTERNAL BEAMS FOR BASE SECTION SIDES   FIG 12

Taking a few notes or photographs of the way buildings are finished in your area will help in creating interesting and realistic finishes to a building (unless you are deliberately re-creating a building located in a part of the world different from your own). In Britain, red brick and tile hanging is very prevalent in the south, soft ashlar smooth-cut stone in the west, roughly shaped blackened stone in some parts of the north and wooden boards in the east.

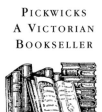

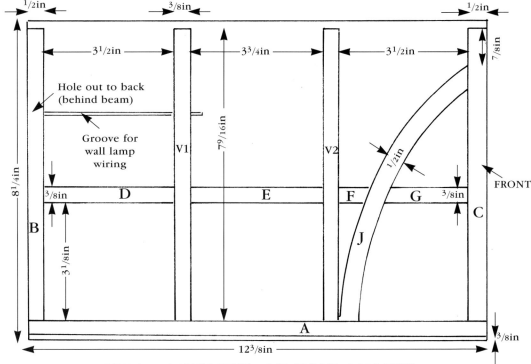

FIG 13

EXTERNAL BEAMS FOR FIRST FLOOR SECTION SIDES (LEFT)

Booksellers often have one glass-fronted cabinet in which they keep valuable books to prevent them being handled too often.

outer edges. Note that there is no top beam and that all those placed vertically are ³/₁₆in short of the top.

Cut and glue the two ³/₈in wide vertical beams V1 and V2 into the positions marked on Fig 13. Follow this by cutting the ³/₈in wide horizontal centre beams D and E, that fit between the verticals and glue these at the distance shown above beam A.

Lay the ¹/₈in thick obeche piece, 3¹/₂in x 7¹/₂in, down onto a flat surface and mark out the ¹/₂in wide curved beam J on Fig 13. As this is meant to resemble a naturally curved piece of wood there is no need to be too accurate with it. However, it needs to be at least 6⁷/₁₆in high and occupy the 3¹/₂in space between beams V2 and C. Trim the ends to match the horizontal and vertical beams.

If you have trouble drawing this beam accurately first cut out the shape from a piece of stiff card, matching it to the space until you are confident it fits, then trace it out onto the obeche and use a piercing saw and a V-block to cut it out.

Cut and fit the horizontal beams F and G, trimming the ends so that they match the curved beam lettered J.

Top Section Carcass

CUTTING OUT THE TOP SECTION

Cut the base from 9mm MDF 14¹/₂in long x 13¹/₂in wide and make sure that all the sides are at right angles to each other. This is especially important if you are using a powered router with side guides to cut the rebates. Lay the base onto a flat surface and mark up the rebates as shown in Fig 14. The top of the first floor section will locate directly into these on both sides and the back. To double check that they are marked correctly lay the base onto the first section and run a line around the top with a pencil.

Cut out the three rebates using a powered router or circular saw and check again for a correct fit onto the section below before proceeding (see Fig 1, page 117). Turn the base over so that the plain side is uppermost and secure it to the work surface while the two long edges are planed to give a 55 degree bevel, allowing the sloping sides of the roof to lay against them. Turn this part over so that the rebates are underneath and draw a line across the back 1¹/₁₆in from the edge. Draw a second line ³/₁₆in from the

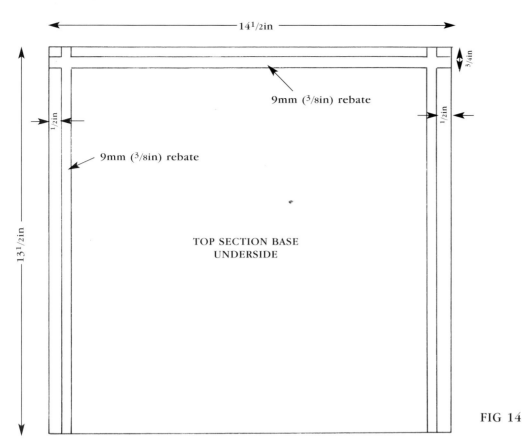

14¹/₂in

9mm (³/₈in) rebate

³/₄in

¹/₂in

9mm (³/₈in) rebate

¹/₂in

13¹/₂in

TOP SECTION BASE
UNDERSIDE

FIG 14

FRONT

front edge. Drill three ¹/₈in diameter holes evenly spaced along each line and counter-sink each of them to take a No.6 screw to fix the gables.

On a sheet of 9mm MDF 14¹/₂in x 9³/₄in, mark up the two shaped gables and cut them out using a sharp saw. Follow the mea-surements given in Fig 15 and the angles should be correct and make sure that they are identical or the roof will twist. Select one of the gables for the front and plane a 5 degree bevel onto the top and bottom edges to allow it to tip forward on assembly.

Cut the roof part A from 6mm MDF 14¹/₂in x 13¹/₂in and part B 14¹/₂in x 13¹/₄in. Use a sharp saw to reduce one end on each part to 14¹/₈in to mimic the slope in the gable when assembled (see Fig 16 overleaf).

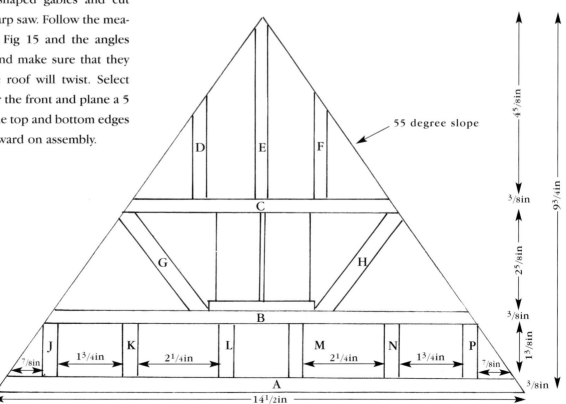

55 degree slope

4⁵/₈in

³/₈in

9³/₄in

2⁵/₈in

³/₈in

1³/₈in

³/₈in

D   E   F

C

G   H

B

J   K   L   M   N   P

A

⁷/₈in   1³/₄in   2¹/₄in   2¹/₄in   1³/₄in   ⁷/₈in

14¹/₂in

FIG 15

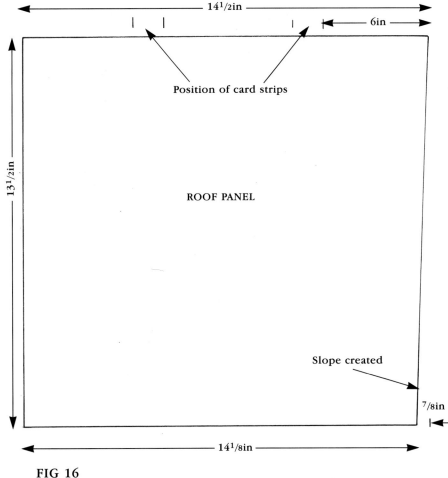

FIG 16

Position of card strips

14½in

6in

13½in

ROOF PANEL

Slope created

⅞in

14⅛in

ASSEMBLING THE TOP SECTION

Fix the back gable into a bench vice with the bottom edge uppermost and lay the top of the base onto it. Locate it so that a sharp awl can be used to mark the position of the three screw holes. Remove the base and pre-drill the holes half the depth of the screws being used. Coat the surface of the gable (still in the vice) with glue and screw the base to it with the rebates exposed. Remove this part-assembly from the vice and secure the front gable into it. Turn the base around and again mark up the screw holes, glue and screw as before with the gable tipping forward, not back.

Lay the part-assembly onto a flat surface and run a line of glue along the edges of the base and both sides of each gable. Pin and glue the roof part B onto the gables with ½in protruding over the gable at the front. The front roof line should follow that of the angled gable. Attach roof part A, overlapping the first at the apex. Panel pins can be placed

through the roof and into the base but care must be taken that they do not come through to the inside. Place the completed assembly to one side and allow all the glued joints to set hard before proceeding.

BEAMS UNDER THE TOP SECTION

To place the beams under the top section, turn the assembly over so that the underside with the three rebates is uppermost and so that the front is towards you and the horizontal rebate is to the back. A 'workmate' type bench with wide jaws is ideal for holding parts shaped this way.

Refer to Fig 17 and mark the position of the long centre beam. With a sharp awl, mark the point where this meets the back rebate and then drill a ⅟₁₆in diameter hole through the base for wiring so that it appears just behind the back gable.

Cut each of the seven oak beams A–G from ½in thick oak x ½in x 12¾in and shape the front ends as shown in Fig 10A on page 125. Each of the parts that you cut need to be stained with old English oak wood stain before they are glued into place.

Take the one marked D on Fig 17 and machine or cut a ⅛in wide x ⅛in deep slot dead centre down 11in of its length (shown by the vertical dotted line), leaving 1¼in at the front uncut. Make a ⅛in wide by ⅛in deep saw cut across the centre slot and the surface of the beam 1¼in from the front edge to form a T-shaped cut. Be sure to do this on the side of the beam that has *not* been shaped, i.e., the side that will be glued to the underside of the floor. Place this beam to one side and glue the other six into place with the intervals shown in Fig 17. Note that the two outer beams A and G run flush with the rebates to give a secure fit when this section lays on top of the first floor assembly.

Following Fig 17, cut the six short cross beams H, J, K, L, M and N from the ½in oak. Glue H, J, M and N into place ¾in from the front edge and between each of the long

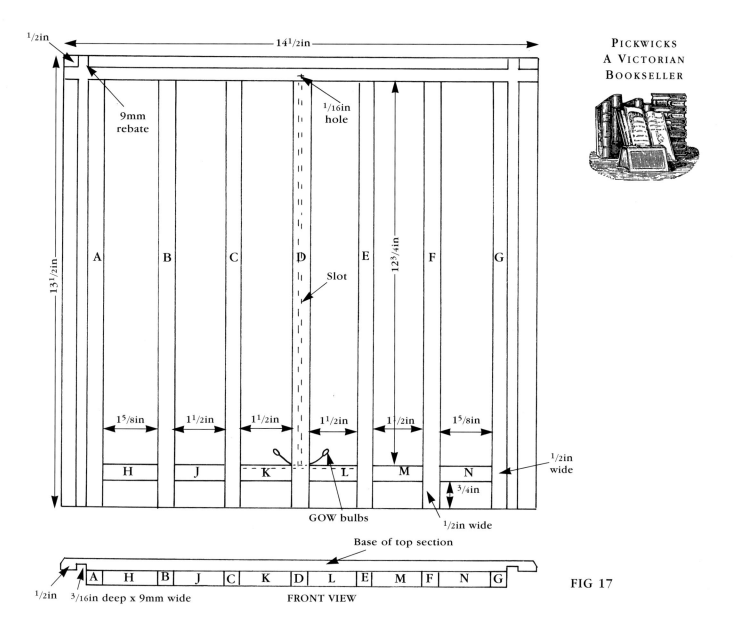

FIG 17

FRONT VIEW

beams. Cut a ¹/8in x ¹/8in rebate on one long edge of K and L, shown on the figure by the dotted horizontal line. (These are fixed either side of the centre beam with the rebates pointing into the shop and this is where the hidden lamps will sit.)

Solder two 12 volt grain of wheat (GOW) bulbs to the ends of a 15in length of twin-wire flex and lay this flex down the centre slot of beam D. Allow each of the two lamps 1in of wire to enable them to turn out at right angles as shown in Fig 17. The centre beam can now be glued into position with the grooved side to the underside of the floor. At this stage the wiring should trail out of the end of the centre beam and be fed through the hole drilled previously. The two short beams K and L either side of beam D

can now be glued into place with their rebates pointing into the shop. Push the two GOW bulbs into the rebates and add a touch of adhesive to hold them in place.

The top section can now be placed onto the first floor section, locating the top walls and back into the rebates.

TOP SECTION
EXTERNAL BEAMS

The beams on this part of the shop are placed on the front gable and are ¹/8in thick x ³/8in wide obeche. Use a clear spirit-based adhesive with a fast grab action to apply all the beams directly to the surface.

With reference to Fig 15 on page 129, cut and glue the beams to the front gable in strict alphabetical order, A through to P. Cut

the parts individually to size and on site as this will give a more exact fit all round.

FITTING THE BARGE-BOARDS

Cut one end of the 5/8in wide decorative moulding strip to fit against (not under) the right-hand front edge of the roof on one side. Trim one end to make a joint with a vertical line and cut the opposite end at a complementary angle to give a horizontal line (see Fig 18). Cut the second piece to match on the left side.

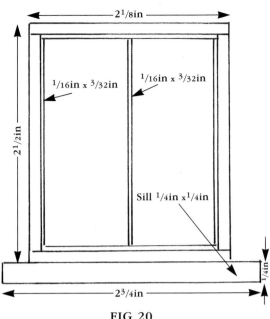

FIG 20

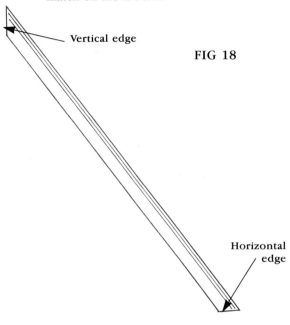

Vertical edge

FIG 18

Horizontal edge

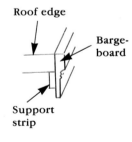

Roof edge

Barge-board

Support strip

FIG 19

From the 1/8in thick x 1/4in wide obeche support strip cut two lengths to fit under the front edge of the roof on both sides – there should be matching angles at the top and complementary ones similar to the barge-boards, at the bottom. Glue this strip into position and when this has set add the barge-boards to the front, gluing to both the roof edge and the supports (see Fig 19).

WINDOW

The window in the top gable section does not have an aperture behind it and is therefore 'blind', being simply glued to the frontage with glazing behind it. From a strip of 1/8in x 1/4in obeche make up a framework 1/4in deep to the dimensions given in Fig 20. Cut a strip of 1/4in obeche x 1/4in x 2 3/4in

long for the sill and glue this onto the bottom of the framework with an overlap at each end. Prepare a strip of 1/32in thick x 1/16in wide obeche and glue it on as a lining to the front edge of the frame. Add a final strip down the centre (the 1/16in edge is to the front).

Cut a piece of 0.7mm acetate to fit the window aperture, locating it behind the lining strip. Lay this down onto a clean surface and using a sharp craft knife incise a 1/4in wide diamond pattern of glass panes (see Fig 20A). Mix a little black and white acrylic

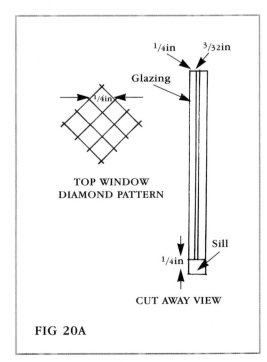

TOP WINDOW
DIAMOND PATTERN

Glazing

Sill

CUT AWAY VIEW

FIG 20A

paints together to give it the colour of lead glazing strips and smear this across the incised lines. Leave for just a few seconds and wipe off the excess with a damp cloth, leaving paint in the lines. Leave this to dry thoroughly and then glue into the frame after decoration. Place the window safely to one side until you have completed the decoration of the front.

CHIMNEY STACK

Cut and prepare a 9³/₄in length of softwood measuring 1³/₈in wide x 1¹/₈in deep. Place this with the width against the back edge of the roof and on top of the base of the top section just 3in from the left-hand side. Draw a line where it meets the slope of the roof, 4³/₈in up from the bottom on the left and 6³/₈in on the right (see Fig 21). Use a sharp tenon saw to cut down both of these lines 7/8in deep x 6mm wide and chisel out the waste to make the location slot. Drill a 3/16in diameter hole at the point shown, 2³/₄in from the base and counter-sink this for a No.8 wood screw in order to fix the stack to the back gable.

Cut two pieces of obeche, A and C, 1/8in thick x 1⁵/₈in x 1³/₈in and glue A to the top of the stack to give a 1/8in overhang on all sides (see Fig 21). Cut and prepare part B from an offcut of 6mm MDF 2in x 1⁵/₈in. Using a sharp craft knife mark up the edges 3/4in apart to indicate joints in bricks. Glue this part on top of A and then glue C on top of B to complete the cap. The completed stack can be decorated and then assembled using the screw to attach it to the gable after the roofing is finished.

Base Section Frontage

CUTTING OUT THE FRONTAGE

With the three sections of the shop assembled, check the measurement between the pavement and the row of beams under the centre section – if the plan has been followed it should be 9³/₈in and a snug fit. The

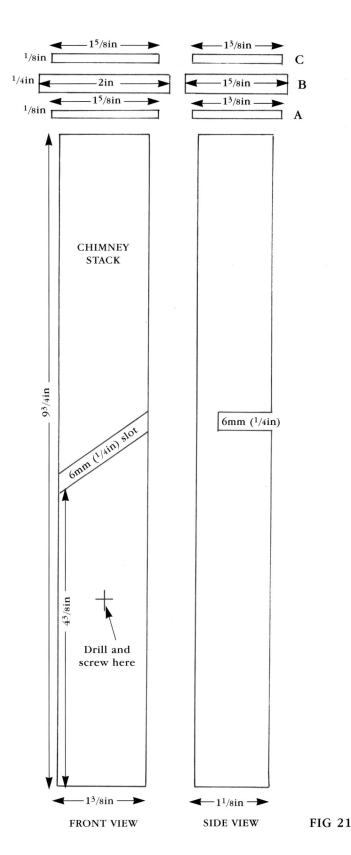

FRONT VIEW   SIDE VIEW   FIG 21

width to the outer edges of the added beams is 13in. Cut and prepare a piece of 9mm MDF to this measurement, checking that the sides are square to each other. Use a powered router or drill and pad saw to cut the main aperture 4³/₄in x 7in, 1in in from the right-hand side and 2in from the bottom

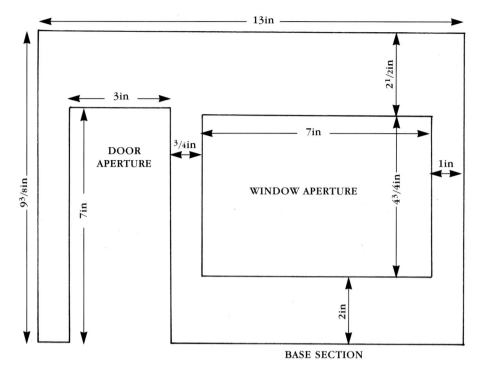

FIG 22

tread $1^5/8$in x 4in from an offcut of $^1/8$in hardboard, cutting notches to match those on the step and leaving a $^1/8$in overlap at the sides and front. Distress the front edge to indicate wear and tear.

MAKING THE BASE SECTION FRONTAGE
Doorway and Surround

Glue the tread onto the step and glue both into the doorway. Cut two upright boards from $^1/8$in thick oak x $^3/8$in wide, each $5^3/4$in long and glue these onto the front of the doorway, overlapping it by $^1/16$in on each side. Cut the two caps from $^1/8$in oak, $^3/8$in wide x $^1/4$in deep, and glue these on top of the uprights.

Prepare the top external lintel from $^3/16$in oak, $3^5/8$in wide x $^7/8$in high, and use a piercing saw and a V-block to mimic the shape in Fig 24. The small, roundel-shaped marks can be indented using a $^3/16$in diameter drill.

edge (see Fig 22). Continue by cutting out the doorway 7in high x 3in wide. Clean up both apertures with fine abrasive paper and remove routed corners with a sharp chisel.

Step

Cut the step from an offcut of 9mm MDF $1^1/4$in deep x $3^3/4$in wide and use a sharp tenon saw to cut out the $^3/8$in wide x 9mm deep notches at each end (see Fig 23). Cut a

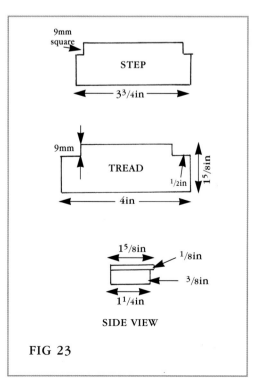

FIG 23

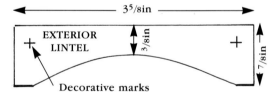

FIG 24

Cut an internal lintel from $^1/8$in thick obeche, $^3/8$in wide x $3^1/2$in long, and glue this on the inside of the doorway directly over and flush to the door aperture.

Door

The door is a typical plank construction supported with ledge and brace struts on the back. The front 'joints' in the planks are covered with thin strips to prevent penetration by the weather.

Cut a piece of $^1/4$in thick oak 3in x $6^7/16$in for the main structure. Prepare a length of $^1/16$in thick x $^3/8$in wide obeche and cut it into three 3in lengths. Lay the door face down onto a flat surface and glue the three ledge strips onto the back, one along the bottom and top edges, the third across the middle. Measure off and cut the two 45 degree braces and glue into place (see Fig 25).

Turn the door over to work on the front. Cut five strips of $^1/_{32}$in thick obeche, $^1/_{16}$in wide x 6$^1/_{16}$in long, and glue these onto the front vertically, following the spacing given in Fig 25, leaving a $^3/_8$in wide gap at the bottom edge. Cut the weather-board from $^1/_8$in thick obeche, $^3/_8$in wide x 3in long. Bevel off the top edge and glue to the bottom edge of the door.

The two handles for this door are made up from a $^3/_8$in long piece of $^1/_8$in square section plastic that is cut and shaped by hand (see Fig 25A). A hole $^1/_{32}$in in diameter is drilled through the handle end with a $^1/_4$in diameter ring made from copper wire threaded through. There are, however, perfectly adequate commercially made handles should you prefer not to make your own.

Hinge the door to the frontage using two $^3/_8$in wide brass strip hinges secured with pins.

Window

The window framework is shown in Fig 26 overleaf (see picture on page 137). Start by preparing a 24in length of $^1/_8$in thick x $^1/_4$in wide obeche and a 7in length of $^1/_8$in thick x $^3/_{16}$in wide obeche to line the window aperture. The strips are glued around the 9mm thick aperture using the $^1/_8$in wide edge and placed $^1/_8$in in from the back (see Fig 26A). Glue in the $^1/_4$in wide strip A along the bottom first. Then glue in the $^3/_{16}$in wide strip B at the top. Follow this with the $^1/_4$in wide strips C and D. Lastly fit a strip as bar E, between A and B at the top.

Cut a strip of $^1/_{16}$in thick obeche x $^3/_{32}$in wide and about 24in long and cut two 7in lengths, E and F. Glue E and F onto the faces of A and B, butting them against the outer edges of the aperture. Cut two further

If you are making up a kit dolls' house shop, it is worth considering the replacement of all the window parts supplied and making your own. We often find those supplied are far too thick for an accurate rendition of $^1/_{12}$ scale and there is no easy way of cutting these down. In $^1/_{12}$ scale, $^1/_4$in is equivalent to 3in full size – far too big for windows. Replacing with $^3/_{32}$in (or 1$^1/_8$in when scaled up) will give a far better appearance and make the shop look more realistic.

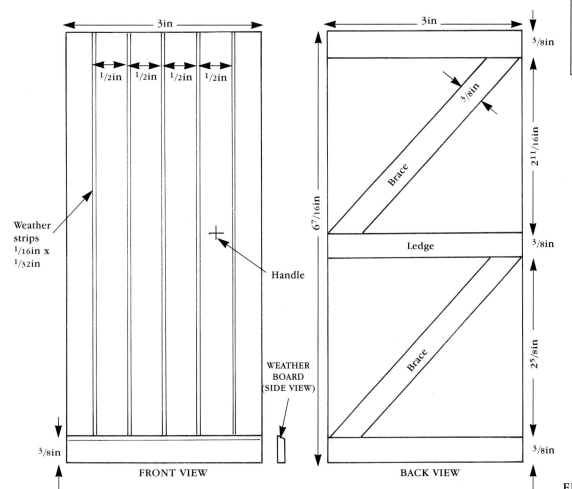

Weather strips $^1/_{16}$in x $^1/_{32}$in

Handle

3in

$^1/_2$in $^1/_2$in $^1/_2$in $^1/_2$in

WEATHER BOARD (SIDE VIEW)

$^3/_8$in

FRONT VIEW

3in

$^3/_8$in

Brace

$2^{11}/_{16}$in

6$^7/_{16}$in

Ledge

$^3/_8$in

Brace

$2^5/_8$in

$^3/_8$in

BACK VIEW

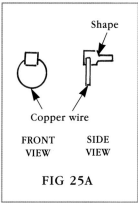

Shape

Copper wire

FRONT VIEW   SIDE VIEW

FIG 25A

FIG 25

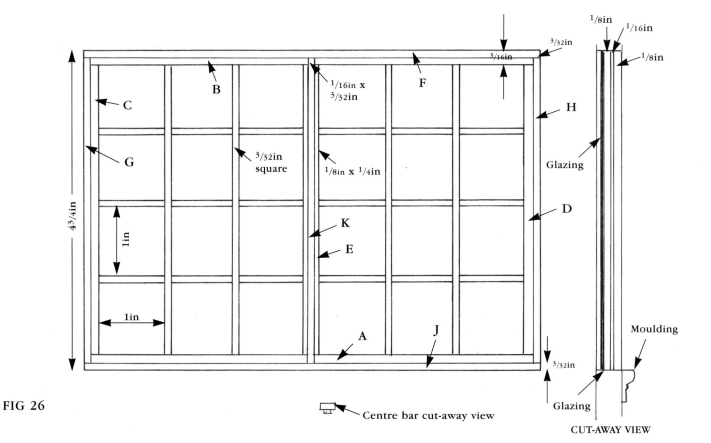

FIG 26

Centre bar cut-away view

CUT-AWAY VIEW

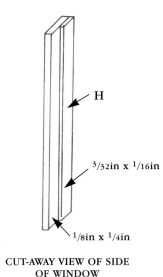

CUT-AWAY VIEW OF SIDE
OF WINDOW

FIG 26A

strips, G and H and glue these to C and D. Finally cut and glue a strip up the centre of the middle bar E.

You will need a 48in length of $^3/_{32}$in x $^3/_{32}$in obeche for the bars that make up the large window. In view of the fact that this is an old building there is no need to make halving joints as a little crookedness on assembly will add to the character of the building.

Cut four vertical bars to fit between strips A and B on the left-hand side, C and D on the right. This height should measure $4^5/_{16}$in but it is best to cut them individually for an exact fit. Each of the apertures, either side of the centre bar, should measure 3in, so space the bars at 1in intervals (see Fig 26). Cut nine horizontal bars each 1in long and trim each of them to fit between the vertical bars. Space them 1in apart to the centres as shown in the figure. To ensure that the bars are all evenly spaced cut a small block of MDF measuring the correct height between the bars and use this as a guide as you work up the window frame. Repeat for the right-hand side of the window.

Cut a length of $^3/_8$in wide window-sill moulding 7in long and glue this to the front immediately under the window aperture. Most commercially available mouldings will be suitable but a plain $^3/_8$in x $^3/_8$in strip could be substituted if you wish.

Finally, cut a piece of clear acetate 0.7mm thick x 7in x $4^5/_8$in and use a clear spirit-based adhesive to fix this behind the bars from the inside after adding the inner window shelf and finishing the decorations.

Inner Window Shelf

Cut the inner shelf from $^1/_8$in thick obeche, $1^3/_8$in wide x 7in long, to match the window aperture. A support is made of $^1/_8$in thick obeche x $^3/_8$in wide strip (see Fig 27). Prepare two brackets from $^1/_8$in thick x $^3/_8$in wide x $1^1/_8$in long obeche, trimming one end of each to 45 degrees. Place the parts to one side ready for assembly after completing the window.

When you are ready to attach the inner window shelf, glue the support onto the inside of the frontage, directly under the window aperture. Then glue the two brackets

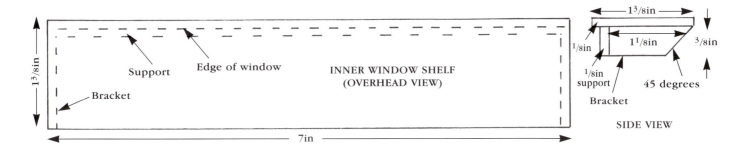

13/8in

Support — Edge of window

Bracket

INNER WINDOW SHELF
(OVERHEAD VIEW)

7in

1³/8in

1¹/8in

1/8in

1/8in
support

Bracket

³/8in

45 degrees

SIDE VIEW

flush to and under the outside edges of the shelf, leaving a ¹/4in gap at the front edge. The shelf can now be glued into position so that it rests on the bottom of the window aperture and the two brackets butt against the support.

Outer Window Shelf

Cut the outer shelf from ³/32in obeche, 1¹/4in wide x 7in long. Cut a support bar ¹/8in x ¹/8in x 7in long and glue this under the front edge of the shelf. Cut two support prop arms from ¹/8in x ¹/8in obeche each 1³/4in long. Use a sharp razor saw to trim both ends to 45 degrees (see Fig 28 overleaf). Place these parts aside ready for decorating. Once decorated the outer window shelf is added as a removable part of the frontage.

When you are ready to fit the outer window shelf, the method is as follows. Use ¹/32in diameter copper wire to make two

FIG 27

The small-paned construction of the late Tudor-style window shows an elegantly dressed customer considering a book from the shelves

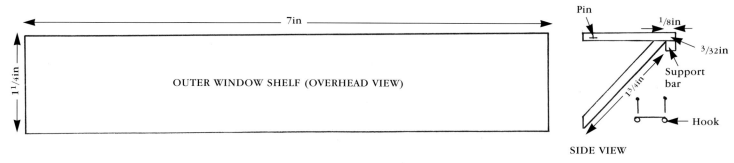

7in

1¼in

OUTER WINDOW SHELF (OVERHEAD VIEW)

Pin

⅛in

3/32in

1¾in

Support bar

Hook

SIDE VIEW

FIG 28

hooks shaped as shown in Fig 28. Pass a ³/₈in long brass pin through one eye of the hook and push it into the edge of the shelf ¼in from the back. Repeat for the other end. Push two pins into each end of the window-sill and swing the hook over this to hold the shelf up, Place the two support prop arms under each end locating them against the support strip and onto the bottom beam A (see below and Fig 28).

Front Beams

All the beams used for the frontage are ¹/₈in thick x ³/₈in wide obeche and should be applied to the surface of the front using a clear, fast-grab, spirit-based adhesive. Cut to the lengths shown in Fig 29 and ensure that where beams butt together the measurements are checked on site before cutting. Work in strict alphabetical order. Cut A as the base beam: it is cut so that it appears on both sides of the door step. Beam B runs across the top and C is placed vertically to complete the frame around the frontage on the left. Cut beam D and then cut a ¹/₁₆in rebate down one long edge to take the wiring for the coach lamp, assembled later. Glue D into place with the rebate to the outside. Beam E is cut neatly around the door hood on the left-hand side. The remaining shorter beams are all cut and inserted between those already placed following the spacing in the drawing. Note that N and P are glued the same height above A.

FIG 29

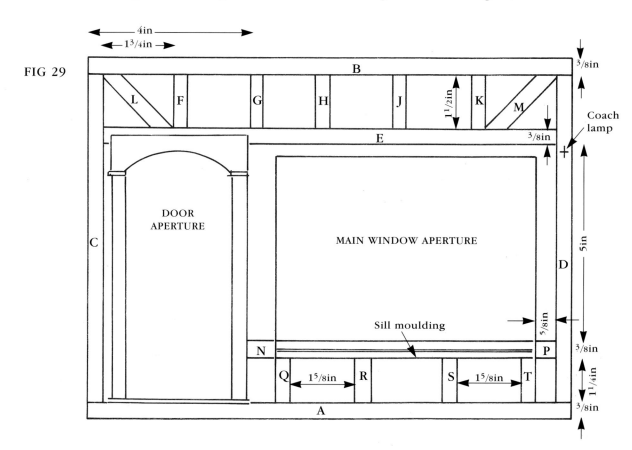

4in

1³/₄in

³/₈in

B

L   F   G   H   J   1½in   K   M

Coach lamp

E   ³/₈in

DOOR APERTURE

MAIN WINDOW APERTURE

C

D   5in

Sill moulding

⁵/₈in

N   P   ³/₈in

Q   1⁵/₈in   R   S   1⁵/₈in   T

1¼in

A   ³/₈in

138

First Floor Section Frontage

CUTTING OUT THE FRONTAGE

With the three sections of the shop assembled check the measurement between the jetted front floor of the first floor section and the row of beams under the top section – if the plan has been followed it should be 6³/4in (see Fig 30). The width to the outer edges of the added beams is 14in. Cut and prepare a piece of 9mm MDF to this measurement, checking that the sides are square to each other. Use a powered router or drill and pad saw to cut the two window apertures each 2¹/2in wide x 3¹/2in tall, 2¹/2in from the right-hand side and 2⁵/8in from the bottom edge. Clean up both apertures with fine abrasive paper and remove routed corners with a sharp chisel.

MAKING THE FIRST FLOOR FRONTAGE
Windows

Instructions are given for one window, simply repeat for the second one. Start by cutting two lengths of ¹/8in thick obeche, ³/8in x 3¹/2in long (A and B), and glue these to the vertical sides of the window aperture as a lining (see Fig 31). Cut two more lengths (C and D), each 2¹/4in long and glue these around the edges of the aperture to complete the lining.

Cut two lengths of ³/32in thick obeche, ¹/16in x 3¹/4in long (E and F) and glue these with the ¹/8in face to the vertical linings, spaced ¹/8in from the back. Cut two further lengths 2¹/4in long (G and H) and glue these to the top and bottom horizontal linings to finish the framework.

Cut two ³/32in x ¹/16in x 3in centre bars J and glue them together vertically to indicate two opening parts of the window. Cut two lengths of ³/16in x ³/16in square obeche 2¹/2in long and glue to the front for the window-sills, placing them flush with the bottom of the window aperture.

To glaze the windows, cut two pieces of 0.7mm acetate, each 3¹/4in x 2¹/4in, and lay on to a clean, flat surface. Prepare a paper template to divide the glazing into ¹/2in diamonds (see Fig 32) and lay the acetate over this. Use a sharp craft knife to incise the lines, being careful though *not* to cut all the way through. Mix a little white and grey acrylic to mimic the colour of weathered lead and rub this into the cut surfaces. Remove some of the excess, leaving sufficient paint to colour the lines and allow to dry. Glue the finished glazing sheets in place after decoration.

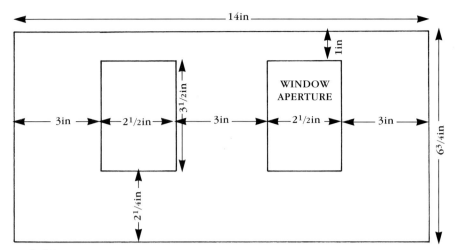

FIG 30

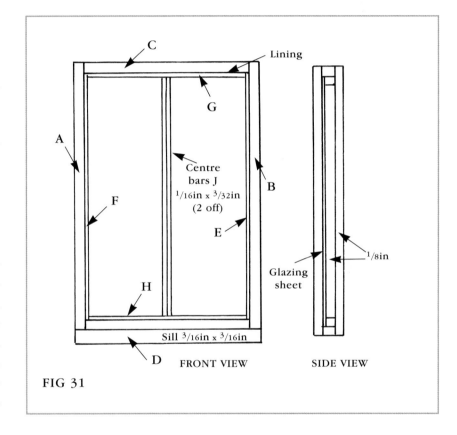

FIG 31

FRONT VIEW   SIDE VIEW

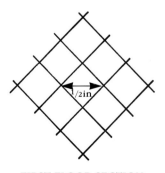

FIRST FLOOR SECTION WINDOW DIAMOND PATTERN

FIG 32

A typical bookseller's desk, full of prints, books and parcels

and are positioned halfway between A and B. Cut M and N to fit neatly from A to C and D respectively.

DECORATING AND FINISHING THE EXTERIOR
Beams

The first stage is to distress the surfaces of all the outer beams to give the appearance of age and weathering. Use a small decorator's wire brush for this, brushing with the grain. Alternatively, you could use some very coarse abrasive paper wrapped around a block the same width as the beam. Be careful not to destroy or break too many of the edges but try to achieve a roughened appearance remembering that you are working in $^1/_{12}$ scale. Proceed on to prepare and paint all the infills, finishing off the beams after this.

Infills

The spaces between the beams on all three sections are all filled using the following technique. Do not fill the area in the front gable section used for the small 'blind' window as this will be painted later.

Pour a little PVA glue into a suitable glass dish and dilute this with 10 percent clean water. Use a small paint-brush to apply the mixture to all the areas and allow this to dry.

Applying the Beams to the Front

All the beams used for the frontage are $^1/_8$in thick x $^3/_8$in wide obeche and should be applied to the surface of the front using a clear, fast-grab, spirit-based adhesive. Cut to the lengths given below and ensure that where beams butt together the measurements are checked on site before cutting. Work in strict alphabetical order as shown in Fig 33. Cut beams A and B 14in long and glue top and bottom of the frontage. Next, add beams C and D, each 6in long, to complete the framework. Cut beams E, F, G and H, all 6in long, and place them flush with the edges of each window frame as shown. Beams J, K and L fit between the verticals

FIG 33

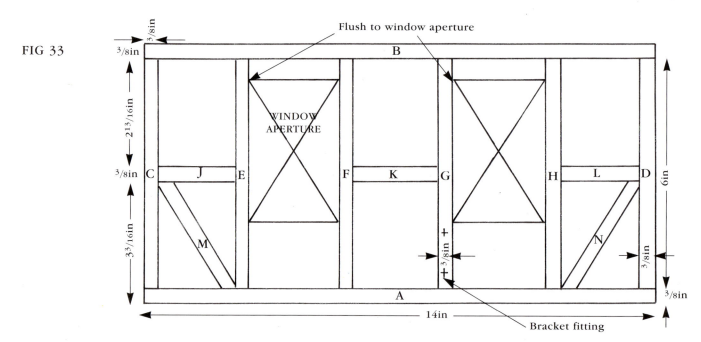

140

Don't worry if a little runs down over some of the beams as it will do no harm. Mix up a proprietary plaster filler and apply a coat of this to all the areas with a small trowel or knife, approximately 1/16in deep. A good tip is to make up a miniature trowel from a scrap of plastic card to the shape and size you want. Don't be too particular about this, as it is not meant to be perfect. As the filler dries, smooth it over with a clean, dampened paint-brush, pushing filler right into the corners and up to the very edges of the beams, taking out any rough edges left by the trowel. Let all this dry thoroughly before proceeding. Mix more of the PVA and water together to the same proportions and paint this over all the plastered areas. Finish by painting all the infilled areas with a matt white emulsion paint.

Paint the area in the gable behind the small window with black gloss enamel paint.

Outer Beams

In real life, the timber used for just about all wooden-framed buildings was oak, and contrary to popular belief these exposed timbers were not stained dark brown or black. This is a modern practice, probably used first by builders of the 'Tudorbethan' houses in the stockbroker belt. In most cases, the beams were originally treated with a lime wash to protect them from the ravages of the weather. This would start off nearly white in colour and gradually weather to a silver grey depending on the prevailing climate and how long they had been exposed.

To paint the beams of this book shop, place some white matt emulsion in a dish and add a little grey and black acrylic paint. Fold the colours together but don't allow them to mix too well – the best result will have a streaky appearance. Use a stiff, narrow paint-brush to apply the paint to all the beams, working with the direction of the grain. Add extra paint by rubbing it on with your fingers to produce an uneven colouring. Use a fine brush to ensure that the edges of the beams where they meet the

infill plaster are also coloured. The woodwork around the door will appear a little different depending on the natural colour of the timber you have used. The barge-boards too can be painted with the same colouring.

Windows and Sills

The woodwork around all the windows, inside and out, is painted very similarly to the beams but a slightly darker mixture of colours was used in order to give a little texture and variation to the front. It would also indicate that these were more recent additions to the old building. Paint the gable window in the same way and when dry fit the diamond paned glazing into the rebate at the back. Glue the completed assembly over the area painted black.

Coach Lamp

The coach lamp is first given a coat of matt black paint and then glued to the right-hand beam using a rapid-set epoxy adhesive. The outer edge beam D is grooved to take the start of the wiring; the remainder is fed and glued into the rebated slot previously cut into the beam (see Fig 29, page 138). The wiring then passes under the building.

Step Tread

The hardboard used for this project has the colouring of naturally weathered stone and so can be left unfinished. However, it could be painted any suitable stone colour.

A box of prints and a globe contribute to a bookish atmosphere

The exterior decoration of a shop should reflect the trade going on inside. For example, practical shops, such as ironmongers and shoe repairers usually had a practical finish to the outside, with rather dull, hard-wearing paint finishes and signs that had often seen better days. Food stores, such as grocers, needed a bright, clean finish if they were to persuade people to come inside and purchase something they intended to eat. You don't need bright colours for this, dark blues and greens are ideal.

Whilst the lady's dog looks on, the bookseller discusses the merits of the latest novel

142

Bracket

A white metal, ornamental cast bracket, available commercially, is painted matt black and glued to the centre frontage using a rapid set epoxy adhesive. Two $^{1}/_{4}$in brass pins are added to give extra strength (see also Fig 34A on page 145).

Roof

Most roof surfaces are smooth and flat, especially when new, however as the timbers used in the Tudor period were unseasoned they tended to warp and twist as they dried out. The result was often an undulating roof surface that no doubt caused many a tile to slip into the street below. Some model makers tend to overdo this effect but it can look effective if it is subtle.

Cut and glue two 1in wide strips of thick card up each slope of the roof, from the bottom to within about 1in of the top, placing them 6in in from either end. On top of these glue a second strip this time $^{3}/_{4}$in wide, followed by a third $^{1}/_{2}$in wide. When the glue has set hard smooth the edges of the three strips using a fine abrasive paper so that they blend together and take on the appearance of an undulation. See Fig 16 on page 130 for the position of the first strips.

The roof was finished with sheets of fibreglass roofing that mimic an old tile finish. Cover the surface of the roof with PVA glue and lay the sheets, one at a time, down onto the surface, working from the front to the back. Smooth the sheet over the undulations as you work until you have achieved a smooth finish. Trim any excess away from the bottom edges using a sharp craft knife or scalpel. Mix up a mixture of white and black acrylic paints and add sufficient water to make the mixture very fluid. With a dry brush pick up a little of the colouring and paint streaks down the roof, especially below the point where the chimney stack will be added. Use a dry cloth to wipe most of this colouring away but leave just enough to indicate a weather stain.

The ridge tiles are made from strip of pliable card cut into pieces 1in wide x 1$^{1}/_{4}$in long. Dampen each cut tile and gently bend each one over a $^{1}/_{2}$in diameter dowel or rod and secure them until they retain their shape. Mix up some plaster filler and fix each tile in place, working from front to back. Mix terracotta, black and grey acrylic paint together in a palette and paint the tiles separately, trying not to achieve a uniform colouring. Paint any filler showing too.

Chimney Stack

The top portion of the stack above the main part, is painted a brick colour using a mixture of acrylic paints to which should be added a quantity of matt black to indicate soot and rain mixed together. The remainder of the stack should be covered with a fibre-glass brick sheeting patterned as old English brick bond. Wrap the sheet around, leaving the join at the back where it will be less noticeable and glue this on using PVA craft glue. Cut away the portion covering the slot for the roof and the entry for the fixing screw using a sharp craft knife.

To finish this stack off properly add a lead flashing using strips of masking tape which have been trimmed to follow the lines of the brick. Colour the tape with a mixture of black and white acrylic paint to indicate the colour of lead.

Pavement

A sheet of embossed wallpaper, used for real houses, and with a pattern very similar to cobblestones, is cut to fit the pavement area. To give it strength, first coat it with PVA glue and allow to dry before gluing it into place. The entire surface can then be painted with a matt white emulsion paint followed by a dark grey acrylic paint. This last coat is applied very roughly allowing the white to 'grin' through.

FINISHING AND DECORATING THE INTERIOR
Base Section

The ceiling between the beams, on the floor above, is painted using a white matt emulsion paint – two coats should be sufficient.

Remove the flooring sheet and the staircase if fitted and paint the walls. We used Farrow & Ball 'Picture Gallery Red', a water-based emulsion paint (see Suppliers). The inside of the base front can also be painted with the same colour, leaving all parts of the window the same colour inside and out. Once this is completed the inside window shelf can be assembled and glued into place. The front edge of the shelf rests on the edge of the window aperture. Paint this to match the walls.

The flooring once removed can be left its own colour but use a soft-leaded pencil to

Reading stands were a popular means of displaying books

emphasise the joints between the stone slabs. Finish by simply polishing with a good quality light brown shoe polish. Buff up using a shoe brush to give only a sheen to the surface rather than a high shine.

Replace the flooring and glue it down if required. Add the staircase and screw this into place from the back. The inner walls A and B can now be placed into position, pinned and glued. Punch down the pin head and colour the hole with a black felt-tip pen. Add wall A with the stud beams, and wall B at this point.

First Floor Section

The ceiling between the beams, on the floor above is painted using a white matt emulsion paint – two coats should be sufficient.

Run a length of masking tape along the bottom of the two walls and the back to protect them from the floor finish. Draw a series of horizontal lines across the floor ⅝in apart using a fine black felt-tip pen to indicate floorboards. Add a few joints at right angles making sure that these are above the beams below. Stain the floor with a dark old English oak spirit-based wood stain, being very careful not to allow it to creep under the masking tape. Follow the manufacturer's instructions regarding naked flames and smoking. Leave the floor to dry in a well-ventilated area, then remove the tape from the walls when the floor has dried out.

Run a length of masking tape along the edges of the floor where it meets the walls. Mix a small quantity of PVA glue and add approximately 10 percent water. Paint this mixture over all the walls. Mix a quantity of a suitable plaster filler in a clean dish so that the mixture is loose rather than stiff. Take a ½in wide paint-brush and apply a very thin, smooth coating to all the walls, carefully avoiding the two wall lamps. When the plaster coating is dry finish off any rough spots with a very fine abrasive paper and remove any dust. Paint the wall surfaces with one coat of Farrow & Ball 'Old White' water-based matt finish emulsion. It is unlikely that you will achieve a perfect finish with one coat and the colour of the white filler will probably 'grin' through. Leave it like that as it will break the solid colour and give the appearance of being old.

The inside of the frontage for this section should first be painted with a matt white emulsion and then over-painted with Old White as for the remainder of the room. Remove any masking tape once the decorating is finished.

Lighting

The wiring for all the lamps connected to the main body of the building should all be gathered together on the back and connected to a suitable 12 volt DC transformer. The coach lamp is attached to the frontage and the wiring passed under the house to make a connection at the back. Alternatively a connection may be made at the base of the frontage and simply disconnected each time the front is removed.

Shop Sign

Cut the hanging sign from a piece of 1/8in thick obeche, 2in x 2in. Glue on a simple frame of 1/16in x 1/16in obeche strip, mitred at the corners (see Fig 34). The lettering can be prepared using a computer desk top publishing package or pressure lettering (e.g. Letraset) using an appropriate font. In this case the title was 'Pickwicks' with the

words 'Books and Prints' below it. Arrange the wording to fit the net amount of space and print up on two pieces of thick paper. Cut out and apply directly to the sign using a PVA craft glue.

From 2³/4in lengths of 1/32in diameter copper wire make two 3/16in diameter swan necked hooks to resemble question marks. Transfer the spacing on the iron bracket loops to the top edge of the sign and push home the hooks so that they are both facing in the same direction. Hook the sign onto the bracket to finish (see Fig 34A).

To complete Pickwicks book shop, fit the lower half of the shop out with as many bookcases as you can (see Shopkeeper's Resource section page 43). Instructions for making shelving can be found on page 87. Tuck in a suitable desk, complete with ledgers, away in the corner under the stairs. Add as many books as you can (see page 45) and pile any extras on the floor. Instructions for making the print holder, ladder and trestle table are in the Shopkeeper's Resource section, pages 42 and 44.

The upstairs part of the shop should have a calmer, less cluttered atmosphere, where prospective buyers of prints and pictures can peruse the stock. The bookseller will almost certainly display an air of faint superiority over his customers and appear to be slightly detached.

Prints and paintings can be clipped from magazines and catalogues, pasted onto stiff card and framed. Printed book covers can be glued over small pieces of foam core board to produce authentic-looking books. Round off one edge for the spine before attaching the cover.

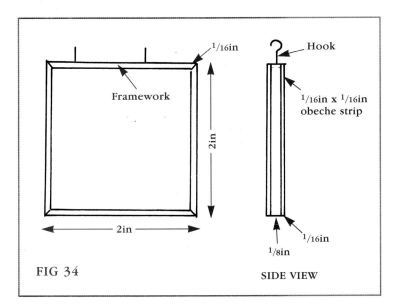

Framework

1/16in

Hook

1/16in x 1/16in obeche strip

2in

2in

1/16in

1/8in

FIG 34

SIDE VIEW

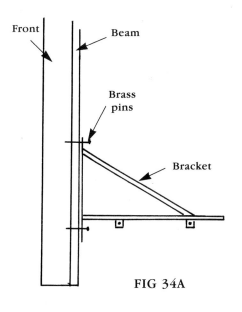

Front

Beam

Brass pins

Bracket

FIG 34A

145

MEADOWS
A 1930s Grocer's Shop

Unlike today's supermarkets, where almost everything is sold under one roof, the lines of produce and trade during the first half of the last century were fairly clearly drawn. In Britain, a grocer's shop in the 1930s would sell tinned goods such as peas, beans and fruits, loose measures and ready-packed goods from household names of oats, rice and biscuits, as well as loose dairy produce such as cheeses, butter and eggs. A range of cooked and cured meats, ham, cured sausages and bacon would be cut and weighed at the customer's request. Fresh and frozen meat would only come from a butcher, bread and cakes from a baker and most fresh vegetables from a greengrocer.

At the turn of the century it was usual to shop at the locally owned corner store. If you lived in one of the larger towns the local grocer might well be part of a national chain such as Sainsbury's, Home & Colonial, Griegs and of course The Co-Operative Stores, but they maintained a local

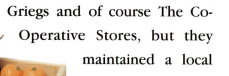

feel and they co-existed on the high street with smaller family concerns. We know now that the chains survived much better than the individual shopkeepers, who could not maintain the economies of bulk buying.

During the 1930s, pre-packaged goods were sold in brightly coloured boxes or tins covered with imaginative and often boastful advertising, but dry goods such as sugar, rice, dried fruit and biscuits, were sold loose in brown or blue paper bags. Dairy produce was sold by weight and would be cut and wrapped in neatly folded greaseproof paper – plastic bags and shrink-wrap would take another fifty years to become the norm.

Very small shops might have just one or two assistants to serve or attend to customers' requirements – a cashier to take the money or enter the bill into the account book, and almost certainly, a delivery boy. He would be equipped with a black bicycle complete with a wicker basket or box on the front although larger establishments might have a driver with a liveried van. Each serving assistant in this type of shop would almost certainly be wearing an apron, both to protect their clothes and give a hygienic appearance. They would also have a pencil to jot down the cost of each item on a piece of wrapping paper or the next paper bag.

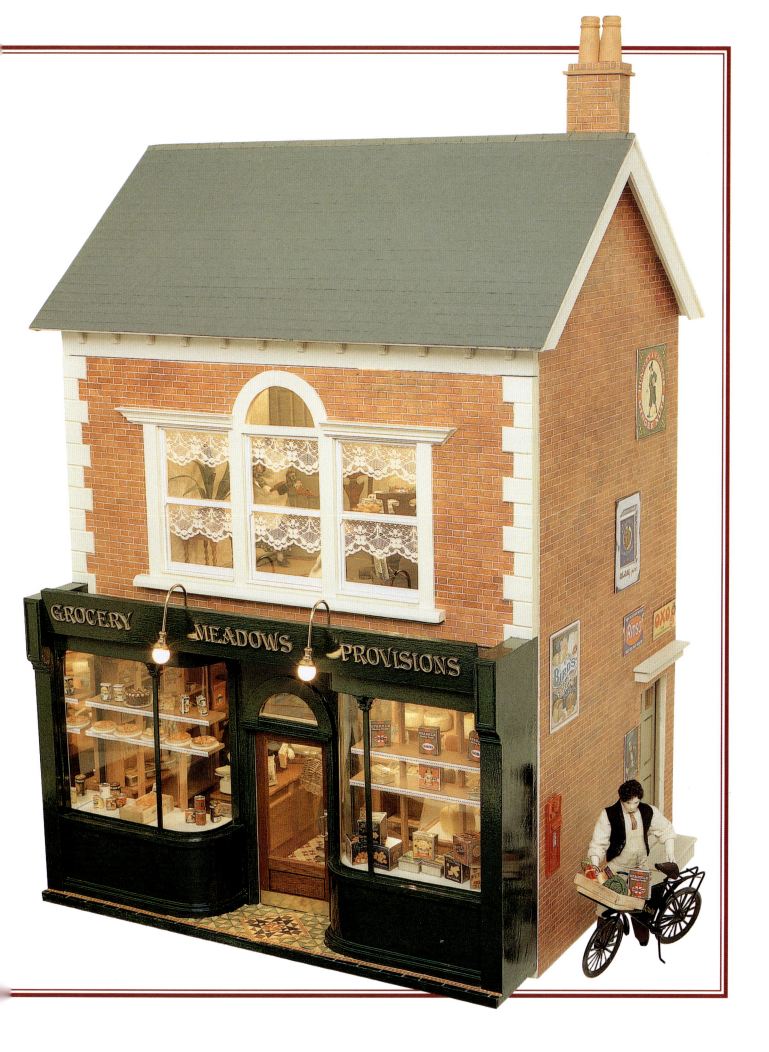

Local deliveries were made by small boys using a large, metal-framed bicycle with a basket or pannier mounted on the front. The bicycles were usually very heavy even before the goods were loaded and it wasn't unknown for everything to be tipped into the road, scattering goods, labels and bills everywhere

Customers of the grocer who were wealthy or respectable enough to enjoy account facilities would be likely to send a cook or a maid with a hand-written shopping list. The order would be made up and delivered, the account being rendered for settlement on a monthly basis. Less wealthy housewives, or their housemaids, would attend the grocers in person and buy sufficient provisions for the next twenty-four hours or so: few people had refrigerators and perishable foods lacked preservatives and soon deteriorated if kept too long. It was usually the job of the assistant to pack the shopping basket for the customer and although a simple task, new boys usually managed to put the un-refrigerated butter at the bottom, under something heavy!

Counters over which cold meats and dairy produce were served often had marble tops as they kept the area as cool as possible and looked clean. The blocks of cheese and hams themselves were usually kept behind a token amount of vertical mounted glass and sometimes within a three-sided glass cabinet, sometimes known as a 'sneeze counter', for obvious reasons. Dry goods would be served over a wooden counter with the packets and tins ranged on shelves behind the assistant. Colourful displays of packets might be added to one end of the counter, biscuits were left in tins along the front to tempt the customer. Broken biscuits,

and there were always some, were usually sold off cheaply. Larger shops would, by their very nature, have a greater number of goods on offer and spread these over more than one or two counters. Each of these counters, with its own assistants, would have its own queue of customers and some of these customers might have to queue three or four times within the same shop. If they forgot to buy cheese after queuing for butter at the cold counter it would be necessary to rejoin the queue and start over again. This was a particular feature of the early Sainsbury's stores.

The decoration of a good and prominent grocer's shop would be bright and clean, possibly with wall tiles around the perishable goods area, and dark wooden shelves and counters in all others. The floors in smaller shops would be wooden floorboards but in larger establishments encaustic tiles would be laid in elaborate patterns and sometimes the name or the initials of the owners would be laid in coloured mosaics. A daily sprinkling of fresh sawdust kept the dirt trodden in from the street in check and was easily swept out at the end of the day. Lighting would not be over-done and in some establishments gas was still in everyday use.

The building and stocking of a miniature shop needs fairly careful attention to date lines: there is little point in insisting that your shop is 1930s if it stocks items unknown at that time. However this hobby is essentially about the fun of creating your own shop and a slight slippage on dates will not matter too much as long as you are aware of it. Remember that the shopkeeper of this period was just as aware of good marketing as shopkeepers today and lots of goods on show and bright and colourful displays worked just as well then as they do now.

This shop is one most likely owned by a family of grocers, long established in the area. Its stock would be aimed at the upper class and those ladies that did frequent it would be certain of the personal attention of Mr Meadows.

MATERIALS

CARCASS

- 9mm MDF pieces as follows:
  Side 12^3/$_4$in x 25^7/$_8$in, 2 off
  Floor 12in x 17^5/$_8$in, 2 off
  Top ceiling 12in x 17^5/$_8$in
  Back 17^3/$_8$in x 19^5/$_8$in
  Pediment A 1^1/$_4$in x 17^3/$_8$in
  Pediment B 1^5/$_8$in x 18in
  Front under skirt 1^1/$_4$in x 17^3/$_8$in
  Filler strip ^{1}/$_2$in x 18in (total)

FRONTAGE

- 9mm MDF pieces as follows:
  Front 18in x 18^3/$_8$in
  Pavement 3in x 18in
  Horizontal fascia support 2^1/$_4$in x 16^1/$_2$in
- Fanlight bar 6mm MDF x 3in x ^{3}/$_8$in
- Fascia board 6mm MDF x 1^1/$_2$in x 16^1/$_2$in
- Pavement face cap ^{3}/$_{32}$in obeche x 9mm x pavement length

SIDE WALLS

- Walls ^{3}/$_4$in softwood x 2^1/$_4$in x 10^3/$_8$in, 2 off
- Column header 9mm MDF 2in x ^{3}/$_4$in, 2 off
- ^{3}/$_{32}$in obeche pieces as follows:
  Top cap ^{3}/$_4$in x 2^5/$_8$in, 2 off
  Front cap A ^{3}/$_4$in x 2^{3}/$_{32}$in, 2 off
  Front cap B ^{3}/$_4$in x 8^3/$_8$in, 2 off
- Moulding ^{1}/$_{16}$in square obeche x 11in (total)
- Cornice moulding ^{3}/$_8$in x ^{5}/$_8$in x ^{3}/$_4$in wide x 2 off
- Quoins in ^{3}/$_{32}$in obeche as follows:
  ^{3}/$_4$in x 1in, 12 off
  ^{3}/$_4$in x ^{3}/$_4$in, 10 off

ROOF

- 6mm MDF pieces as follows:
  A 19in x 9^1/$_4$in
  B 19 x 9^1/$_2$in
- Barge-boards ^{1}/$_8$in obeche as follows:
  1in x 10in, 4 off
  ^{1}/$_8$in x ^{1}/$_8$in, 4 off
- Chimney breast 18mm MDF x 4^1/$_2$in x 9^5/$_8$in

- Chimney stack 1^1/$_8$in softwood x 1^7/$_8$in x 3^1/$_2$in
- Stone cap ^{1}/$_8$in obeche x 2^1/$_8$in x 1^3/$_8$in
- Top 6mm MDF x 1^1/$_8$in x 1^7/$_8$in
- Terracotta chimney pots 1^1/$_2$in, 2 off
- Dentil corbels, 12 off

UPPER FLOOR INTERNAL WALLS

- 9mm MDF pieces as follows:
  Wall A 8^7/$_8$in x 9^5/$_8$in
  Wall B 8^3/$_4$in x 9^5/$_8$in
  Wall C 2^3/$_4$in x 9^5/$_8$in
  Arch A 3in x 2in
  Arch B 2^3/$_4$in x 2in
- Plaster corbels ^{3}/$_4$in, 2 off

SHOP INTERNAL WALLS

- 6mm MDF pieces as follows:
  Wall A 14in x 9^5/$_8$in
  Wall B 5^5/$_8$in x 2^3/$_4$in
- Architrave moulding ^{3}/$_8$in x 18in

STAIRS

- 18mm MDF x 2^3/$_4$in wide x 2in, 14 off

SHOP SIDE DOOR

- ^{1}/$_4$in obeche or pine pieces as follows:
  Vertical stiles ^{3}/$_8$in x 6^1/$_8$in, 2 off
  ^{3}/$_8$in x ^{3}/$_4$in
  ^{3}/$_8$in x 1^3/$_4$in
  ^{3}/$_8$in x 1^7/$_8$in
  Cross rails ^{1}/$_2$in x 2in, 2 off
  ^{3}/$_8$in x 2in, 2 off
- ^{1}/$_{16}$in obeche pieces as follows:
  Panels A & B ^{7}/$_8$in x 1^7/$_8$in, 2 off
  Panels C & D ^{7}/$_8$in x 2in, 2 off
  Over-panels E & F ^{5}/$_8$in x 1^5/$_8$in, 2 off
  Over-panels G & H ^{5}/$_8$in x 1^3/$_4$in, 2 off
- Glazed panels 0.7mm acetate ^{7}/$_8$in x ^{7}/$_8$in, 2 off
- Lintel 6mm MDF x ^{3}/$_8$in x 2^3/$_4$in
- Door surround ^{1}/$_8$in obeche x ^{1}/$_8$in x 18in
- Door step ^{5}/$_8$in softwood x 1^1/$_8$in x 3^1/$_4$in
- Tread ^{1}/$_8$in thick obeche x 1^1/$_4$in x 3^1/$_2$in
- Door hood 9mm MDF x 4in x ^{1}/$_2$in
- Top ^{1}/$_8$in obeche x ^{5}/$_8$in x 4^1/$_4$in
- Brass door knob ^{1}/$_4$in diameter, 2 off

Adding machines were almost unknown but a cash register might be found in a more up-market establishment. Instead the assistant would write each amount down on a paper bag, adding up the bill in his head and it was up to the customer to spot if the same item was entered twice or the addition was incorrect. The customer would then be expected to go to the cashier's booth and settle the amount immediately, in cash.

Shop Front Door

- Mahogany pieces as follows:
  Upright stile A $1/4$in thick x $3/8$in x $6^3/8$in, 2 off
  Centre horizontal rail D $1/4$in thick x $3/8$in x $2^1/4$in
  Top & bottom horizontal rails B & C $1/4$in thick x $1/2$in x $2^1/4$in, 2 off
  Centre panel $1/8$in thick x $2^3/8$in x $7/8$in
  Semicircular arch $1/8$in x 4in x 2in
- Brass strip $1/32$in x $1/2$in x 3in
- Glazing sheet 0.7mm thick acetate
- Doorway trim $3/8$in wide architrave moulding x 6in, 2 off
- Lintel $1/8$in thick obeche x $3^1/2$in x $3/8$in
- Brass door handles, 2 off

Main Shop Window

- 9mm MDF pieces as follows:
  Support blocks (3 per side) $11/16$in x $2^1/4$in
  Former A 2in x $6^1/8$in, 2 off
  Formers B & C $2^3/8$in x $6^1/8$in, 4 off
- Brass glazing bars $1/8$in thick x $1/4$in x 6in, 2 off
- Glazing support strips $3/32$in obeche x $1/4$in x $5^7/8$in, 4 off
- Decorative 'ears' $5/8$in wooden cornice, 10 off
- Inner retaining strips 0.6mm aero plywood $1/4$in x 36in (total)
- Facings 0.6mm aero plywood:
  Bottom $2^3/4$in x $7^3/4$in, 2 off
  Top $1^1/16$in x $7^3/4$in, 2 off
- Moulding bars as follows:
  Bottom A $3/32$in thick x $7/16$in x 8in
  Bottom B $3/32$in thick x $1/4$in x 8in
  Top C $1/8$in thick x $1/4$in x 8in
- Glazing 0.3mm thick acetate (measured in construction)
- Mirror 'glass' $1^5/8$in x 6in, 2 off

Upper Windows (3 off)

- Window framework from obeche pieces as follows:
  Window-sill $5/16$in thick x $1/2$in x 12in
  Vertical facing columns $3/32$in x $1/2$in wide x $5^1/8$in, 4 off

Under-arch bar $3/32$in x 3in x $1/4$in
Arch $3/32$in x $3^3/4$in x $1^3/4$in
Upper lintel understrip $3/32$in x $4^1/2$in x $1/2$in, 2 off
- Cornice over moulding $1/2$in x $4^3/4$in, 2 off
- Styrene sheet, bar and U-channel (sufficient for one window) as follows:
  A $1/16$in thick sheet x $3/16$in x $2^7/8$in
  B $1/16$in thick sheet x $2^{13}/16$ x $1/8$in wide
  C $3/32$in square bar x $2^{13}/16$in
  D $3/32$in square bar x $2^1/4$in
  E $3/32$in square bar x $2^1/4$in
  F $3/32$in square bar x $2^3/16$in, 2 off
  G $3/32$in square bar x $2^3/8$in
  H $3/32$in square bar x $2^3/8$in
  J $3/32$in thick sheet x $2^{11}/16$in x $1/4$in
  K $1/16$in thick sheet x 3in x $1/2$in
  L $3/32$in U-channel x $5/16$in x $4^{15}/16$in, 2 off
  M $3/32$in square bar x $1/4$in, 2 off
- Glazing 0.7mm thick acetate, cut to fit
- Plastic weld adhesive

Lighting

- Hall ceiling light with shade
- 12 volt grain of wheat bulb and shade
- Fine twin-flex wire
- Copper tape
- Ceiling rose $1^1/2$in diameter
- Overhanging globe lamps, 2 off

Miscellaneous

- Standard 4-panel door kit complete with architrave (see Suppliers)
- Skirting board (Victorian pattern) $5/8$in high x 72in (total)
- Picture rail $3/16$in x 72in (total)
- Shop floor tiled flooring paper, 2 sheets
- English bond brick finish facing x 10 sheets
- Slate roof fibre-glass sheet, 2 sheets
- Free standing fireplace
- Brass 2in butt hinges, 2 off
- Wallpaper as required

Where 'glue' is referred to, it means a PVA adhesive unless otherwise stated. You will also need No.6 counter-sunk wood screws 1in and 1¼in long, panel pins ½in and 1in long, No.3 ¾in brass screws, some mapping pins and dress-making pins.

Measurements in the book are imperial, however, as MDF is only sold in the UK in metric sizes, these thicknesses are given with approximate imperial equivalents, e.g. 6mm (¼in), 9mm (³⁄₈in) where appropriate.

A selection of commercial paints were used for this project and wherever possible we have given the company's names and colours so an exact match can be made. You could, of course, choose your own colours from other paint brands. The inner walls and stairs are best cut and assembled after the main carcass is completed, although they are shown here immediately after cutting out the main parts. Working *after* the carcass is built allows you to adjust the heights of parts to match those of your assembly should it vary even slightly from the plans.

CUTTING OUT THE CARCASS

Cut out two sides from 9mm MDF, 12³⁄₄in wide x 25⁷⁄₈in high. This height includes the sides of the roof, which slope at a 50 degree angle – see Fig 1 for dimensions (Fig 5 on page 154 also shows the overall shape of the side). Check that the sides are at right angles with a try square and place the two sides together to make sure that they match perfectly. Mark the front edge on both pieces to avoid confusion later.

Mark up and cut out the four 9mm (³⁄₈in) wide rebates to a depth of ³⁄₁₆in, using a powered router or pad saw – two for the floors, one for the ceiling and one for the back. Check that the width of the cut is correct by inserting an offcut of 9mm MDF. Ideally the fit should be snug but not so tight that it needs to be forced home. When

all the rebates have been cut these two parts should be mirror images of each other.

Mark up the right-hand side only with the aperture for the side door and cut this out too. Be careful not to cut it too low or it will foul the rebate for the bottom floor. Clean up the edges and the corners of the aperture with a sharp chisel or abrasive paper wrapped around a suitable block.

The next step is to cut out from 9mm MDF the two floors and the top ceiling, all of

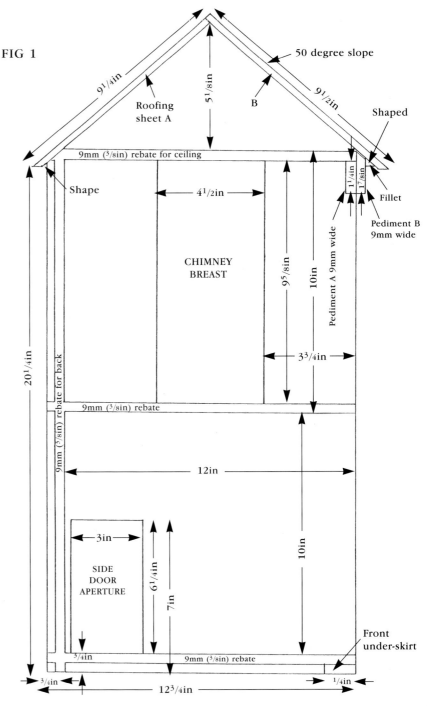

FIG 1

INSIDE VIEW OF SIDE OF SHOP

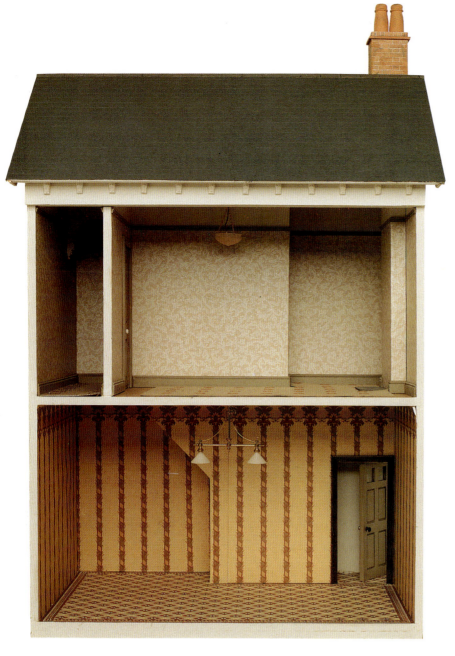

which have identical measurements of 12in x 17⅝in. Again, it is important that all these parts are identical and that all the edges are at right angles to each other. Place the ceiling and one floor to one side. The one remaining floor piece will be placed in the centre, so following Fig 2, cut out the stairwell from the back edge with a tenon saw. With a sharp craft knife cut the ¹/₁₆in x ¹/₁₆in groove for wiring, shown by dotted lines on the figure. It is a good idea here to score two lines ¹/₁₆in apart in the surface with a sharp knife or scalpel and then chisel the waste out using a sharpened watchmaker's screwdriver. Drill a ¹/₈in diameter hole for the main shop light, as marked.

Drill a ¹/₈in diameter hole in the ceiling for the upper floor light 4¹/₂in from the front and 7¹/₂in from the right-hand wall. The roof will hide the wiring for the upper floor and there is no need to cut grooves.

Now, take both of the sides and mark a centre line along the reverse faces of all the rebates and drill two equally spaced ¹/₈in diameter holes through each line to take No.6 screws. Counter-sink each of these holes so that the heads of the screws when inserted will sit below the surface.

Place the centre floor into a bench vice with one edge uppermost, dry fit the correct

Finished by the decorators, the shop is now ready for Mr and Mrs Meadows to move in

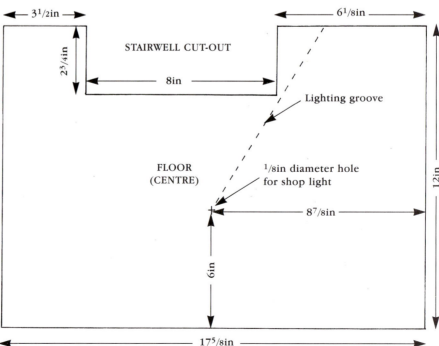

FIG 2

side rebate onto this and use a sharp awl to make starter holes into the floor edge for both of the screws (the stairwell cut-out should be at the back). Increase the depth of these with a 1/8in diameter drill bit to about two-thirds of the screws' final depth and then remove the piece. Now place the bottom floor into the vice and treat this in the same way as the centre floor. Repeat for the ceiling and then for all the floors, this time for the second side.

Cut the back from 9mm MDF, 17³/8in x 19⁵/8in, being very sure that the sides are square to each other as this will determine whether or not the carcass stands correctly. Check with a try square and use a block plane to correct any errors.

From 9mm MDF cut inner pediment A 1¹/4in x 17³/8in, outer pediment B 1⁵/8in x 18in and the front under-skirt 1¹/4in x 17³/8in (see Fig 1).

Dry fit all the parts without adhesive to ensure that they all fit each other in the correct manner. Mark the position of all the floors on the outside of the back with a straight line and use this as a guide for the accurate placing of panel pins on assembly.

CUTTING OUT THE FRONTAGE

Cut the blank for the front 18in wide x 18³/8in high from 9mm MDF and square up all the edges. Lay this on a flat, clean work surface and mark up the apertures for the three top rectangular windows and the separate arched fanlight over the centre (see Fig 3).

Next, mark up the two main window apertures and the one for the central front doorway with the arched fanlight. This aperture can be cut in one pass with the doorway and the fanlight bar inserted after. Use a

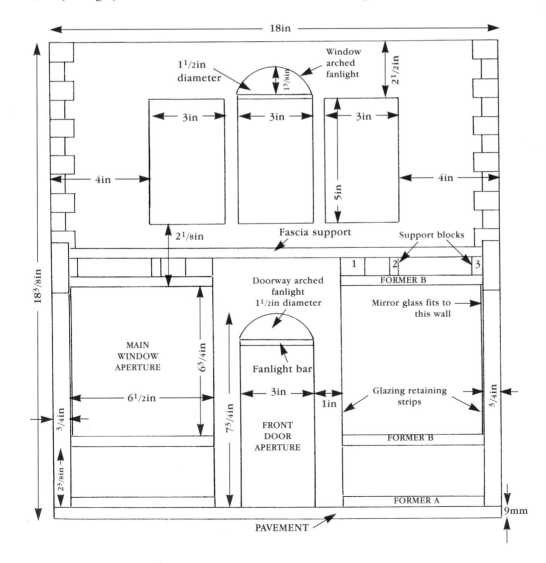

FIG 3   153

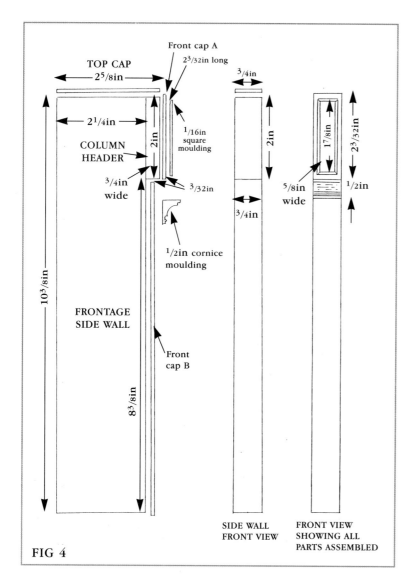

FIG 4

TOP CAP 2⁵/₈in

Front cap A
2³/₃₂in long

³/₄in

COLUMN HEADER 2¹/₄in

2in

¹/₁₆in square moulding

³/₄in wide

³/₃₂in

¹/₂in cornice moulding

FRONTAGE SIDE WALL

10³/₈in

8³/₈in

Front cap B

2in

³/₄in

1⁷/₈in

2³/₃₂in

⁵/₈in wide

¹/₂in

SIDE WALL FRONT VIEW

FRONT VIEW SHOWING ALL PARTS ASSEMBLED

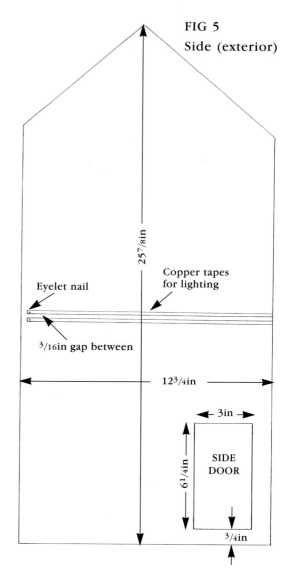

FIG 5 Side (exterior)

25⁷/₈in

Eyelet nail

Copper tapes for lighting

³/₁₆in gap between

12³/₄in

3in

SIDE DOOR

6¹/₄in

³/₄in

---

powered router or drill and pad saw to cut out all the marked apertures and clean up all the faces and corners. Use a sharp chisel or a piece of fine abrasive paper wrapped around a cork block to ensure that everything is kept as square as possible and that routed corners are squared off.

Cut the fanlight bar for the shop doorway from an offcut of 6mm MDF 3in x ³/₈in.

Cut the pavement from 9mm MDF, 3in x 18in, the width matching the frontage. The front of the building is built up from a number of component parts, some of these can safely be cut before the assembly but others are better cut to fit, particularly if your model is likely to vary even slightly from the drawings here.

Cut the two frontage side walls from ³/₄in thick softwood 2¹/₄in wide x 10³/₈in long and check that they both match each other

perfectly, then lay each to one side. Cut two column headers from 9mm MDF, each ³/₄in wide x 2in long (see Fig 4).

The fascia board and the fascia support can be cut at this stage but we suggest that they are cut ¹/₄in oversize in length and trimmed later to fit the final assembly – see the Materials list on page 149 for the dimensions. The wiring for the two lamps over the fascia board is run along the back of this board and out to the side of the carcass with the hinges. Connection for these lamps is then made with a 'loop' of wire to a copper tape run from the back (see Fig 5). If you wish to use another method, especially one that will require cutting grooves, do so now to avoid unnecessary work later.

Fix the fascia support board into a bench vice and plane the front edge to 60 degrees so as to allow the fascia board to tilt for-

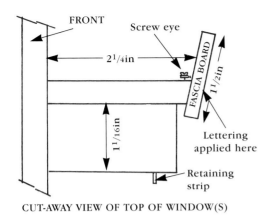

FRONT

Screw eye

FASCIA BOARD

2¹/₄in

1¹/₂in

1¹/₁₆in

Lettering
applied here

Retaining
strip

CUT-AWAY VIEW OF TOP OF WINDOW(S)

FIG 6

wards on assembly (see Fig 6). Fit three ¹/₈in diameter brass screw eyes into the back of the board ⁷/₈in from the top – one dead centre and the other two 1in in from each end. Place the board in position so that it rests on the screw eyes and mark through these with a sharp awl. Drill a ¹/₃₂in diameter starter hole at each of these points to take a ³/₈in long No.3 brass screw and use these to fix the board into place when everything has been painted and the signage letters applied.

Cutting Out the Window Formers

Now that you have cut the apertures for the windows, the next stage is to cut and groove the six window formers. Note that there are two lettered 'A' and these are placed one either side, at the bottom. They do not sit inside the aperture but flat against the front. Mark up and cut out the six blanks using a fretsaw and V-block to shape the curves shown in Fig 7.

Cut out the notches on the four B formers so that they fit snugly into the apertures. Mark out the ¹/₃₂in wide grooves using a sharp pencil, making two mirror image pairs. To make every curve identical first make up a template from stiff card and trace around this. Cut out the grooves to a depth of ³/₃₂in and this is best achieved using a drill mounted on a drill stand or fixed head router fitted with a suitably sized cutter. It may be advantageous to make up a temporary jig with a fixed stop to do this but it can

also be achieved with a sharp knife and small chisel.

Cut out the small window bar slots to take the brass bars in the same formers by drilling two ¹/₁₆in diameter holes at each point and chiselling out the waste. Note that the slot in the bottom formers is only ³/₁₆in deep whilst that for the top formers passes completely through.

ASSEMBLING THE CARCASS

Secure the centre floor in a suitable bench vice with one edge uppermost, checking that it will assemble with the stairwell cut-out to the back. Coat this upper edge with PVA glue and lay one of the sides onto this. Fit the floor into the centre rebate, again checking that everything that should points towards the back. Tap down gently to make a secure fitting and finish off with two No.6 screws, then remove both parts from the vice. Fix the bottom floor into the vice and assemble the same side onto it as you did for the centre. Repeat the procedure for the top ceiling.

Lay the assembly completed so far onto its side with the floors uppermost and run a bead of PVA glue along the back edge of all three floors and place to one side. Before the adhesive starts to set, take the back of the carcass, coat one long edge with glue and tap this down into its rebate. Screw in from the side through the rebate, to make a good fit. Check that each of the floors are at right angles to the side and use panel pins to fix the back to each of these in turn.

FIG 7

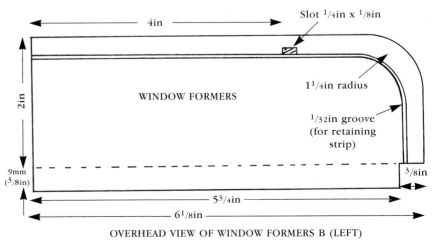

4in

Slot ¹/₄in x ¹/₈in

2in

1¹/₄in radius

¹/₃₂in groove
(for retaining
strip)

WINDOW FORMERS

9mm
(³/₈in)

³/₈in

5³/₄in

6¹/₈in

OVERHEAD VIEW OF WINDOW FORMERS B (LEFT)

155

Now lay this large assembly, comprising of one side, two floors, back and a top ceiling onto a flat, clean work surface with the edges of the floors uppermost. Take the second side and coat each and all the inner edges of the rebates with glue and fit onto the assembly. Tap down using a mallet shielded with a piece of waste wood until all the parts are fitted together and then fix with screws as before. Double check that all parts are square and leave the adhesive to set hard, probably overnight. Large sash cramps are very useful for this type of assembly as the correct pressure can be applied to joints.

Fix the front skirt and under-pediment in place with adhesive and panel pins.

In order to make the wiring for the top lamp easy to connect after the roof has been assembled, cut a small notch into the upper side of the ceiling dead centre on the back

FIG 8

edge to allow the wiring to pass through. Pass a spare piece of 'pull-through' wire up through the centre hole in the ceiling, over the top and down the back and tie a knot in the end left inside the room so that it will not pass through the hole until you want it to. When fitting the lamp in place join the ends of its wiring to the pull-through. Alternatively, make the pull-through a double flex and use this to join the lamp to the wiring circuit on the back, tucking any spare up through the hole and into the ceiling void.

The second lamp used upstairs is located behind the hallway arch and is a ceiling fitting. Again, drill a $^1/_{16}$in diameter hole in the ceiling dead centre of the hallway and 1in into the hall from the back wall. Cut a notch in the back to allow the wiring to pass through to the outside using the same 'pull-through' method.

ROOF

From 6mm MDF cut the two roofing sheets, A 9$^1/_4$in x 19in, and B 9$^1/_2$in x 19in. Shape the outer edges with a small wood plane, as shown in Fig 1. Fit sheet A into place using PVA glue and $^1/_2$in panel pins – it should lie flush with the top edge of the shaped sides.

Cut and shape roofing sheet B and dry fit so that it lies flush at the top with the one at the back and plane off any overhang where the two sheets fit together. Lay a bead of glue along the edges of the two sides and the back roof and glue and pin into place. Use masking tape laterally and horizontally to make a firm joint between the back and the front along the top edges. You can use panel pins for this but 6mm is quite thin for fixing in this way and the material may split and spoil the joint. The roofing material will cover any gap at the top where the two sheets join but it should be filled before this.

Add the outer pediment B at this stage shaping the top edge with a sharp plane to give a neat fit against the underside of the roof. Cut a 9mm MDF offcut $^1/_2$in wide x 18in long (marked fillet on Fig 1) and use a

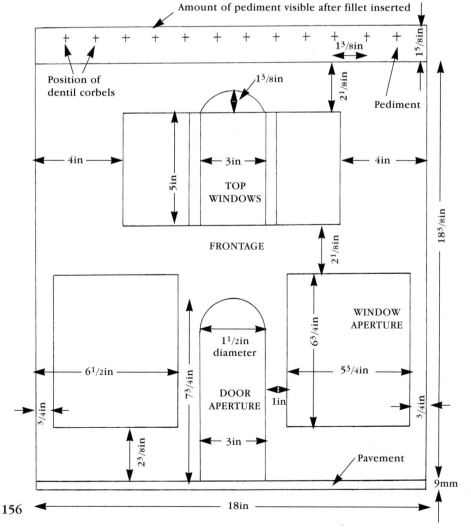

Amount of pediment visible after fillet inserted

Position of dentil corbels

$1^3/_8$in

$1^5/_8$in

$1^3/_8$in

$2^1/_8$in

Pediment

4in

3in

4in

5in

TOP WINDOWS

FRONTAGE

$2^1/_8$in

$18^3/_8$in

$6^3/_4$in

WINDOW APERTURE

$1^1/_2$in diameter

$6^1/_2$in

$7^3/_4$in

DOOR APERTURE

1in

$5^3/_4$in

$^3/_4$in

$^3/_4$in

$2^3/_8$in

3in

Pavement

9mm

18in

sharp plane to shape it so that it fills the void between the pediment and the underside of the roof.

Cut sufficient 1/8in thick x 1in wide obeche strip to make the barge-boards and trim the angles so that they meet vertically in the centre when placed under the roof edge. Trim the outer edges to a complementary angle. Prepare sufficient 1/8in x 1/8in obeche strip to glue down the outer edge of each of the barge-boards. Cut the angles to match and glue these strips onto the boards to increase the width of the top edge, using a clear, spirit-based adhesive. Glue the completed boards under the edges of the roof at either end.

With reference to Fig 8, mark the positions of the twelve dentil corbels at 1 3/8in intervals under the pediment and then glue a dentil corbel to the centre of each mark.

UPPER FLOOR INTERNAL WALLS

Check that the height from your floor to ceiling is the same as the drawings and amend if necessary. Note that no flooring other than carpet was laid on this floor and as this was fitted after the work was completed no height allowance for it was necessary. If you intend to lay fitted floorboards before fixing the walls you will have to make the adjustments now.

Cut out walls A, B and C according to the dimensions in the Materials list on page 149 and with reference to Fig 9 for the cut-outs on wall A. Test fit the parts following Fig 10 before proceeding.

Using Fig 11, on page 158 which is actual size, trace the shape of the archways A and B and cut them out from 9mm MDF using a piercing saw and bench V-block, cleaning up the edges.

Mark out and then cut out the aperture for the door kit in wall A and test fit. The door and its architrave can be painted and finished away from the carcass and assembled after decorating.

Fix wall B into a bench vice with one long

side uppermost and glue wall C onto it in a dog-leg assembly, checking that they are at right angles (see Fig 10). Secure the parts together with masking tape until set. For a more secure fixing, pre-drill 1/32in diameter holes to take 1/2in panel pins and use these to make stronger joints.

Glue arch A onto the back of wall B to provide an even space between the wall and

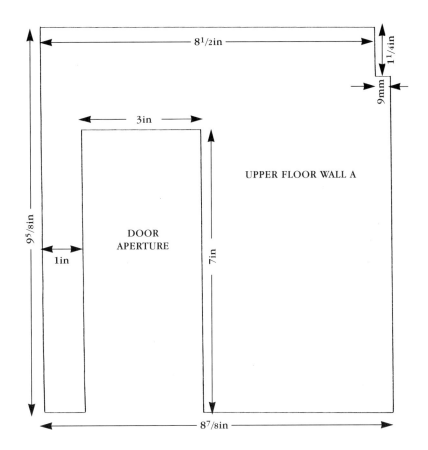

FIG 9

FIG 10

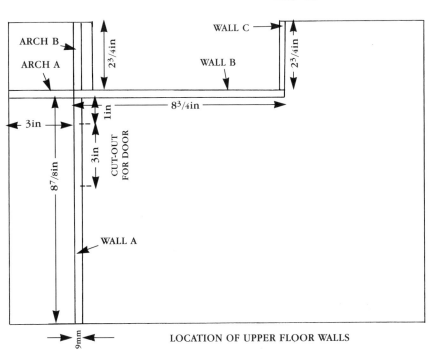

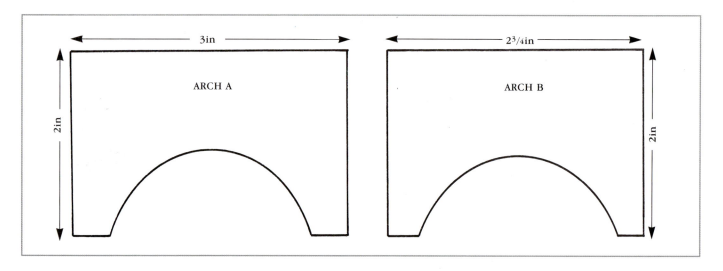

ARCH A

3in

2in

ARCH B

2³/₄in

2in

FIG 11 (actual size)

The comfortable living quarters of the family reflects their affluence

the back (see Fig 10). Place the assembled walls into position and check that they can be easily removed later for decoration.

CHIMNEY BREAST

Chimney breasts in real houses of this type are usually between 15–18in deep, however this would tend to dominate a room built in ¹/₁₂ scale and we have therefore reduced this to ³/₄in (18mm) for purely visual reasons.

Cut a piece of 18mm MDF 4¹/₂in wide x 9⁵/₈in, checking the height of your room

before you do this and adjusting if necessary. Clean up all the cut edges. Position this piece 3³/₄in from the edge, as shown in Fig 1 and mark this on the right-hand wall. Drill two ¹/₈in holes through this wall to the outside and counter-sink them on the outside to take No.6 wood screws. Fix into place with adhesive and screws or leave separate until after you do the decorating later.

All the internal picture rails and skirting boards (see Materials list page 150) for the upstairs room can now be cut to fit, remem-

bering to cut around the chimney breast. The skirting is best continued around the front of the breast once the size of the fireplace is known.

Lay all the picture rail and skirting pieces out and mark on the back of each the order in which they should be glued into place. Keep them safe until it is time for painting.

STAIRS

Cutting Out the Stairs

If you have the use of a mechanical bench or table saw it would make this job much easier.

The stairs for this project are made from a single strip of MDF 18mm thick. There is no need to buy a large sheet as most timber merchants have boxes of MDF offcuts that they will sell you cheaply. Find a piece that measures no less than 36in long x 2½in wide or, if you are using a mechanical circular saw, at least 3in wide. You will need to produce fourteen treads all with identical measurements and the easiest way to do this is to cut it as one long strip at least 36in long to give at least two spares.

You will see on Fig 12 that the back edge of each tread is angled at 45 degrees, and again it will be easier to cut this angle on one long strip in one pass rather than separately for each tread. The first step is to cut the angled back edge of the treads at 45 degrees along the entire length of the 18mm thick strip. The second step is to reduce the strip to 2in wide, leaving one edge at 90 degrees and the other at 45 degrees.

Whilst the treads are still in the strip form, set the saw to give a ⅛in wide cut from the front edge to leave a ⅛in nosing at the top. Run this through the saw and reset it to make right-angled cuts across the strip at 2¼in intervals, so producing separate treads.

Assembling the Stairs

Stack the treads one on top of the other as a dry fit to check the height against the carcass. No adjustment should be necessary but if you need to reduce one tread do so

now. Any small addition of height can be achieved using a 2¼in wide packing strip of obeche of the necessary thickness. Although the staircase is not a visible feature from the front of this building you should still make any adjustments as neatly as possible. Trim the back edge of the top tread at 90 degrees to enable it to fit flush to the upper floor where it abuts (see Fig 12). If you intend to use a spirit-based wood stain on these stairs rather than paint, it is a good idea to do this before gluing them together as any spots of glue will prevent stain finishes from taking properly.

Mark each tread ¾in from the front edge of the nosing and draw a straight line across using a small try square. Finally, glue the treads together to the dimensions in Fig 12 to produce a staircase with fourteen treads. You will find it easier to do this by starting with just two treads, clamping them together until the adhesive has set and adding more treads. Several blocks of treads can be built up separately and added together to make the complete staircase. Lay the staircase in position and check that there is sufficient clearance for the side door to open – you will need at least 3in. Make any adjustment necessary by trimming more material off the back edge of the top tread.

FIG 12

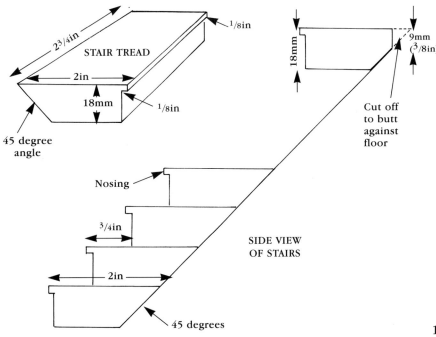

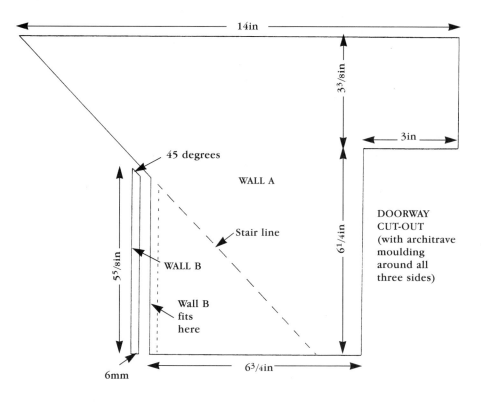

FIG 13

Now lay the completed staircase into its final position and mark the back wall at the fourth tread up and fourth tread down. Remove the staircase and drill a 1/8in diameter hole through the back in both places, dead centre of the edge of the tread position. From the back of the carcass countersink each of the holes for a No.6 wood screw. Fix the stairs into place with the screws and make any adjustments required at this stage. Leave them in position until the walls for the shop area are cut and shaped, then remove and set them to one side for painting later.

SHOP INTERNAL WALLS

Cut the larger wall A from 6mm MDF, 14in x 9⅝in after first checking that the height on your shop area measures the same as Fig 13.

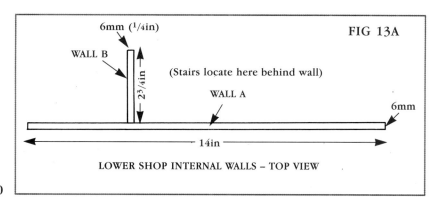

FIG 13A

LOWER SHOP INTERNAL WALLS – TOP VIEW

We suggest that you cut this as a rectangular blank first and lay it against the stairs at the back. Reach around the left-hand side of the wall and, using a sharp pencil, mark the line of the stairs. Alternatively, you can mark the point at which the stairs start at the top and draw a line at 45 degrees to the point the angle changes to 90 degrees. Mark both lines on the front surface of the wall and cut out this shape. Lay the wall against the stairs and check that it fits and that no stair treads can be seen.

Mark and cut out the doorway to the right. There is no door for this aperture but it is still trimmed with a moulded architrave on the shop side of the wall.

Cut wall B from 6mm thick MDF, 2¾in x 5⅝in. Secure in a vice and use a sharp wood plane to shape the top edge to 45 degrees. This wall fits behind the left-hand edge of the main wall A and the 45 degree cut butts flush against the stairs (see Fig 13A). Glue this into position after fixing the stairs and wall A into place.

SHOP SIDE DOOR

Side entrances and enclosed stairways are by their very nature dark and this building is no different. As there is no fanlight, the side door has the two top panels glazed.

Cut all the main parts for this from 1/4in thick obeche or pine following the Materials list on page 149 and Fig 14. The two outer stiles and the top and bottom cross rails have a 1/16in groove cut centrally along their length on one side only (see end view detail in Fig 14). The two centre stiles and rails have the grooves cut in both of the longest sides for the panels. Following the dimensions in Fig 14, cut the panels A and B, and C and D from 1/16in thick obeche as accurately as possible to avoid distortion on assembly. Cut the two top glazed panels from 0.7mm thick acetate, each 7/8in square. You will find it easier to assemble the door if you use a bench jig with at least one set right angle and a facility for clamping parts together.

Assemble the door as shown in Fig 14, and glue together using a PVA glue for all the wooden parts. Cover both of the acetate-filled panels with masking tape to protect them when they are painted later.

To give the door panels a raised or 'fielded' appearance, a second set of over-panels, E, F, G and H, is cut from 1/16in obeche (see Fig 14 for dimensions). These are glued on top of the first set of panels, with an evenly spaced gap all round each.

Drill a 1/32in hole in the right-hand stile, top and bottom, for the dressmaking pins used to hinge this door. Insert and glue the bottom pin in place at this stage. Drill a 1/16in diameter hole in the left-hand stile for the door knobs.

Cut a lintel from 6mm MDF 3/8in wide x 2 3/4in long and lay this on to the top edge of the door, flush to the front. Drill a 1/32in hole for a pin matching the position of the pin in the top of the stile and assemble the door onto this by inserting a pin through the lintel. Place the door inside the hall, with the lintel placed against the wall. Note where the bottom pin meets and drill a corresponding hole into the floor. When the door has been decorated, simply place the door into the hall and drop the bottom pin into the hole. Apply a little clear, spirit-based adhesive to the lintel and glue it over the doorway, on the inside, to hold the door in. Check that the door will open.

Finish off by gluing 1/8in x 1/8in obeche strip around the door aperture, and a 3/8in wide doorstop to prevent it from opening outwards. It will be necessary to cut a neat notch in the right-hand back edge to allow the door to swivel on its pin hinge. The door knobs are fitted later after decoration.

Side Door Step

From 5/8in thick softwood cut a door step 1 1/8in wide x 3 1/4in long (see Fig 15 overleaf). This should just be high enough to reach the back door aperture when the tread has been added. Cut a tread from 1/8in thick obeche, 1 1/4in wide x 3 1/2in long – it

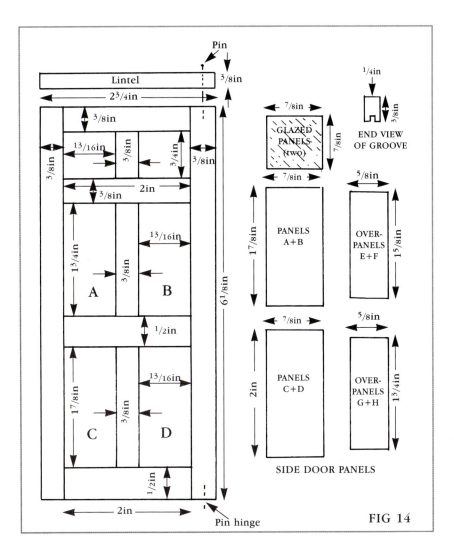

FIG 14

should produce a 1/8in overlap on three sides. Glue the tread to the top of the step, flush at the back. As this part protrudes from the body of the shop it can be left loose or glued into place after decorating.

Side Door Hood

From an offcut of 9mm MDF cut this part 1/2in wide x 4in long and then add a top of

Tins of biscuits, not packets, displayed to tempt the shopper

161

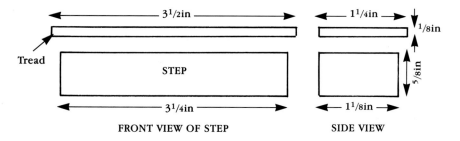

FRONT VIEW OF STEP

SIDE VIEW

Tread

STEP

3¹/₂in

3¹/₄in

1¹/₄in

1¹/₈in

1/8in

5/8in

FIG 15

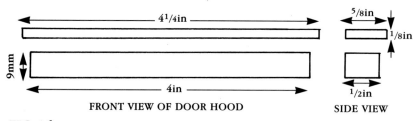

FRONT VIEW OF DOOR HOOD

SIDE VIEW

4¹/₄in

4in

9mm

5/8in

1/8in

1/2in

FIG 16

sink a ¹/₈in diameter hole through from the longest side to fix the stack to the roof.

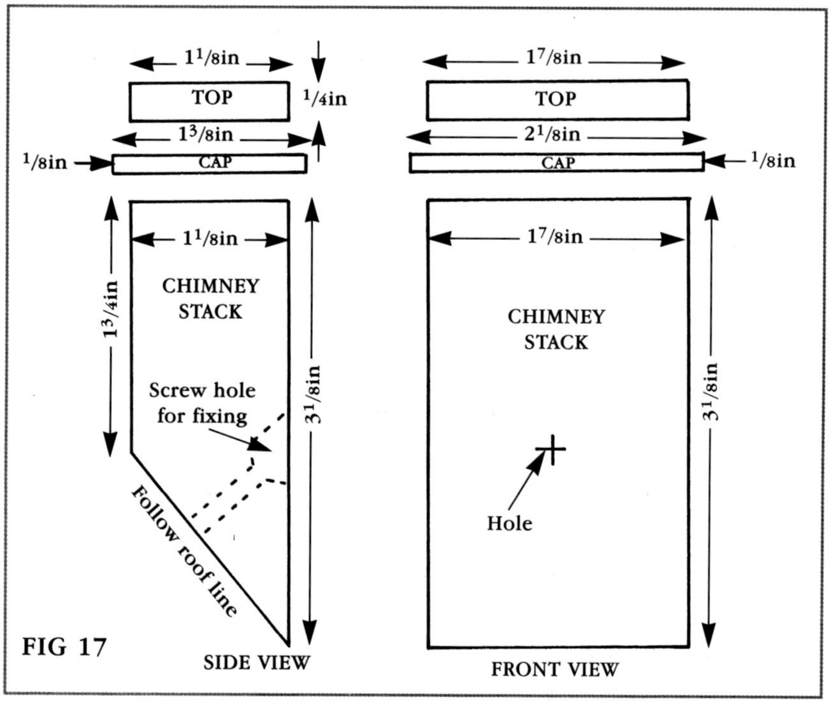

Cut the stone cap from ¹/₈in thick obeche, 2¹/₈in x 1³/₈in, and glue this dead centre on top of the body of the stack. Now, cut and shape the top from a 6mm MDF offcut, 1¹/₈in x 1⁷/₈in, and glue this in place. We suggest that both of the chimney pots are added after fixing the stack in place and decorating has taken place. Fix the stack to the back roof ¹/₂in from the apex and 1in from the outer edge.

FRONTAGE ASSEMBLY

It is most important that in building this assembly you keep all the parts as square to each other as possible as this will avoid distortions showing up later.

Pavement

Take the pavement piece you cut out earlier when cutting out the parts for the frontage and ensure that the length is exactly the same as the width of the front. Draw a line ³/₁₆in in from one long edge and measure 3in in from each end. Drill and counter-sink ¹/₈in diameter holes to take No.6 wood screws at these points.

Fix the front in a bench vice with the bottom uppermost and place the pavement on to it, marking the position of the screw holes with a sharp awl. Remove the pavement and make starter holes for the No.6 screws about ³/₁₆in deep. Whilst the front is still in the vice, glue and screw the pavement to the bottom edge, checking that it sits at right angles and then put to one side to allow the adhesive to set. Cut a pavement cap from ³/₃₂in thick obeche x 9mm x the length of the pavement, and glue it onto the front edge of the pavement to hide the MDF.

Side (Column) Walls

Each of these walls (cut earlier) sit on the pavement with their backs flush to the frontage, one each side. Dry fit each in turn and mark the positions with a sharp pencil. Drill through from the underside of the

obeche ¹/₈in longer and wider (see Fig 16). Glue them together and mark the position the hood will take ¹/₂in above the doorway. This will be glued into place after decorating and the brick sheet must be cut to fit around the marks.

CHIMNEY STACK

Cut the main body of the stack from a 1¹/₈in thick softwood offcut, 1⁷/₈in x 3¹/₂in long. Now trim this down at the correct angle shown in Fig 17 to 3¹/₈in long. Place in a secure soft-jawed vice and drill and counter-

SIDE VIEW

FRONT VIEW

TOP

CAP

CHIMNEY STACK

Screw hole for fixing

Follow roof line

TOP

CAP

CHIMNEY STACK

Hole

1¹/₈in

1³/₈in

1/8in

1³/₄in

3¹/₈in

1⁷/₈in

2¹/₈in

1/8in

1⁷/₈in

3¹/₈in

1/4in

FIG 17

pavement and the frontage with a 1/8in diameter drill bit and counter-sink each to take No.6 wood screws. Glue, screw and clamp the walls into place.

Pin and glue the headers into place at the top of each of the side walls, which should now appear from the front as columns (see Fig 4, page 154).

Prepare a strip of 3/32in thick obeche at least 30in long and from this cut two each of the following lengths: 2³/32in (front cap A), 8³/8in (front cap B), and 2⁵/8in (top cap). Glue these into place to cover the front of the columns and headers. Cut two lengths of 1/2in x 1/2in cornice x 3/4in and glue these under the column headers. Cut a 12in length of 1/16in x 1/16in obeche strip and cut with 45 degree mitres to form the moulding at the top of each column as shown in Fig 4.

MAIN SHOP WINDOWS

You will need to refer back to Figs 3, 6 and 7 when making up these windows. The six window formers prepared earlier are divided into two sets comprising one A and two B's (see Fig 7, page 155). Check that all the parts are identical, especially in each set. Glue and pin formers A onto the pavement, one under each window aperture, butting up against the side wall and the frontage (see Fig 18). Now glue and pin one former B onto the bottom edge of the window aperture with the groove uppermost, so that the small cut-out locks it into place – again the outer end should butt against the side wall. Check that this sits square and at 90 degrees to the front. Repeat this procedure for the second B former placed at the top of the aperture so that it sits directly over the first this time with the groove pointing down. All three formers must line up vertically. Allow all of this to set into place and when it is dry smooth off any slight overlap on the inside of the frontage. Repeat for the second side. Glue and clamp the support blocks, three each side, into place above the top former as shown in Fig 3, page 153.

The fascia support board can now be cut to

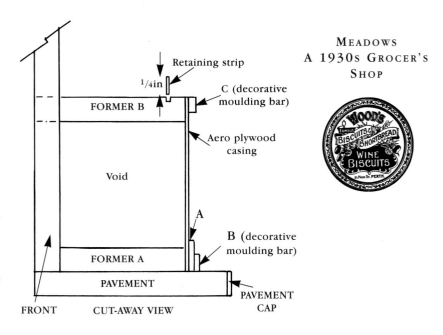

FIG 18

fit exactly between the two side walls and glued into place onto the support blocks. Make sure that the bevelled edge points to the front and down, not up (see Fig 6, page 155).

Building up the Main Windows

At this stage you can attach the thin aero plywood facings onto the formers, working on one side at a time. This material is very pliable and very strong but it will offer some resistance to bending and some restraint is necessary whilst the adhesive sets: we found small mapping pins with round glass heads to be very useful for this purpose. Check the measurements between the bottom and top former and cut a length of plywood to this width, trimming to the length given in the Materials list on page 150. If you are not sure just how long this should be, make up a template using a length of good quality paper or card. It is better to cut it too long and trim it than to cut it too short. Keep a note of this measurement as it can be used when preparing the top and bottom moulding bars.

Use a PVA wood glue and pins to fix each strip onto both of the formers (see Fig 18) and leave until set, preferably overnight. Repeat this procedure for the top facings, measuring between the bottom face of the former and the fascia support board, pinning

Window display was something of an art and as many products as possible were crammed in. Several reference books were available to grocers to perfect the art, using simple materials such as card and crêpe paper.

and gluing these to the top former and the support blocks. Fill any pin holes with a suitable plaster filler at this stage and, when this is dry, smooth down the surface with a very fine abrasive paper.

The moulding bars on the lower facings, three per side, are bent around the curve, however the thickness of the strip and the sharpness of the curve will not allow you to do this without some work. Cut the bars to length, again too long rather than too short. The trick to this is to make a series of fine saw cuts across the bar (see Fig 19). Do this throughout the length of the curve plus $1/4$in to about 50 percent of the bar's thickness. The spacing of these cuts need to be quite close but not so close that you remove all material between them. Ideally the result will look just like a dentil or toothed moulding. If you have a small circular saw with a fine blade you can do this quite easily. If you only have hand tools it can still be achieved with a little patience. Glue the moulding bars in place and use the mapping pins to hold them whilst the adhesive sets. Smooth off the resulting mouldings with fine abrasive paper and fill the edges of the cuts with fine filler.

Cut four strips of the aero plywood $1/4$in wide to retain the glazing and glue these into the slots made in the top and bottom formers (see Fig 18). You can check the length of the slots with a strip of paper. It will be seen that the two brass glazing bars are too long to fit between the top and bottom formers. This is quite deliberate as they are fitted by passing the bar up through the top former into the void and then dropping it down into the blind slot cut into the B former at the bottom (see Fig 7).

In order to hold the glazing sheet, which will be under pressure from the curve, you need to glue in two vertical obeche strips

per side, each $3/32$in thick x $1/4$in wide x $57/8$in. Glue one each side on the outside edge of the window against the side wall (or column) so that the glazing is prevented from coming through to the front. The second pair of retaining bars is also fixed on the outside, this time at the curved end of the window and positioned $1/8$in in from the outer edge of the aperture. We recommend that you cut and test fit the glazing sheets at this point but then remove them until after the painting is completed.

You will find it easier to cut the acetate sheet for each window separately rather than both together. Carefully measure the height at both ends – this should be identical but you will have to take into account any variance. It is virtually impossible to measure around the curve for the length so we suggest you cut a strip of card about 1in wide and trim this until it fits. Transfer both measurements to the card and cut this shape out to produce a template. Offer the template to the window from the inside and check for fit. When you are happy with the result, transfer the shape to 0.3mm thick acetate sheet. Place the curved end in first against the bottom and top strips and the other end should then snap into place against the retaining strip placed on the outside. The pressure derived from the curve will hold it in place.

A third vertical obeche strip $1/16$in thick x $1/4$in wide is fitted against the opposite inner edge of the window aperture to frame the mirror each side.

The decorative 'ears' are cut as $5/8$in wide slices from a strip of standard $5/8$in cornice moulding. Glue one at each corner and one either side of the brass glazing bar. A fifth is added at right angles to the bar, on the outside.

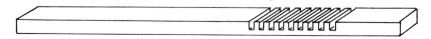

FIG 19   CUTTING THE BACK OF THE MOULDING BARS TO FACILITATE BENDING

SHOP FRONT DOOR

As befits a shop of this type the main door is made of polished mahogany with a brass kick bar at the bottom and a large glazed centre panel.

Doorway

Begin by preparing the doorway, gluing the fanlight bar into the doorway 6in from the bottom, as shown in Fig 3 on page 153. Then cut two 6in long strips of 3/8in wide architrave for either side of the door and glue these into place so that they overlap the doorway by 1/16in either side to prevent the door opening outwards.

Cut the lintel from 1/8in thick obeche, 3/8in deep x 3 1/2in wide and glue it on top of both of the two 3/8in wide architrave mouldings.

Use a piercing saw and V-block to cut the semicircular arch for the fanlight from a sheet of 1/8in thick mahogany, 4in x 2in, so that it overlaps the inside of the arch by not less than 1/16in to hold the fanlight glazing in place. Glue the arch in place over the lintel.

Front Door

Start the construction of the door by preparing the two upright stiles (A) and the three rails (top B, bottom C and centre D) from 1/8in thick mahogany (see Fig 20), making sure that the width of the rails are all exactly the same width or the door will not assemble correctly. See the Materials list on page 150 for the sizes.

Use a small circular saw to make a centre slot 1/32in wide down one side of each stile and across one side of the top and bottom rails (see Fig 20A). The centre rail is then grooved on both sides to take both the glazing and the panel (see Fig 20B).

Cut the centre panel from 1/8in thick mahogany, 7/8in wide x 2 3/8in long, and chisel or machine off 1/8in all round x 1/16in deep. Remove a further cut to leave 1/32in wide x 1/32in thick back edge to locate into the slots in the rails and stiles (see Fig 20C).

Stain all the wooden components of this door with a light mahogany spirit-based wood stain and allow this to dry thoroughly. Clean up any rough edges and assemble and glue together all the parts, except the top rail, in a suitable jig.

Cut and polish the 3in x 1/2in wide brass strip and glue into place on the face of the bottom rail using a rapid set epoxy adhesive. Clamp together with light pressure until set.

Check that the door fits the aperture and adjust as required. Round off the left-hand stile with a sharp wood plane and fine abrasive paper so that it will open and shut when the pin hinge is fitted. Apply a dark coloured wax polish to all surfaces of the wood (except the two ends of the top rail and the top 1/2in of the two stiles).

Cut and fit the acetate glazing sheet so that it fits into the grooves and is locked into place by gluing in the top rail.

Drill 1/32in diameter holes into the top and bottom of the left-hand stile, as shown in Fig 20, for pin hinging later.

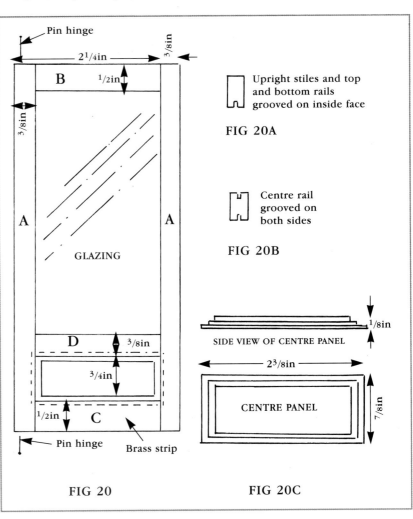

Upright stiles and top and bottom rails grooved on inside face

FIG 20A

Centre rail grooved on both sides

FIG 20B

SIDE VIEW OF CENTRE PANEL

1/8in

2 3/8in

CENTRE PANEL

7/8in

Pin hinge

2 1/4in

3/8in

B

1/2in

3/8in

A

A

GLAZING

D

3/8in

3/4in

1/2in

C

Pin hinge

Brass strip

FIG 20

FIG 20C

UPSTAIRS WINDOWS

Each of the three windows is made up separately and simply dropped into the apertures previously cut in the frontage, and provided you have cut all of these exactly the same it will be possible to make the windows away from the frontage. If you have any doubts regarding the accuracy of the cut-outs you made it might be better for you to build the actual windows in situ. Start by making the wooden framework.

Window Framework

Cut the main window-sill that runs along the bottom $1/2$in wide x 12in long from $5/16$in thick softwood or obeche and machine a $1/32$in drip slot on the underside, $1/8$in in from the front edge (see Fig 21). Bevel the leading edge 30 degrees and glue this into place $1/8$in below the three apertures.

From $3/32$in thick obeche prepare the four vertical facing columns, $1/2$in wide x $5^1/8$in long and glue these into position with one either side of the outer window aperture and the others between them. They must sit on top of the sill and reach to the top of the apertures.

Next, cut the bar covering the lintel that sits under the arch, from $3/32$in thick obeche $1/4$in wide x 3in long, and glue this into place over the centre aperture with the top $1/16$in over the bottom edge of the arch. Cut the arch from the same thickness material,

$1^3/4$in x $3^3/4$in, using a piercing saw and a bench V-block. Notch the outer edges to locate onto the bar and glue into place so that it overlaps the centre arched aperture by $1/16$in all round.

The two upper lintel mouldings over the two outer windows are made from a standard $1/2$in deep cornice moulding mounted onto two strips of $3/32$in thick obeche. Cut the two strips each $4^1/2$in long x $1/2$in wide (or the same width as the cornice moulding you are using) and shape the inner end to match the arch using a piercing saw for a neat fit. Cut the outer edge at 45 degrees and glue this into place flush with the top of the window apertures.

Cut two lengths of cornice moulding $4^3/4$in long and shape the outer ends to 45 degrees, matching the strips. The inner edge should be shaped with a piercing saw to mimic the curve of the arch that they overlap by $1/4$in at the centre. Glue the cornice pieces onto the obeche strips.

Windows

All three windows are made up from white polystyrene sheet and mouldings that are glued together using a proprietary plastic weld adhesive (see page 13 for handling). This adhesive works by literally dissolving the styrene sheets and fusing them together and is drawn into the joints by capillary

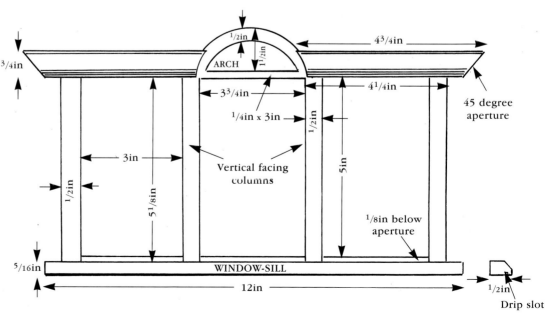

action. Do not allow this adhesive to get onto your fingers whilst you are handling the parts or you may find fingerprints indented into the surface. Follow the instructions from the manufacturer regarding working with this product and obey those concerning smoking or using near naked flames.

It will be seen that these are sash type windows, meaning that the top sash overlaps the bottom one and is therefore placed to the front of the channel moulding at the side. The bottom sash is placed to the back.

Making up this assembly will be much easier if you use a small bench jig with at least one fixed right angle. Cut the parts A–M following the sizes given in the Materials list on page 150. With reference to Fig 22, which shows one window, start by gluing up a framework beginning with the two L parts (the U-channels left and right), K and A. To make the bottom sash, glue G and H to the back of the channel and lock these into place with J and F1. Next make up the top sash by adding parts C, D, E and F2. Glue on part B to lock in the top sash. Note that parts F1 and F2 are glued together along their length. The two horns M are added to the bottom corners of the top sash on the outside and the top corners of the bottom sash on the inside. Cut and fit the glazing from 0.7mm acetate: this can be held in place with additional bars placed under F1 and over F2, but this is optional. Make the other two windows in the same way.

QUOIN STONES

To make the quoin stones first cut a 24in length of $^3/_{32}$in thick obeche x $^3/_4$in wide and from this length cut twelve pieces 1in long and ten further pieces each $^3/_4$in long. Bevel three edges of each quoin at 45 degrees and glue them onto the front at the outer edges (see Fig 23). Start with a 1in quoin at the top and work down with alternate lengths. The bottom quoin on either side will need to be trimmed to fit around the top of the side walls.

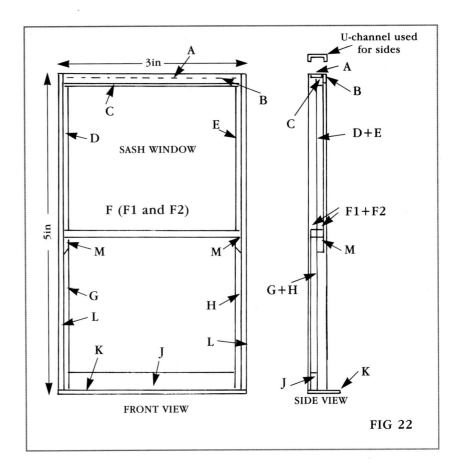

FIG 22

FINAL ASSEMBLY OF FRONTAGE

The frontage can now be fixed to the right-hand side wall with two 2in brass butt hinges, fixed with screws and positioned 4in above the bottom floor and 4in below the pediment. Ensure that you drill starter holes for the screws, especially into the edge of the MDF or it may split. (You will notice that no hinges are visible in the photographs accompanying this chapter, this was simply to make photography easier.)

INTERIOR DECORATION

We realise that this part of the book is very much a personal choice but in order to provide some guidance we give below details of the schemes we used.

At this stage the internal walls, top and bottom, have not been fixed into position so this will allow you to work around them away from the carcass and in some cases assembling them almost at the last. Begin by punching down any nail heads and filling all the holes, inside and out, with a suitable plaster filler. Rub down with a fine abrasive

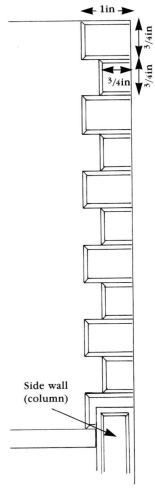

FIG 23 Quoins

paper to a smooth finish, then use a damp cloth to remove all plaster dust.

Decorating Main Body and Walls

It is assumed that the front will be hinged on the right-hand side in which case run two parallel strips of single copper tape keeping them 3/16in apart from front to back. The position of these should be 11in above the bottom and they should extend from the centre of the carcass back, around to the front to within 3/8in of the front edge of the side. Smooth them down firmly and insert a brass eyelet, or nail, into each strip at the front to enable a connection for the two front lamps (see Fig 5, page 154).

Thread the top light pull-through wire through the ceiling rose and glue the rose to the surface of the ceiling directly over the drilled hole. Paint both ceilings, including the rose, with a matt white emulsion and continue this down the upper walls by 13/8in to meet the line for the picture rail. Paint the internal walls and arches for the top floor to the same depth with the same colour.

The edge of the carcass and the pediments are coloured with Farrow & Ball's cream eggshell finish emulsion. The outer edges of the roof and the barge-boards should be painted with a matt white emulsion. Using a matt cream or white, paint the inside back wall, up the line of the staircase from the bottom to the top and all that part hidden behind the top internal wall. Leave the width of the hallway at the back bare as it is to be papered.

The staircase can be treated in a number of ways: a centre strip of masking tape will allow you to decorate the outer edges with emulsion paint or it could be gloss painted or stained. The underside of the staircase was painted a matt cream emulsion. Screw the staircase to the back wall when all this area has been decorated.

The wallpaper can now be applied to all the upper floor walls, fixed or otherwise, using a standard wallpaper paste or a PVA

craft glue for stronger results. Take care to ensure that any pattern drops in the carcass match those on walls not yet fixed into place. For a really neat finish, the chimney breast can be papered separately and screwed to the wall after.

Paint all the upstairs skirting boards, picture rails and the internal door with Farrow & Ball's 'Drab' colour emulsion and set aside to dry thoroughly. Most of these parts can be glued to the main walls as soon as the papering is completed. However, we suggest that you do not fix any of them to the internal walls until these are finally fixed into position as this will allow you to line up some of the smaller pieces with those already in place. The exception to this rule is the hallway side of wall A, as this will be out of reach once assembled. The skirting board covering the exit hole for the wiring connecting the shop lamp should not be glued into position until the wiring is connected and tested.

Drill 1/16in diameter holes into the opening stile of the internal door and add two 1/4in diameter door knobs that have first been painted with cream enamel to simulate ceramic fittings. This is also a good opportunity to assemble the hallway light and run the wires out to the back. Check the circuit and that the bulb is working before proceeding.

To fix the walls in place run a line of PVA wood adhesive along the top floor in front and to the left of the stairwell, then run a second line along the rear side of arch B and the right-hand wall. Push the walls into place and hold until the glue has set. If necessary turn the carcass onto its back and place a suitable weight onto the upturned wall assembly. Add the second arch A between the two walls and add the two 3/4in supporting plaster corbels. Add the door and its architrave mouldings to wall A, and then fit this wall into position, locating it behind the inner pediment. It may be necessary to insert this at an angle of 45 degrees and stand it up into position after a line of adhesive has been run. Check that it is straight and if necessary use one or two panel pins inserted through pre-drilled holes from the ceiling below to fix more securely.

Stain the $3/8$in mouldings that are to be placed around the shop wall aperture with a dark mahogany wood colour and set aside to dry thoroughly.

Glue and pin the inner shop wall onto the staircase making sure that it butts against the right-hand wall.

The shop walls can now be papered, carefully matching the pattern where one wall joins another. Add the doorway mouldings to complete this.

EXTERIOR DECORATION

The two sides of the main carcass were finished off with a pre-printed English bond brick finish supplied in sheets (see Suppliers). The size of the carcass meant that several sheets had to be joined together and although this can be tricky they do come with instructions on how to achieve a neat finish. It is a good idea to lay the sheets out on a flat surface before deciding which ones are best butted together as colours and shades may vary across the sheet – placing them all in the same direction can lead to the pattern repeat being very obvious. Apply the sheets using a good quality PVA craft glue and smooth down from one edge to remove any trapped air.

As one of the sheets will cover the two runs of copper tape we suggest that you remove about $1/2$in x $1/2$in from the end of the sheet where it lays over the two eyelets. Keep this small piece and punch a small hole through it for the wires to pass through. Once they are soldered or connected to the tape this can be glued into place using a clear, spirit-based adhesive.

Roof

Glue a strip of thin card $1/2$in wide along the two leading edges to lift the covering slightly and mimic a real roof. Both sides can then be covered with a fibre-glass slate sheet

applied using a PVA craft glue. Smooth down all over, especially at the sides. To complete the roof, run two strips of $3/4$in wide masking tape, one on top of the other, along the top of the roof apex, where the two sides meet. Paint this with a mixture of white, brown and grey acrylic paints to mimic a coping stone colour and finish off with a fine black felt-tip pen to indicate the joints between them at $1 1/4$in intervals from the front.

Chimney

The chimney stack can be removed whilst the sheets are glued down but we suggest that you carefully cut around the shape of the stack base and remove this to give a neat finish.

Paint the top and cap with terracotta coloured emulsion or craft paint, adding a few darker streaks to give a little life to the finish. Cut the shape, from the base to the stone cap, from an oddment of the English bond brick sheeting used for the sides. Score the corners to make a neat finish and

Dressed in her overalls, the cleaner arrives to tidy up the fireplace

169

glue on, after fixing the stack to the roof, using PVA glue. Add a second piece of brickwork sheet to the cap, carefully selecting the position and direction of the bricks and glue on two terracotta chimney pots. Finish this off by using a dark grey acrylic paint to add the appearance of a lead flashing strip around the base of the stack and the roof.

Frontage Interior

Rub down and paint the inside surface of this part with cream water-based eggshell finish emulsion and leave to dry. The inner surfaces of the window formers can also be painted at this stage. Colour the two top formers with cream emulsion and for the bottom two forming the window bases mix a marble finish with a white emulsion and apply thin grey streaks, brushed over with a stiff, dry brush whilst the paint is still damp.

Shop Exterior

Paint all the woodwork around the three top windows and the quoins with Humbrol cream enamel paint, running this around the edges of the quoins. The remainder, which includes the side walls, the fascia board, fascia support and around the windows, is primed and undercoated before finishing with a proprietary British Racing Green coloured gloss paint to give a high finish. Apply paint to all the surfaces of the fascia but keep it separate from the building at this stage so that you can add the lettering more easily. The area above the fascia is covered with the same English bond brick sheeting used for the sides. Take care to cut around the window mouldings and quoins and match any joins.

Shop Lettering

The words on the front of the shop fascia – Grocery, Meadows, Provisions – were assembled using wooden laser-cut letters to give a bold three-dimensional effect (see Suppliers). These are really excellent and quite robust, although care must be taken

with any thin sections, such as the letter V. Check that you have the correct letters and lay them out onto a flat surface to check the spelling and the spacing. Find the centre of the word by measuring, do not take the middle letter, and also locate the centre of the fascia. Use a straight edge, a steel ruler will do, and practise building up the words. It may be necessary to remove the straight edge if some of the letters have tails that fall below the base line. Remember that letters are not all spaced apart by the same distance, the spacing also relies on balance, appearance and the nearness of the preceding letter. Check the spelling and make a note of all these measurements – if necessary plan it out on paper, drawing the board and letters full size. When you are happy, remove the letters ready for painting.

To do this first fix a piece of masking tape to a flat board with the adhesive side uppermost. Press each of the letters onto the tape to keep them in place and use a car spray enamel to provide a grey undercoat as this method gives even coverage. Avoid overspraying and building up too many coats of paint as it will show at the edge of the letters when they are removed from the tape. If you need more than two coats we suggest that you carefully remove the letters from the masking tape once dry and then repeat the above method using a second piece of tape. We painted ours with a metallic gold car spray paint.

When you are confident that you can lay the letters out correctly, proceed to apply them by brushing a very thin coat of clear, spirit-based adhesive on to the back of the first letter and press it into position. Build up the wording slowly and carefully, checking by eye and ruler as you go.

When the lettering is complete, the fascia board can be fixed to the shop front by inserting screws through the eyelets.

(Picture, right) *Mr Meadows personally attends to a customer while an assistant brings in more stock*

Flooring and Pavement

The upstairs floor was finished with a coat of wax furniture polish and then buffed up. A carpet was then laid and fitted to the main room and the hallway, although the alcove was left as 'bare boards'.

The shop floor is decorated with tiled flooring paper – we used one based on an old encaustic tile pattern. It was laid to all of the ground floor including the small area at the base of the stairs. These papers are supplied with a printed border and you will need to trim this carefully so that it runs around the outer edges of the floor where it meets the walls, to ensure that the pattern still matches. Dry fit all the pieces first and then fix into place using a PVA craft glue. Smooth down and wipe off any residue.

The tiling along the front pavement area was copied from colour plate of a sample of Victorian tiling. This was scanned into a computer and printed out in several pieces that were each trimmed to fit the shape.

Front Door

Fix the front door using the pin hinge method. The bottom pin is drilled up through the pavement while the top pin is first fixed to the door and then is inserted into a pre-drilled $1/32$in diameter hole. Glue the brass handles to both sides of the door stile using rapid set epoxy glue, first removing any polish from the area.

Lighting

The large double lamp in the shop (see Suppliers) is supplied with a relatively short length of wire, so you may need to solder sufficient twin-flex wire on the ends to reach the back. Thread the wires up through the centre hole and glue the wiring down into the pre-cut groove, out through a pre-drilled hole in the back and glue on to the skirting board. Check that the light is working and use a silicone sealant or rapid set adhesive to fix the lamp in place. We found that as the lamp we used was quite substantial it need support whilst the sealant set.

The two globe lamps outside on the frontage are placed so that they do not obscure the lettering. They both have quite large bases and were glued into place, using rapid set epoxy glue, as close to the fascia board as possible. The wiring was trailed off to the side that has the copper tape runs on the carcass. Solder an extra length of twin-flex wire onto the four tails from the lamps, then use a PVA glue to fix this behind the fascia board and along the top of the side wall. Drill a neat and unobtrusive $1/16$in diameter hole from the outside through the side wall and into the void behind, pass the wiring through this to the outside and leave enough to connect onto the tape strips to make a connection at the back of the carcass. Paint over any visible wires with matching colour paint so that it will blend in.

Glazing the Main Windows

Replace the glazing sheets as detailed earlier. Add two sheets of plastic 'mirror glass' (see Suppliers) to either side of the main window, cutting the pieces to fit.

Side Door

Paint this with Farrow & Ball's 'Drab' colour into which has been added a little grey

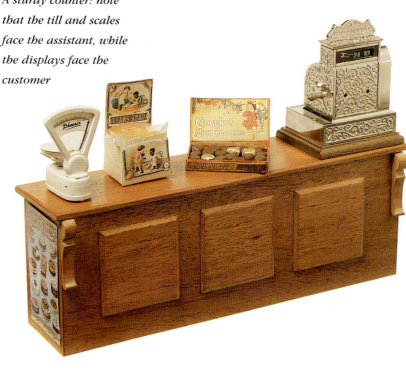

A sturdy counter: note that the till and scales face the assistant, while the displays face the customer

acrylic. Add ¼in diameter brass knobs that have been pre-painted black to simulate cheap iron fittings.

Paint the side door step and door hood with two coats of Farrow & Ball's Old White emulsion and finish off by streaking it with a grey acrylic to produce a distressed and worn finish.

Finishing Off

Now that the main part of the building is complete, the loose shade and grain of wheat bulb can be fitted to the ceiling centre lamp in the upstairs room. We chose a round glass shade evocative of the period and this was attached to the ceiling rose by three short brass chains fixed to a hook glued to the rose. However, any light fitting or shade could be used if this type is not available to you.

The fireplace surround used is a typical ¹⁄₁₂-scale miniature and is free standing. Simply place it at the centre of the chimney breast, adding a touch of glue if required. Trim and place the small pieces of skirting board either side of the surround, to match those on the outer edges of the chimney breast.

WINDOW DISPLAY BOARDS

The importance of a good window display cannot be emphasised enough. These simple shelf fittings will enable you to show the goods to best advantage and are an ideal way to give your display height.

MATERIALS

- ⅛in mahogany x ¼in x 5⁷⁄₈in, 4 off
- ⅛in mahogany x 1in x 5¼in, 4 off

Cut four vertical bars, two per side, from ⅛in thick mahogany ¼in wide x 5⁷⁄₈in long.

These are designed to be a tight push fit between the lower and upper window formers so it is a good idea to check the height on your model before cutting. This will

allow their removal for dressing the window, however they can be fixed if desired. Cut three notches ⅛in wide x ⅛in deep into one edge of all four bars. Position these at 1in, 2¹⁄₈in and 3¼in from the top. Place the two bars into each of the windows so that there is an evenly measured space between them and each side, the notches to the outside.

Cut four shelves, two per side, from ⅛in thick mahogany 1in wide x 5¼in long. These should just sit into two of the notches and be held in position. If your notches are too large the shelves will drop forwards in which case we suggest that you glue them into place. Trim the front of the shelves with paper lace.

Meadows the Grocers is now ready for a final fitting out with counters, shelves and high-class stock. If you refer to the Shopkeeper's Resource section pages 29, 31 and 33, you will find special counters for both dry goods and foodstuffs to be found in a delicatessen, including one with a sneeze top. Use a paper template to organise the layout and amend some of the sizes to suit your taste. Choose your stock with care and arrange it as artfully as you can. You can also use some of the grocery packaging stacks found in the Shopkeeper's Resource section on page 46 to bulk up the displays. Keep stock signs as small as possible and remember to keep currency in the correct period. If your shopkeeper is also going to have a boy assistant, complete with bicycle, remember to stock this as well.

Cold meats and pies were usually cut by hand with a sharp, long-bladed knife, and a sharpening steel was usually nearby. Keep produce such as cheese or cold meats to their own part of the counter as it is most unlikely that they would be placed together except in the most untidy and unhygienic of shops.

Bicuits supplied in tins were sold loose by weight

173

SOURCES OF INFORMATION

The authors are happy to provide what information they can on receipt of a stamped self-addressed envelope to: The Mulberry Bush, 9 George Street, Kemptown, Brighton, UK BN2 1RH. Tel: 01273 600471 or send e-mail to: enquiries@mulberrybush.com

Magazines

In recent years the hobby has grown so rapidly that there are now more dolls' house magazines and directories published in the UK than in any other country in the world.

All of the magazines published in the UK are available from your local newsagent and those published in America can be obtained from some bookshops. Most of those published within the UK are also available from outlets in both Europe and America. The magazines provide readers with a good source of international advertisers offering shops, houses and miniatures, many of these have mail-order catalogues.

Fairs

The number of fairs taking place has grown proportionately to the size of the hobby and it would be impossible to list all the organisers and venues here. In order to find specialist miniaturist fairs new collectors would do well to purchase one or two magazines, from different publishers, as we feel that it would be unfair of us to mention just a few.

SUPPLIERS
Names and Addresses

Jill Bennett, Mendip Lodge, 8 Bathwick Hill, Bath, BA2 6EW
Tel: 01225 420828

Box Clever, 8 Meadow Road, Meadow Rise, Dunston, Lincoln, LN4 2ES

Sue Cook, Unit 5, Arundel Mews, Arundel Place, Kemptown, Brighton BN2 1GD
Tel: 01273 603054

Country Treasures, Rose Cottage, Dapple Heath, Admaston, Nr Rugeley, Staffs WS15 3PG
Tel: 01889 500652

Farrow & Ball Ltd, Uddens Estate, Wimborne, Dorset BH21 7NL
Tel: 01202 876141

C. A. Hooper, 3 Bunting Close, Ogwell Cross, Newton Abbot, Devon TQ12 6BU
Tel: 01626 360628

Wendy Jackson, 38 Lansdowne Road, Purley, Surrey, CR87 2PA.

Robert Longstaff Workshops, Appleton Road, Longworth, Nr Abingdon, Oxon OX13 5EF
Tel: 01865 820206

The Mulberry Bush, 9 George Street, Kemptown, Brighton BN2 1RH
Tel: 01273 600471

Tina Newman, J Designs, 95 Westgate Road, Beckenham, Kent BR3 5TX
Tel: 0181 650 4031

Quality Dolls House Miniatures, 55 Celandine Avenue, Locks Heath, Nr Southampton SO31 6WZ
Tel: 01489 578420

Angela and Laurence St Leger, 17 Stuart Way, Bridport, Dorset, DT6 4AU
Tel: 01308 424 709

Ann Underwood, 20 Park Lane, Glemsford, Sudbury, Suffolk, CO10 7QQ
Tel: 01787 281372

Pat Venning, Pineways, Faircross Avenue, Weymouth, Dorset, DT4 0DD
Tel: 01305 773325

Paul Wells, 18 Kingswood Road, Colchester, Essex CO4 5JX
Tel: 01206 851620

Wood & Wool, 555 AIA Enterprise Park, Rendlesham, Woodbridge, Suffolk IP12 2TW
Tel: 01294 460836

Specialist Supplies used in the Shops

Items seen within the shops but not listed below are from the authors' collection unless referred to in the text as in the Shopkeeper's Resource section.

THE SHOPKEEPER'S RESOURCE
The Mulberry Bush
Centurion Balusters No. 7202.

JINGLES TOY SHOP
J Designs
Dolls.
The Mulberry Bush
Fort, rocking horse, boxed games, books, toy shop, grille, decorative panel, brackets and trim strip (North Eastern), lights.

LUSCOMBE'S IRONMONGERS
Robert Longstaff Workshops
Fascia lettering.
A. & L. St Leger
Flue brush, mop, feather duster, bath brush, pastry brush, funnel, mouse traps, washing tongs.
Box Clever
Calendar.
Quality Dolls House Miniatures
Garden tools and equipment.
The Mulberry Bush
Lights, wire and asphalt rolls, tin-ware, rubber boots, brassware, pots of paint, staircase, newel posts, bannisters (Houseworks), brick wall cladding, wooden flooring, decorative brackets and fascia trim strip.
J Designs (Tina Newman)
Dolls.
Country Treasures
Warming pan.

THE CLARENCE TEA ROOMS
Jill Bennett
Dolls.
Pat Venning
Art Deco china and mask.
Wendy Jackson
Mirror.
Box Clever
Menus, carrier bags.
The Mulberry Bush
Cutlery, sandwiches, tables and chairs, trays.

PICKWICKS BOOK SHOP
Jill Bennett
Dolls.

Box Clever

Maps, print folio, sheet music, country atlas, specialist books, map bin.

The Mulberry Bush

Lights and bulbs, globe, books, Xacto furniture kits, roofing.

MEADOWS THE GROCERS

Wood & Wool

Main shop and outside lights.

J Designs (Tina Newman)

Dolls.

Country Treasures

Biscuit tins.

Ann Underwood

Hen and eggs, display shelf.

Sue Cook

Plaster corbels and dentil corbels.

C. A. Hooper

Fireplace, door handles.

Wendy Jackson

Mirrors, mirror glass.

Robert Longstaff Workshops

Fascia lettering.

The Mulberry Bush

Bicycle, lights, slicer, scales, tins, tills, clock, bottles, roofing, chairs, side board, mirror, dustpan, flooring, roofing, door kits.

Paul Wells

Brick wall sheets.

GENERAL

Farrow & Ball Ltd

Specialist paints as used on all projects.

BIBLIOGRAPHY

For a wide-ranging stock of new and second-hand books on dolls' houses, miniatures, architecture and crafts, contact:
The Mulberry Bush, 9 George St, Kemptown, Brighton, BN2 1RH.
Tel: 01273 600471

ADBURGHAM, Alison
Shops & Shopping 1800–1914
(George & Allen Unwin, 1964)

ADBURGHAM, Alison (Intro)
The Army & Navy Stores Catalogue
(David & Charles reprint, 1980)

BARNARD Lionel & HINCHCLIFFE Michael *The Dolls' House Gardener*
(David & Charles, 1998)

BEECHING, C.
Modern Grocery Display
(Caxton Publishing Co. *c.*1933)

DAVIDSON, Craig *Sam Smith, Grocer Extraordinary*
(Kellog & Co GB, *c.*1930)

DOLPHIN, Tracy
Biscuit Tins (Shire Publications, 1999)

EVANS, B. & LAWSON, A.
A Nation of Shopkeepers (Plexus, 1981)

JACKSON, W. A.
The Victorian Chemist and Druggist
(Shire Publications, 1981)

KLEIN/McCLELLAND, HASLAM,
In the Deco Style
(Thames & Hudson, 1987)

KRAMER, Ann *The Victorians*
(Dorling Kindersley, 1998)

LUCAS & BEDFORD
The Book of Shops (Forum Books, (1899) reprinted 1990)

MASON, Laura
Sweets & Sweet Shops
(Shire Publications, 1999)

OPIE, Robert
Sweet Memories (Pavilion, 1998)

OPIE, Robert *Remember When*
(Mitchell Beazley, 1999)

OPIE, Robert *The Art of the Label*
(Simon & Schuster, 1987)

POWERS, Alan *Shop Fronts*
(Chatto & Windus, 1989)

RIESSER, Ingeborg
Les Maison de Poupees
(Massin Editeur, 1993)

ROUNDTREE, Susan
Dollhouses, Miniature Kitchens and Shops
(The Colonial Williamsburg Foundation, 1996)

WARNER, Barbara *Dollhouse Lighting*
(Boynton Ass.,1986)

WILLIAMS, Bridget *The Best Butter in the World – A History of Sainsbury's*
(Ebury Press, 1994)

MEADOWS, C. A.
Victorian Ironmonger
(Shire Publications, 1978)

ACKNOWLEDGEMENTS

The authors would like to thank the following people: Jill Bennett, Janet and Paul Brownhill, Sue Cook, Farrow & Ball Ltd, Martin Butler, Tony Hooper, Elaine Howard, Wendy Jackson, David & Audrey Johnson, Robert Longstaff, Ken Mainwaring, Tina Newman, Angela & Laurence St. Leger, Ann Underwood, Pat Venning and Paul Wells.

Linda Clements our editor for her help and attention to details and Jeremy Thomas for all the photography, especially the lighting effects. And to any others we may have forgotten to name who have contributed to this book – our sincere thanks.

175